IMPERIALIST REALISM

POLITICS AND CULTURE AT THE END OF THE AMERICAN CENTURY

What People Are Saying About

Imperialist Realism

Daniel Bessner's *Imperialist Realism* rises out of the ruins of traditional international relations theory and diplomatic history, offering a new, clear-eyed conception of U.S. power that feeds off chaos, global conflict, and domestic polarization. An indispensable book that brings clarity to confusing times. Highly recommended.
Greg Grandin, Peter V. and C. Vann Woodward Professor of History at Yale University and author of *The End of the Myth: From the Frontier to the Border Wall in the Mind of America*, winner of the Pulitzer Prize in General Nonfiction

Daniel Bessner is one of the sharpest analysts of U.S. foreign policy writing today. *Imperialist Realism* asks how a democratic society can regain control over decisions made in its name abroad. It's a powerful argument for connecting our foreign policy to the same ideals of participation and accountability we expect at home.
Bhaskar Sunkara, president of *The Nation* and founding editor of *Jacobin*

Daniel Bessner knows how to ask the big questions: about empire and war, American political culture and national identity. Imperialist Realism — the book and the concept — helps us make sense of the contradictions so often at the heart of U.S. foreign policy.
Beverly Gage, John Lewis Gaddis Professor of History at Yale University and author of *G-Man: J. Edgar Hoover and the Making of the American Century*, winner of the Pulitzer Prize in Biography

IMPERIALIST REALISM

POLITICS AND CULTURE AT THE END OF THE AMERICAN CENTURY

Daniel Bessner

London, UK
Washington, DC, USA

First published by Zer0 Books, 2026
Zer0 Books is an imprint of Collective Ink Ltd.,
Unit 11, Shepperton House, 89 Shepperton Road, London, N1 3DF
office@collectiveinkbooks.com
www.collectiveinkbooks.com
www.zero-books.net

For distributor details and how to order, please visit the 'Ordering' section on our website.

Paperback ISBN: 978 1 80341 480 5
eBook ISBN: 978 1 80341 481 2
PCN: 2026932668

A CIP catalogue record for this book is available from the British Library.

Design credit(s): Lapiz Digital
Cover image by Justin Hantz

UK: Printed and bound by CPI Group (UK) Ltd, Croydon, CR0 4YY
Printed in the US by S&S

The manufacturer's authorised representative in the EU for product safety is:
eucomply OÜ - Pärnu mnt 139b-14, 11317 Tallinn, Estonia,
hello@eucompliancepartner.com, www.eucompliancepartner.com

To Courtney and Leo Bessner
and
my editors

TABLE OF CONTENTS

ACKNOWLEDGMENTS

There's an old joke in academia that in the acknowledgments section of a scholar's first book, one winds up thanking everyone from their preschool teacher to their mail carrier, but as time goes on, and as one publishes more books, the acknowledgments sections get shorter and shorter. So let's keep this brief.

Since I began writing for public audiences, I've had the pleasure of working with a number of excellent editors who have improved both my writing and my thinking. I'd like to thank them all, especially Mark Krotov of *n+1*, David Marcus of *The Nation*, and Laura Marsh of *The New Republic*. They have made me a better writer, and I appreciate that.

I'd also like to thank Alex Aviña, Justin Boyd, Frank Smecker, and Tom Strand for reading the entire manuscript and catching several spelling, grammatical, and syntactical errors.

All essays in this volume, save for the opening chapter, "Imperialist Realism," originally appeared in other venues. I'd like to thank the various publications that first released these pieces for letting me republish them. Please note several things. First, I kept references to historical events or phenomena that have now ended—e.g., the U.S. occupation of Afghanistan—as well as references to specific time periods—e.g., "earlier this year," "last April," or what have you—as they appeared in the original text. Second, I have slightly revised many of these pieces, though their cores remain the same. Third, I have added scholarly footnotes to these essays.

"Imperialist Realism," while containing mostly new material, also contains parts of "An Empty Tale: The Foreign Policy Establishment Is Responding to Trump-Era Brutalities by Demanding More, Not Less, Aggression and Empire," originally published in *Jacobin* in August 2019; "Antony Blinken and the Triumph of Zombie Liberalism: The New U.S. Secretary of State Does Not Seem Inclined to Question Washington's Conventional Foreign Policy 'Wisdom,'" originally published in *Foreign Exchanges* in February 2021; "First-Person Shooter Ideology: The Cultural Contradictions of *Call of Duty*," originally published in *The Drift* in February 2021; "The End of Mass Politics: If Americans Feel Disconnected from Their Government and Their Communities, Perhaps That's Because They Are," originally published in *Foreign Exchanges* in January 2022; and "*The Rings of Power* Is a Saga for a War-Hungry Nation: In Amazon's Take on *The Lord of the Rings*, the Hero Is a Fanatic, Ceaselessly Seeking Out Potential Threats," originally published in *The New Republic* in September 2022.

"The Principles of a Democratic Socialist Foreign Policy" was originally published as "What Does Alexandria Ocasio-Cortez Think About the South China Sea? The Rising Left Needs More Foreign Policy. Here's How It Can Start" in *The New York Times* in September 2018.

"Empire Burlesque" was originally published as "Empire Burlesque: What Comes After the American Century?" in *Harper's Magazine* in July 2022.

"Barack Obama and the Process Presidency" was originally published as "The Barack Obama Memoir: Don't Trust the Process" in *Jacobin* in February 2021.

"George Soros After the Open Society" was originally published as "The Globalist: George Soros After the Open Society" in *n+1* in June 2018.

"The Discontents of Francis Fukuyama" was originally published as "A Bad Breakup: The Discontents of Francis Fukuyama" in *The Nation* in April 2023.

"H.R. McMaster and the Tragedy of American Empire" was originally published as "A Very High Degree of Certainty in Future Military Operations: H.R. McMaster and the Tragedy of American Empire" in *n+1* in May 2017.

"Robert M. Gates and America's Forever Foreign Policy" was originally published as "Argument Without Argument: Robert M. Gates and America's Forever Foreign Policy" in *n+1* in February 2021.

"Samantha Power and the Fog of Intervention" was originally published as "The Fog of Intervention: Samantha Power Did Not Set Out to Justify War" in *The New Republic* in September 2019.

"The Worlds of Noam Chomsky" was originally published as "Empire's Critic: The Worlds of Noam Chomsky" in *The Nation* in January 2025.

"On John J. Mearsheimer and Michael Walzer" was originally published as "Foreign Policy for the Twenty-First Century: It Is Time to Develop a New Geostrategy Unencumbered by Past Traumas" in *Boston Review* in October 2018.

"Ending Primacy to End U.S. Wars" was originally published by the Quincy Institute for Responsible Statecraft in April 2022.

"Ukraine and the Return of the United States" was originally published as "The Return of the United States: Ukraine and the 'Rules-Based International Order'" by the Alameda Institute in April 2023.

"America Has No Duty to Rule the World" was originally published as "America Has No Duty to Rule the World: The Story of the Country's Rise to Dominance Shows How It Can Step Back" in *The New Republic* in October 2020.

"The Case Against Humane War" was originally published as "The Case Against Humane War: How the Turn Toward 'Precision' Combat Promoted Endless War" in *The New Republic* in September 2021.

"Mass Destruction" was originally published as "Mass Destruction: How Democratic Participation in Foreign Policy Became Unthinkable" in *Boston Review* in March 2023.

"Whose Fault Was the Cold War?" was originally published in *The Ideas Letter* in August 2025.

"It Didn't Happen Here" was originally published as "Does American Fascism Exist? For Nearly a Century, Americans Have Been Throwing the Term Around—Without Agreeing What That Means" in *The New Republic* in March 2023.

"This Is America" was originally published as "This Is America: Donald Trump's Authoritarian Second Term Has Led Critics to Describe Him as a Fascist in the Mold of Adolf Hitler. But Trump's Reactionary Politics Are All-American—and the Path to Defeating Him Runs through Reform of America's Antidemocratic Institutions" in *Jacobin* in March 2025.

Finally, I'd like to thank my family, Courtney and Leo Bessner, for their unwavering support. I do it for them, and I couldn't do it without them—thank you for improving my life immeasurably and for making it worth living.

November 2025
Seattle, WA

PART I
THEORY

INTRODUCTION
IMPERIALIST REALISM

The United States is an empire and has been since its inception. From the settlement of the eastern seaboard and the oppression, expulsion, and genocide of Indigenous peoples; to the Monroe Doctrine and the search for hemispheric hegemony; to "Manifest Destiny" and the conquest of the American West; to the seizure of territories in the wake of the Spanish–American War and the establishment of formal colonial regimes; to the embrace of a global grand strategy during World War II and the establishment of an "empire of bases" during the Cold War; to the "unipolar moment" of the 1990s and the "Global War on Terror" of the 2000s and 2010s; and to the return of neo-mercantilist imperialism under President Donald J. Trump, U.S. policymakers have pursued an imperialist foreign policy whose political, economic, cultural, and geographic purviews inexorably grew over time.

Despite recent talk of American "decline," in pure economic and military terms the United States remains the dominant world power. At the time of writing, Trump has requested $962 billion in funding for the U.S. Department of Defense, which Congress is likely to approve.[1] This domestic military spending undergirds a global network that consists of approximately 750 military bases operating in 80 foreign countries, territories, and colonies.[2] U.S. primacy is likewise evident in the international political economy, where the dollar continues to serve as the global reserve currency. And, despite a track record of military failures abroad, the United States retains a significant degree of so-called "soft power." A 2025 survey by the Pew Research Center that polled people in 24 foreign countries, for instance, discovered that "a median of 49% of adults have a favorable overall view of the U.S."[3] Meanwhile, on a global level, the nation faces no serious challengers. Though China and Russia clearly desire to become regionally hegemonic—China's ever-expanding military presence in the South China Sea and Russia's 2022 invasion of Ukraine demonstrate as much—neither of these nations appears willing, or capable, of threatening the United States' preponderant planetary position. Thus, while the United States is no longer as relatively powerful as it was in the postwar, Cold War, and unipolar eras, discussions of its absolute decline are overblown.

The fact of U.S. Empire has had a profound effect on American life; it shapes our language, culture, and quotidian experiences. Think of the martial metaphors that permeate U.S. discourse, from the "war on drugs" to the "war on cancer" to the "war on crime" to the "war on poverty" to the "war on COVID" to the "war on woke" to the "war on disinformation." Or consider the "flyovers" of military aircraft that sometimes augment "The Star-Spangled Banner" at National Football League (NFL) games, which the NFL describes as "a symphony of high powered supersonic capable jet engines blazing across the sky at the conclusion of America's beautiful anthem."[4] Meanwhile, at airports across the country, anyone who enters a passenger boarding area must undergo invasive searches of their belongings and bodies as airlines allow active-duty military personnel to board before everyone else. Finally, appreciate how Americans believe it's their right and duty to have opinions on what their country "should do" abroad, from Afghanistan to Zimbabwe. To live in America is to live an imperialist life.

Empire is all around Americans, whether we know it or not. Take, for instance, Los Angeles (LA) county, where I first began this essay. While LA is primarily known as the headquarters of Hollywood, since the early 1920s it's also been home to a significant portion of the nation's defense industry—blue skies, after all, are good for two things: filming movies and flying planes. In Fiscal Year 2023, LA county received $12 billion in defense contracts (the third highest in the country and the highest in California) and housed five military installations: Air Force Plant 42, the Long Beach Fuel Complex, the Los Angeles Air Force Base, Norwalk 2, and the San Pedro Fuel Depot.[5] Boeing, Lockheed Martin, Northrop Grumman, and Raytheon have LA offices, while the county also hosts the RAND Corporation (founded in 1948), the nation's first national security think tank and among the most influential. In addition to these installations and organizations, LA's built environment, famously constructed around the automobile, was made possible by imperialism: cars need oil to fuel them and rubber to make the tires that propel them, and for much of U.S. history, these raw materials could only be extracted in quantity from abroad. As the case of Los Angeles indicates, empire is all around us and has become, as historian William Appleman Williams aptly put it, "a way of life" we barely notice.[6] Nevertheless, when Williams deployed the phrase "empire as a way of life" in 1980, he did so in a context very different from our own. In effect, Williams was arguing that a defining belief of American life was "our *a*historical faith that we are not now and never have been an empire."[7] Though this might have been true 45 years ago, in 2025 it no longer is; the disasters of U.S. foreign policy are just too great to ignore. In fact, when one uses the Google Books Ngram Viewer to trace the use of the term "American Empire" in American English over time, it's clear that in the past four decades—and especially since the United States initiated the Global War on Terror (GWOT) in 2001—Americans have begun to acknowledge the imperial nature of their country.[8]

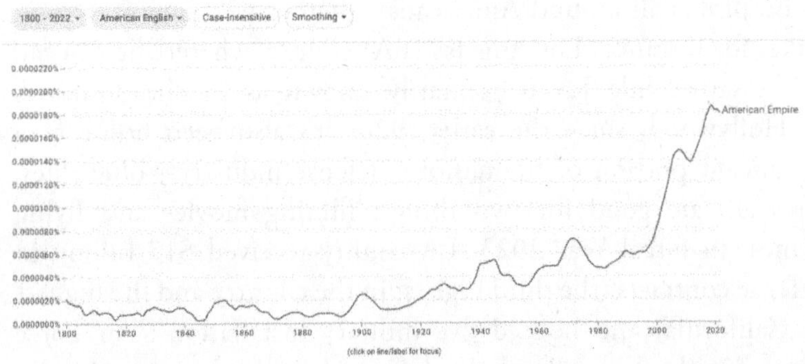

But, if Americans are now willing to name their empire as such, two questions remain: Why has there been so little opposition to it? Are Americans imperialists?

The available data suggest that the answer to the latter question is no, or at least not uniformly; a significant minority of Americans have become skeptical of the notion that the United States should dominate global politics. A recent poll by the Chicago Council on Global Affairs, for example, reveals that "fewer than six in 10 Americans think the United States should play an active role in world affairs."[9] "This reading," the council notes, "is one of the lowest levels recorded since the survey question was first asked in 1974."[10] Another poll, this time by Gallup, similarly has discovered that only "sixty-six percent of Americans want the U.S. to take either the leading role (19%) or a major role (47%) in trying to solve international problems," which, the company reports, "remains lower than Gallup readings between 2001 and 2009, which averaged 75%, and is essentially tied with 2023 (65%) and 2011 (66%) as the low in the trend."[11] Meanwhile, an earlier poll by the Chicago Council shows that 70 percent of Americans "express confidence in the United States' ability to deal responsibly with world problems," down from 82 percent in 2015.[12] Clearly, there is a growing skepticism about U.S. power. Why, then, is there so little opposition to American Empire?

To answer this question, this essay introduces the concept of *imperialist realism*—the notion that it is easier to imagine the end of the world than it is to imagine the end of the U.S. Empire.[13] Simply put, I argue that the primary reason Americans accept and make use of their empire is their belief, whether consciously or unconsciously held, that they are unable to change it. Americans, in a sense, have become alienated from their empire—it appears as something outside their control—even as they deploy it abroad. It is the seeming immovability of U.S. Empire, its apparently obdurate character, that is the primary reason Americans accept it. As General George S. Patton told his troops in the Third Army before the 1944 D-Day invasion of Normandy, "Americans love a winner and will not tolerate a loser."[14] If a political struggle seems unwinnable, a mass of Americans will not pursue it—just ask those who advocate for government-ensured healthcare, a policy most Americans endorse but which has never engendered a broad-based popular movement.[15] This is the situation in which those skeptical of U.S. primacy find themselves today.

Imperialist Realism

Before exploring the specific content of imperialist realism, it's crucial to appreciate what the concept is not. Above all, imperialist realism is not an ideology; it should not be understood as a coherent, if dynamic, system of ideas, ideals, and preferences that shapes how one understands reality. Imperialist realism is not as systematic as that; it exists at a deeper, more affective and emotional, level. It is also not a *Weltanschauung*—a philosophy of life—that gives direction to individual and collective actions. Instead, imperialist realism is most like what the critic Raymond Williams termed a "structure of feeling"—"a specific structure of particular linkages, particular emphases and suppressions" that "cannot without loss be reduced to belief-systems, institutions, or explicit general relationships."[16] In short, imperialist realism is a structure of feeling that provides a sense of what is possible and what is not when it comes to the present and future of U.S. Empire.

Imperialist realism has three fundamental features that shape the concept's contours.[17] First, it is cynical. After the GWOT's failure to achieve any of its goals—to end "terrorism," to spread democracy abroad, to improve the United States' global image—many Americans no longer believe their country has the capacity to move the world in a positive direction. At the same time, they also don't believe that anything can truly change because the forces in favor of the empire are too powerful, too entrenched, to be challenged. This engenders a cynicism that permeates American political and popular culture. Second, imperialist realism is defined by a sense of mission, or what I term *missionism*, which insists that, despite its manifold foreign policy failures, the U.S. Empire is here to stay and must therefore act in the world. In effect, Americans are so embedded in an imperial context that they can't imagine *not* acting. Third, imperialist realism is saturated with a sense of tragic guilt that emerges from the tension between its cynicism and missionism. While Americans appreciate that U.S. global "leadership" has resulted in terrible outcomes, they nonetheless avow that, because they have an empire and because the world is brutal, they still must direct global politics. This results in feelings of tragic guilt—guilt because Americans appreciate that they have not been benevolent stewards of international relations, tragic because they insist that they have no other choice but to dominate them—feelings that are ever-present and never reconciled. These three features—cynicism, missionism, and tragic guilt—constitute the essential elements of imperialist realism in twenty-first-century America.

To explicate how imperialist realism functions, this essay interweaves analyses of decision-makers' statements with analyses of several massive spectacles that in recent decades have come to define American popular culture, including the *Call of Duty: Black Ops* video game series and a film from the Walt Disney Company's Marvel Cinematic Universe. I focus on foreign policymakers' remarks and pop culture artifacts because these are rich texts that embody the performance of imperialist realism's cynicism, missionism, and tragic guilt. Carried in elite and popular discourses, the assumptions of imperialist realism sediment in the minds of domestic and international publics, shaping what ruling classes and ordinary people alike understand to be politically "realistic." If we hope to create a world in which change is imaginable, we must denaturalize the present, imperialist-realist common sense.

As we head into the main body of this introduction, I want to make clear that this essay is meant in the original sense that the French philosopher Michel de Montaigne used the term—as an initial attempt to apprehend a subject, not the final word on it. There are themes and components of, and tensions within, imperialist realism that I do not explore. Above all, imperialist realism, like all contemporary phenomena, is shaped by race, gender, and class relations; these, however, remain outside the scope of my analysis. Moreover, other scholars will have to examine what it means for imperialist realism that, though the U.S. military plays a substantial role in American culture and discourse, the United States is not a "militarist" society in the manner of, say, Israel, South Korea, and Singapore, countries where most male citizens are required to serve in the armed forces.[18] In sum, there remains significant work to be done on imperialist realism that I hope future historians, critics, and theorists will undertake.

This essay proceeds as follows. First, I explore the two most important structuring conditions that made imperialist realism possible—the end of mass politics and the GWOT's failure. I then turn to analyzing imperialist realism's three primary features. Finally, I conclude with a reflection on imperialist realism's present and its possible future.

The End of Mass Politics and the Failure of the Global War on Terror

Imperialist realism is a function of several structuring conditions. The most basic of these is the fact that, since the early 1940s, U.S. elites have sought global military and economic primacy.[19] Nevertheless, the pursuit of primacy is a necessary, but not sufficient, condition for imperialist realism's emergence. Imperialist realism became the common sense of an era as the result of two other factors: first, the end of mass politics, and second, the failure of the Global War on Terror.

Genuinely *mass* politics is a relatively recent phenomenon. Beginning in the nineteenth century and continuing into the twentieth, intertwined processes of urbanization, industrialization, and technological development reshaped politics across the North Atlantic world, giving ordinary people more power than they ever had before. In effect, as people moved from rural areas to cities, became industrial wage workers, and organized in unions, and as new technologies such as the telegraph and radio enabled leaders to communicate directly with large groups of citizens, a novel type of political formation—the "mass public," which was considered to have an "opinion"—arose. For the first time in history, government officials started to conclude that their policies needed to have some relationship to what the mass public desired. Predictably, the emergence of the mass public as a political force engendered significant discussion among intellectuals about the proper role "public opinion" should play in policymaking. In the 1920s United States, two prominent thinkers, the journalist Walter Lippmann and the philosopher John Dewey, engaged in a debate that continues to define how American elites understand the public's political function.

On one side, Lippmann argued that ordinary people were simply too ignorant and too easily manipulated to be given the reins of public policy.[20] In place of the public, Lippmann affirmed that social scientists needed to attach themselves to institutions that directly provided the government with advice. Lippmann thus presented technical expertise as the solution to the problem of mass politics. On the other side, Dewey averred that, though Lippmann was correct to doubt the public's wisdom, elites should not ignore the masses but must instead educate them.[21] Through education, Dewey claimed, ordinary people could eventually gain the knowledge necessary to make astute political choices.[22]

Initially, most American intellectuals embraced Dewey's position over Lippmann's: democracy, they maintained, relied on an educated mass public. Nevertheless, by the late 1930s, historical events in the United States and abroad led many thinkers to change their minds and endorse Lippmann over Dewey. First, the Great Depression, which witnessed bank runs, labor militancy, and other "irrational" mass behaviors, suggested to many intellectuals that the public was innately unreasonable. Second, and more important, the ascendance in Germany of the Nazi Party—whose power, Americans believed, rested on the masses—demonstrated to many observers that ordinary people could easily be duped to support destructive dictators such as Adolf Hitler. Together, the domestic responses to the Great Depression and the rise of Nazism persuaded an emergent majority of American elites that the masses could not be trusted. Mass politics and public opinion became things to be tamed and manipulated rather than improved.[23] The stakes of the debate over public opinion became especially high during and after World War II. Following the fall of France in the summer of 1940, American elites concluded that the future of their nation, "Western civilization," and humanity as a whole depended on the United States' triumphing over Nazi Germany, a country whose fascist politics represented an illiberal attempt to address the problems of mass industrial society.[24] In essence, U.S. elites began viewing international relations as a sphere of life defined by a zero-sum struggle between Manichaean enemies, the winner of which would determine the fate of the world.[25] Luckily for those who endorsed this position, the Japanese attack on Pearl Harbor and other U.S.-controlled territories in December 1941 made it easy for the United States to go to war; in the days after the attack, 97 percent of Americans approved Congress' declaring war against Japan and 91 percent said that President Franklin Delano Roosevelt should have also asked Congress to declare war on Germany.[26] For the remainder of World War II, most Americans accepted that their country needed to defeat the Axis.

The situation, however, was not so simple in the early Cold War. While, after World War II, manifold American elites rapidly transferred their anxieties about Hitler and Nazism onto Joseph Stalin, Bolshevism, and "international communism" writ large, they didn't trust that the public—which, they worried, had proven itself ignorant and capricious in the past—would necessarily do the same. Indeed, as late as May 1947, 35 percent of Americans said they had "friendly" "feelings" toward Russia (i.e., the Soviet Union).[27] This presented elites with a problem: How could they ensure that the irrational mass public would allow its leaders to prosecute a potentially decades-long "cold war" against the Soviet Union, a nation that had only recently been an ally? American elites developed a clever solution to their conundrum: to guarantee that ordinary people didn't stand in the way of the Cold War, they constructed a governance apparatus designed to limit the public's impact on foreign policy. The creation of executive branch groups such as the National Security Council, Central Intelligence Agency, and Department of Defense, as well as parastatal organizations such as the RAND Corporation and other national security-focused think tanks and academic centers, institutionalized a system in which elites, not the masses, made the important foreign policy decisions. Put another way, in the late 1940s the United States embraced two distinct "containment" policies. Internationally, U.S. elites sought to contain the Soviet Union by preventing it from improving its global power position; domestically, they sought to contain the American public by preventing it from shaping U.S. foreign policy. From its inception, the U.S. pursuit of global primacy was accompanied by a domestic democratic deficit.

Since World War II, the public has had at best a minor influence on the conception and execution of U.S. foreign policy. All the major strategic decisions made by U.S. elites after 1945—to spend an enormous amount on the military; to build a global empire of bases; to deploy hundreds of thousands of troops abroad; to intervene repeatedly in the politics and economies of other countries—have been made with only passing reference to public opinion. This is not to say that American politicians and officials have always ignored the public; they've often paid attention to, and tried to manipulate, it. Still, the public was rarely, if ever, the driver of U.S. foreign policy. Even Congress, the institutional representative of the people's will, has been a secondary player in U.S. foreign policy- and war-making. Indeed, the last time Congress declared war was on June 4, 1942, against Bulgaria, Hungary, and Romania despite the fact that, as the political scientists Monica Duffy Toft and Sidita Kushi have discovered, between 1946 and 2019 the United States intervened abroad with "the threat, display, or direct usage of force" 216 times.[28] Though the language of mass politics continues to permeate U.S. discourse and influence how Americans conceive of their political role, when it comes to foreign policy, we do not live in a mass democracy and haven't for almost a century.[29]

The powerlessness of the masses in the realm of foreign affairs is one of the two key structuring conditions that make imperialist realism possible. While the organizations and practices of the age of mass politics remain extant—Americans still vote for mass political parties; we still engage with politics through mass media; we still participate in mass protests—these are not effective vehicles for the will of the *demos*. Ours is an individualistic, atomized, and alienated era overlaid with atavistic institutions unable to influence the power elite. Indeed, research suggests that wealthy capitalists are the only people capable of shaping policy. According to the political scientists Martin Gilens and Benjamin I. Page, "multivariate analysis indicates that economic elites and organized groups representing business interests have substantial independent impacts on U.S. government policy, while average citizens and mass-based interest groups have little or no independent influence."[30] Is it any surprise that Americans have become cynical about politics? In fact, a recent report by NORC at the University of Chicago revealed that, when polled, "barely one in ten Americans thought the government represents them well"; 70 percent "thought politicians were only out for themselves"; and just 19 percent "said people in government could be trusted to do what's right."[31]

The other necessary condition for imperialist realism's emergence is more proximate: the failure of the Global War on Terror. For those who don't remember the early 2000s, it's difficult to overstate how patriotic, jingoistic, and—importantly—*hopeful* Americans became once the George W. Bush Administration committed the United States to fighting a war on "terror." In January 2002, for example, 93 percent of Americans believed that the United States made the correct decision to send military forces to Afghanistan and 66 percent said the United States was "winning the war against terrorism."[32] To many Americans, the GWOT was a world-historical project that united the country in a moment when the United States lacked an existential enemy and thus lacked an organizing principle for both domestic life and U.S. foreign policy. This conviction was perhaps best reflected in Bush's 2002 State of the Union address, in which the president declared that the 2000s "will be a decisive decade in the history of liberty" because Americans have "been called to a unique role in human events"—to eliminate "terrorists" and all those who supported them.[33]

But the GWOT did not proceed as planned. Instead of marching to triumph, the United States lurched from disaster to disaster. Above all, Americans fought, and lost, a twenty-year war in Afghanistan and an eight-year war in Iraq. The GWOT, which expanded beyond Afghanistan and Iraq to Pakistan, Syria, and other countries, cost around $8 trillion, engendered the displacement of 38 million people, resulted in at least 940,000 direct deaths and 3.6–3.8 million indirect deaths, witnessed the deaths of over 7,000 U.S. troops, and helped impel police militarization, political polarization, and the erosion of civil liberties at home.[34] Without putting too fine a point on it, the GWOT was one of the most significant failures in the history of U.S. foreign relations: the disconnect between the hopes placed in the GWOT and its vicious, violent, and counterproductive reality undermined Americans' belief in themselves and their country. Because of it, the United States is a more cynical place. It is to this cynicism that we now turn.

Imperialist Realism in a Cynical Age

In the past decade, as demonstrated earlier, more and more Americans have become skeptical about U.S. global power. Nonetheless, few believe they have the capacity to encourage, let alone force, the United States to be less domineering in world affairs. On an intuitive level, Americans understand that mass political action, whether street protests or voting, does not have a decisive impact on U.S. foreign relations. This tension, between a desire for change and an inability to make it, has engendered a cynicism about U.S. foreign policy that is one of the defining features of the imperialist realism that permeates American culture. Even mainstream consumer objects that allow Americans to play at war—such as the best-selling video game *Call of Duty: Black Ops Cold War*, which sold over 30 million copies and which one might imagine would adopt at least a semi-patriotic perspective—evince and promote a remarkable pessimism about U.S. foreign policy.[35]

The *Call of Duty* video game series is one of the most popular media franchises in modern history; between 2009 and 2024, a *Call of Duty* game was the best-selling or second-best-selling video game in the United States.[36] For the uninitiated, *Call of Duty* games are "first-person shooters" (FPS), a video game genre in which players assume the perspective of a "shooter" who travels through varied environments, killing enemies. The *Call of Duty* series is broken up into three subseries: World War II, Modern Warfare, and Black Ops. Where the World War II and Modern Warfare subseries are self-serious, the Black Ops strand of the *Call of Duty*-verse is lurid and kooky. The games star grizzled reactionaries with tenuous government allegiances doing whatever's necessary to protect the American way of life. Like the protagonists of a John Milius film, for these men the vicious immorality of that violent project is its own reward.

Released in November 2020, *Call of Duty: Black Ops Cold War* (which became among the highest-selling entries in the entire *Call of Duty*-verse, which at the time consisted of 19 games) begins just after Ronald Reagan's inauguration in January 1981.[37] Mindful of the humiliation the United States recently suffered during the Iran hostage crisis, the new president has "authorized a black operation to take down two [of the crisis'] suspected masterminds." The player plays as various members of the CIA team charged with this and other operations. After a number of twists and turns that take the player from Amsterdam to Turkey to the German Democratic Republic, the player learns that a Soviet secret agent, codenamed "Perseus" (and presumably based on a hypothetical spy whose real-life existence was rumored but never confirmed), plans to detonate several neutron bombs placed earlier by the United States under European cities to ensure that those cities not fall into communist hands.[38] Perseus hopes that, when he triggers the nukes, the international public will assume that the United States was responsible for the destruction, which will turn the nation into global enemy number one and spur the Soviet Union on to victory in the Cold War. Upon discovering this false-flag operation, the player spends the rest of the game trying to locate Perseus. Eventually, after infiltrating the Lubyanka Building (better known as KGB headquarters), the player learns that Perseus is hiding on the White Sea's Solovetsky Islands. In the game's final mission, the player travels to the islands and prevents Perseus from detonating the nukes, though the spy escapes to fight another day.

In *Black Ops Cold War*, players spend most of their time as "Bell," the codename of the game's protagonist. By the game's end, the player learns that Bell was an associate of Perseus, whom one of the Iranian "masterminds" from the very first mission had tried, and failed, to murder. Indeed, the CIA saved Bell's life and used mind-altering drugs taken from the top-secret Project MKUltra to trick him into thinking he was a long-standing CIA operative. Bell eventually learns the truth, and though the CIA manipulated him, he helps the Americans save the day.

In telling this story, *Black Ops Cold War* repeats, and refigures, one of the classic tropes of Cold War-era fiction: brainwashing. As the literature scholar Scott Selisker notes in his *Human Programming: Brainwashing, Automatons, and American Unfreedom*, during the Cold

War, thinkers and intellectuals across the political spectrum regularly deployed the idea of brainwashing in their work.[39] On one side, centrists and conservatives claimed that their communist enemies, whether Soviet, Korean, or Vietnamese, were brainwashed "masses of human automatons, will-less and therefore less than human."[40] Such a perspective allowed centrists and the Right to present the battle between capitalism and communism as a necessary struggle between a "free" world and a "slave" world that needed to be won at all costs—the enemies of liberal capitalist democracy, after all, were barely human.[41] Against these Cold War hawks, who presented so-called "totalitarians" as programmed simpletons, stood more progressive thinkers such as Ralph Ellison and Betty Friedan. Both Ellison's *Invisible Man* (1952) and Friedan's *The Feminine Mystique* (1963) turned the idea of the "brainwashed totalitarian" on its head, claiming that it was actually American institutions that transformed people, be they Black Americans or bourgeois housewives, into automata.[42] According to Friedan, Ellison, and others, the true struggle for freedom was found not in the geopolitical arena but at home.

Black Ops Cold War combines elements of both the hawkish and the progressive approaches to brainwashing, highlighting how the imperialist realism of the present moment flattens the distinctions that previously constituted Cold War-era politics. According to the game, Bell began his career an avowed "totalitarian," a stalwart ally of Perseus bent on eradicating the United States and its freedoms. One imagines that the hawks would be just fine with Bell's brainwashing at the hands of the CIA; even if his transformation occurred without his consent, at least Bell was pushed to the right side of history. But *Black Ops Cold War* simultaneously takes pains to present the CIA as morally corrupt; at base, it's an organization willing to kill innumerable Europeans if this would ensure that Central and Western Europe do not fall into Soviet hands. Furthermore, the CIA's brainwashing of Bell suggests that the group is perfectly willing to upend the norms of liberal capitalist democracy—which by definition depends on the ability to think freely—themselves. In *Black Ops Cold War*, there are no heroes.

Black Ops Cold War reflects the cynicism of our imperialist realist moment. Today, few Americans will proudly assert, as Madeleine Albright did in February 1998, that the United States is the world's "indispensable nation" because "we [Americans] stand tall and we see further than other countries into the future."[43] But, at the same time, few are able to affirm an alternative vision to U.S. Empire. As the second Trump Administration's first few months demonstrate, the only alternative on serious offer is a neo-mercantilism that relies on tariffs and gunboat diplomacy. Put another way, the choice before Americans is twentieth-century empire or nineteenth-century empire; hardly a choice at all. The character of Bell embodies the tensions of an age in which the negative consequences of empire are understood and admitted, but in which there is little political will, or even a strategy of how, to transform the system. Bell is both a perpetrator of violence and a victim of institutions beyond his control, neither a good guy nor a bad guy, just a soldier fighting wars that will one day be forgotten, based on decisions over which he had no say, made by people who have total power over him. There's no reason for Bell to ponder the larger context within which he operates, because that context doesn't affect whether he lives or dies. This notion is clearly expressed in Bell's trigger phrase—"We've got a job to do"—which implies that all a soldier can do is put their head down and get to work. No other world is possible. Taken as a whole, *Black Ops Cold War* can't justify American actions abroad, but it also can't imagine a post-imperial world.

If God died in the nineteenth century, ideology died in the twentieth. In almost every way, *Black Ops Cold War* is a post-ideological product. The gamers who beat *Black Ops Cold War*, for example, never even learn what, exactly, the United States and Soviet Union are fighting over; the words "capitalism" and "communism" are barely uttered. Instead, the game presents geopolitics as being about nothing but power, accepting the rather blinkered vision of "realists" who reduce international relations to a struggle of might. Like the realists, in fact, *Black Ops Cold War* offers an incredibly pessimistic theory of human nature, in which people fight because fighting is what people do.[44] In the final analysis, the game argues that the United States is a powerful empire, and by dint of this fact, it runs amok around the world. Conflict is inevitable, and you can choose how to act within this inevitability, but you can't do much else.[45] That's the beginning, and end, of *Black Ops Cold War*'s politics. Its cynicism is boundless.

The post-ideological imperialist realism of *Black Ops Cold War* enabled Pentagon officials to embrace the game as a recruiting tool. In 2019, in collaboration with the Call of Duty Endowment—a 501(c)(3) nonprofit cofounded by the CEO of Activision Blizzard (the company behind *Call of Duty*) to aid veterans—the military established the CODE Bowl, in which military eSports teams played *Call of Duty* against each other.[46] Though the game presented CIA operatives as, in effect, psychopaths, the military didn't seem to mind, likely because it also presented U.S. domination as an unchanging feature of geopolitics. Simply put, American primacy is perfectly consonant with imperialist realism's cynicism. If nothing can really change, might as well fight for the United States. After all, we've got a job to do—who really cares why we're doing it?

The cynicism reflected in *Call of Duty: Black Ops Cold War* has recently emerged as a central feature of U.S. foreign policy discourse, albeit in a somewhat different key. Where *Black Ops Cold War* is cynical about individuals' ability to push the system in new directions, the speeches and remarks of elite policymakers reflect a cynicism about the U.S. imperial project itself. In essence, decision-makers have abandoned the post–Cold War, "unipolar moment"-era faith that the United States could remake the world in its liberal, democratic image and have instead embraced a framework that considers U.S. hegemony a necessary means to protect American "interests."[47]

In the Joseph R. Biden Administration's October 2022 *National Security Strategy* (NSS), for example, the term "interests" is deployed around 42 times; compare this to the 2006 *National Security Strategy* of President George W. Bush's second term, which was produced at the height of the unipolar moment and Global War on Terror, and in which the term "interests" is used only about 20 times.[48] Furthermore, the 2022 NSS does not mention democracy promotion once; the 2006 NSS, in contrast, declares that "the most effective long-term measure for conflict prevention and resolution is the promotion of democracy."[49] Similarly, in speeches President Biden gave in August 2021, as the United States prepared to retreat from Afghanistan, the only thing the president said about Afghan democracy was that "our mission in Afghanistan was never supposed to have been nation building" and that "it was never supposed to be [about] creating a unified, centralized democracy."[50] Indeed, Biden asked those who wanted "a third decade of war in Afghanistan" to weigh this desire against "the vital national interest," which he defined as "to make sure Afghanistan can never be used again to launch an attack on our homeland."[51] Predictably, Trump in his second term has totally disregarded ideals and has instead embraced a vulgar, materialist, and interest-based nationalism. At the time of writing, Trump has shuttered the United States Agency for International Development; withdrawn from the Paris Agreement, World Health Organization, and United Nations Human Rights Council; renamed the Gulf of Mexico the Gulf of America; instituted numerous tariffs; threatened Greenland with invasion; and, as stated earlier, requested an enormous defense budget—"the largest peacetime increase in the defense topline since the Reagan Administration."[52]

The Biden Administration's emphasis on interests is especially ironic given that the administration came into office claiming that international relations was defined, as the October 2022 NSS insisted, by "the competition between democracies and autocracies."[53] Despite such rhetoric, however, administration officials rarely acted as if they believed this to be the case. Take, for instance, the remarks members of the Biden Administration offered to justify U.S. assistance to Ukraine in the wake of Russia's February 2022 invasion of the country, an event that would appear to fit perfectly into the democracy-versus-autocracy framework. Two months after the invasion, Secretary of Defense Lloyd Austin told reporters that one of the United States' major goals in the war was to ensure that "Russia [was] weakened to the degree that it can't do the kinds of things that it has done in invading Ukraine." While Austin did say he hoped Ukraine would remain "a democratic country," he immediately connected the notion of democracy to the desire to guarantee that Ukraine was "able to protect its sovereign territory."[54] Austin's remarks indicated that what was most important to the United States when it came to Ukraine was diminishing Russian power so as to ensure that the latter was unable to become the predominant power in its near abroad. This is why U.S. aid to Ukraine focused on providing matériel; "nation-building" efforts similar to those pursued during the Vietnam War of the 1960s and the Afghanistan and Iraq Wars of the 2000s and 2010s were nowhere to be found.

Secretary of State Antony Blinken's statements on the Russia–Ukraine War reflected a similar concern for guaranteeing U.S. security, as opposed to ideological, interests. In remarks Blinken gave in early March 2022, for example, the secretary never once mentioned the idea of democracy or democracy-promotion, instead affirming that the United States would aid Ukraine because the invasion was:

> an assault on some very basic principles that we established together after two world wars to make sure that we wouldn't see another one, principles that are at the heart of an international system that has a responsibility to preserve peace and security among nations, principles like the notion that one country can't simply commit acts of aggression on another, changing its borders by force; that one country can't dictate to another its choices, its decisions, its policies, with whom it will associate; principles like one country can't exert a sphere of influence to subjugate its neighbors to its will—each principle now under assault by the aggression against Ukraine committed by President [Vladimir] Putin and Russia.[55]

Notice that none of the principles Blinken referred to focused on defending, promoting, or strengthening any ideological interest. After two decades of a failed war on terror, U.S. officials, even those who claimed to care about democracy, seem in practice to have shed their concern with the concept. Now what matters, above all, is security and, implicitly, maintaining U.S. hegemony.

The cynicism about the United States acting as a force for good in the world that currently permeates U.S. foreign policy discourse was further reflected in decision-makers' remarks about U.S. and Israeli policy in Gaza. To take one depressing example, at a June 2024 conference called to insist on an "Urgent Humanitarian Response for Gaza," Blinken avowed that Israeli Prime Minister Benjamin Netanyahu—the individual most responsible for initiating and continuing the Israel Defense Forces' genocide of the strip—had "reaffirmed [to Blinken] his support and his commitment to bringing [a ceasefire] proposal across the finish line."[56] Moreover, there was the incredible, and undeniable, gap between the declarations of U.S. foreign policymakers, such as Biden and Blinken, who affirmed that they desired independent Palestinian statehood, and the fact that the United States provided Israel with untold numbers of bombs that not only killed countless innocents but also obliterated much of Gaza's civilian infrastructure and, in effect, made an independent Palestinian state that would incorporate the strip an impossibility.[57] Indeed, Biden Administration officials and other Democrats seem to have lied when they declared that the administration was working "tirelessly" toward a ceasefire.[58] In April 2025, Michael Herzog, who served as Israel's ambassador to the United States during Biden's term in office, revealed that "we [Israel] fought [in Gaza] for over a year and the administration never came to us and said, 'ceasefire now.' It never did."[59] In terms of U.S. foreign policy toward Israel and Palestine, the cynicism of Biden Administration officials was mind-boggling.

The Biden Administration's cynicism as regards the Russia–Ukraine War and Israel's war on Gaza reflects a broader cynicism that presently lies at the center of U.S. foreign relations. American officials no longer believe, as Madeleine Albright and others during the unipolar moment did, that their country can move the world in a positive, more liberal, and more democratic direction. The Global War on Terror has proven that hope a fantasy; the dream has curdled into a nightmare. But at the same time, officials don't trust that they can transform how their empire acts on the global stage. The conviction that no other reality is possible is why Blinken runs cover for war crimes; after all, like Bell from *Call of Duty: Black Ops Cold War*, he's got a job to do.[60] A more cynical—a more imperialist realist—perspective is difficult to imagine.

There Is No Alternative: U.S. Foreign Policy and Its Mission

The cynicism that permeates imperialist realism exists comfortably alongside the concept's next defining feature: the belief that there is no alternative to American global hegemony and that, for this reason, the United States must play an active role in world affairs. Despite U.S. foreign policy's manifold and manifest failures—failures that gave rise to the cynicism described above—few within the establishment argue against what they euphemistically refer to as U.S. global "leadership."[61] In an October 2023 speech given to persuade Americans to continue to spend money on the Russia–Ukraine War and to address the then-recent Hamas attack on Israel, for example, Biden asserted that "American leadership is what holds the world together."[62] A similar tune was sung by Blinken in 2020, when, during a conversation at the Hudson Institute with the neoconservative thinker Walter Russell Mead, he maintained that if the United States was:

> not doing a lot of ... organizing in terms of shaping the rules and the norms and the institutions through which countries relate to one another, then one of two things [happens], either someone else is doing it and probably not in a way that advances our own interests and values or maybe just

> as bad, no one is and then you tend to have chaos and a vacuum that may be filled by bad things before so by good things."[63]

More recently, when *The Atlantic* asked Trump in early 2025 how his second term felt different from his first, the president responded that this time around he envisions himself as "run[ning] the country and the world."[64] Thus, while Trump is less likely to speak in glowing terms about U.S. hegemony, it's fairly clear he sees this hegemony as necessary. To Biden, Blinken, and Trump, U.S. dominance is the assumed condition of geopolitics, the *sine qua non* of international relations—no other world is desirable or even imaginable.

Because elite decision-makers consider U.S. hegemony both indispensable and valuable, they embrace the idea that the United States has a global mission to dominate international relations. This idea was evident in the aforementioned October 2022 *National Security Strategy* released by the Biden Administration, which avowed in no uncertain terms that "around the world, the need for American leadership is as great as it has ever been."[65] For American officials, only the United States can put the globe on the right path. As Biden remarked at the U.S. Coast Guard Academy's 140th Commencement Exercises in May 2021, "the United States of America has always been able to chart the future in times of great change."[66] Even Trump has insisted that the United States has a global mission, declaring in 2016 that the nation needed to "focu[s] on creating stability in the world" and was dedicated "to bring[ing] peace to the world."[67] Almost 400 years after the Puritan leader John Winthrop affirmed in 1630 that he and his fellows "must consider that we shall be as a city upon a hill," shining light unto other nations, American officials continue to believe that only the United States, despite its many, many failures, has the correct answers to the problems of geopolitics.[68]

A primary reason elites are able to champion the U.S. Empire and its mission is that they misunderstand, and distort, this empire's actual history. Take, for instance, Ivo H. Daalder and James M. Lindsay's 2018 *The Empty Throne: America's Abdication of Global Leadership*.[69] Daalder and Lindsay are about as high up in the foreign policy establishment as one can get. Daalder, the former U.S. ambassador to NATO, is presently the chief executive officer of the Chicago Council on Global Affairs. Lindsay, for his part, is currently the Mary and David Boies distinguished senior fellow in U.S. foreign policy and director of Fellowship Affairs at the *Ur*-establishmentarian Council on Foreign Relations. Their coauthored book embodies how foreign policy elites misread history as a means to justify an American-centric global order that has done profound damage to the world.

Consider, for example, how Daalder and Lindsay recount the history of the Cold War. In the mid-1940s, they claim, American policymakers correctly concluded that international peace and prosperity depended on the United States' "advancing collective security; opening free markets; and promoting democracy, human rights, and the rule of law" throughout the globe.[70] To accomplish these goals, the two authors continue, decision-makers "created a system based on the logic of cooperation—countries willing to follow America's lead would flourish, and as they did, so too would the United States."[71] (Cooperation doesn't usually mean that countries just follow what the most powerful nation does—that's gangster logic—but let's move forward.) Daalder and Lindsay admit that this U.S.-led world order had its problems—it only applied to "the West"; the United Nations and other international organizations were never especially effective; "human rights were often sacrificed to political expediency"; and some mistakes, such as the Bay of Pigs invasion and the Vietnam War, were made.[72] On balance, however, the two aver that the order "was a historic success" because the United States successfully reconstructed Western Europe and Japan; "the reach of democracy and human rights was extended"; and the Soviet Union disintegrated without a major war on the European continent.[73] For these reasons, Daalder and Lindsay insist that the United States must continue to occupy the global "throne," preventing any other nation—namely, China—from replacing it as hegemon.

To say that Daalder and Lindsay embrace a sanguine view of the Cold War's history would be an understatement. Here's another, more accurate way to tell the story that Daalder and Lindsay narrate. In the mid-1940s, U.S. policymakers decided to construct a world order based not on liberal principles of cooperation, reason, and law but on imperial principles of military, political, economic, and cultural supremacy. Americans, in effect, arrogated to themselves the right to act on behalf of humanity writ large. As such, for much of the twentieth century's second half, the United States repeatedly intervened in foreign countries, distorting organic developments and engendering mass death and displacement. The political scientist Lindsey O'Rourke has shown, for instance, that during the Cold War the United States attempted to covertly overthrow foreign regimes 64 times, and that "states targeted in a covert regime change operation appear less likely to be democratic afterward and more likely to experience civil war, adverse regime changes, or human rights abuses."[74] The historian Paul Thomas Chamberlin has likewise shown that more than 20 million people perished in Cold War–era conflicts.[75] Finally, the political scientists Sidita Kushi and Monica Duffy Toft have crunched the numbers and discovered that between 1946 and1989, the United States militarily intervened in foreign societies 104 times, at the rate of 2.42 interventions per year.[76] One can hardly call this a "rules-based world order," as Daalder and Lindsay do.[77]

This raises the question: Why do Daalder and Lindsay embrace a Pollyannaish view of American history disconnected from what U.S. hegemony meant for much of the globe? The two authors do so not because they're evil or ignorant, but because they can't imagine a world absent American domination. For them, the United States has a holy mission forged in the fires of World War II—to lead the world. No countervailing evidence that illuminates the actual consequences of that "leadership" can be brokered because Daalder and Lindsay's arguments are based on faith, not reason. Theirs is a religion, and unfortunately, it's the religion of the foreign policy establishment.

The conviction that the United States has a mission to "lead" the world is further expressed in American popular culture. A salient recent exemplar of this belief is the first episode of Amazon's *The Rings of Power* streaming series, which debuted in 2022 and is a prequel to the story told in J.R.R. Tolkien's three-volume fantasy epic *The Lord of the Rings* (LOTR).[78] *The Rings of Power* is the most expensive television series of all time, costing a whopping $1 billion. As *Time Magazine* reported, "no other series in the history of television has been this sprawling, this cinematic, this massive." Indeed, according to Jennifer Salke, the head of Amazon Studios at the time the series was released, *The Rings of Power* "is the crown jewel" of Amazon's entertainment content.[79] It is also a prime example of the missionism at the heart of imperialist realism.

The Rings of Power begins with a prologue in which viewers learn that the elves—the most powerful race living on Middle-Earth, the world where LOTR takes place—have defeated Morgoth, an evil primordial spirit. Unfortunately for the elves, Sauron, Morgoth's lieutenant and the soon-to-be eponymous lord of the rings, has escaped the elves and is in hiding, presumably gearing up for an attack. Despite this potential threat, at the start of *The Rings of Power* most of the elvish elite is intent on placing its figurative head in the proverbial sand. Only one elf—our hero Galadriel (played by Welsh actress Morfydd Clark)—is committed, even obsessed, with finding and killing Sauron. Galadriel's brother Finrod perished in the war against Morgoth, and she refuses to abandon her search for the future dark lord, as this would mean her brother's death was for naught.

While *The Rings of Power* tells the same basic story as *The Lord of the Rings*—a hero tries to defeat Sauron—that story's meaning has changed over time. In the 1960s, when LOTR first became popular in the United States, the children of the counterculture imagined themselves as weed-smoking, pacifistic hobbits.[80] In the 2000s, when films based on LOTR became massive hits, feverishly vengeful Americans reeling from the 9/11 attacks imagined themselves as "humble folk" defying Osama bin Laden/Sauron.[81] In the latter instance, the threat that readers and audiences wanted to depose was clear.

But at the beginning of *The Rings of Power*, there is as yet no definite threat. Morgoth has been defeated, and Sauron is nowhere to be found. The violence that the dark lord and his minions pose is theoretical. Galadriel, however, remains steadfastly devoted to finding and annihilating them. Her sense of mission is unabated, and it's here that *The Rings of Power* embodies imperialist realism. For Galadriel, who serves as the commander of the northern armies, Sauron provides a reason for being; if he didn't exist, she would have to invent him. Galadriel cannot accept peace, just as the United States cannot accept peace, because conflict is what makes her life meaningful (and, in the case of the United States, it's what justifies hegemony). One senses that even if Galadriel located and murdered Sauron, she'd keep searching for the next evil, lurching from crisis to crisis, from war to war, like the United States has done since World War II, when new "existential" threats—the Soviet Union, "terrorism," Russia, China—have emerged time and again.

Predictably, *The Rings of Power* is decidedly on Galadriel's side. From the text, we, the audience, know that Sauron is, indeed, planning his return; the show depicts Sauron's forces torching towns and killing innocents. In the meta-text, we also know that Galadriel and the elves will find and defeat Sauron because he will retreat and come back later in Middle-Earth's history to be defeated again by Frodo, Sam, Gandalf, Aragorn, and the rest of the fellowship of the ring. Galadriel, the audience is forced to conclude, is correct to go after Sauron. It's never really a question.

In this way, *The Rings of Power* affirms Galadriel's commitment to rooting out any potential evil wherever it might theoretically arise. Contra *The Lord of the Rings*, whose heroes were joint-passing, pacifistic hobbits and a ranger dedicated to destroying an enemy that has revealed himself, *The Rings of Power* makes a military fanatic its protagonist. It's thus the perfect embodiment of imperialist realism's missionism. Though Americans face no existential enemies—and haven't since Nazi Germany's defeat in 1945—we are constantly searching for one, justifying our search with reference to a mythologized past in which good guys defeated bad. If in 1968 Americans liked to imagine ourselves as the chill Frodo, and if in 2001 we preferred to imagine ourselves as the righteous Aragorn, today all we can imagine ourselves as is the zealot Galadriel. And like Galadriel, we will continue to prosecute our mission, no matter how damaging it has been and no matter how quixotic it might appear.

A final example from American popular culture that embodies the missionism of imperialist realism is found in HBO's *Game of Thrones*. The primary antagonists of this series, one of the most popular in television history, are the White Walkers, zombies intent on breaching The Wall, the sole barrier protecting the kingdom of Westeros from destruction. At the beginning of the series, the White Walkers have been mythologized, with many Westerosi claiming they never even existed.[82] Suffice to say that the White Walkers do in fact exist, and one of *Game of Thrones*' major themes is that good people must never let down their guard, because if they do, they will confront annihilation.[83] The message of the show is clear: there is always an existential enemy out there, waiting to pounce, and one must therefore never abandon the proverbial barricade. This is imperialist realism in a nutshell.

The Tragedy of U.S. Empire

Imperialist realism is ultimately a product of the Global War on Terror, the failed, ongoing, and quixotic war waged, as George W. Bush declared in October 2001, "against all those who seek to export terror" and "against those governments that support or shelter them."[84] Put simply, this war was too destructive, and too unsuccessful, to ignore—though it was also too destructive and too unsuccessful for many Americans to confront head-on, as doing so would require them to rethink the foundations of U.S. global power. The result of this tension is that, while Americans have not truly reconsidered U.S. hegemony, they have become more diffident about it. Indeed, there is now a resigned quality to the statements of those who defend American domination. In his July 2020 conversation with Walter Russell Mead, for example, Antony Blinken apologetically insisted that, "whether we like it or not, the world tends not to organize itself," which means humanity requires "American leadership."[85] As this suggests, unipolar-moment-era arguments that justified U.S. hegemony with reference to American superiority have been replaced by arguments that justify U.S. hegemony with reference to necessity. Though both claims are steeped in notions of American exceptionalism, the difference in confidence between them is striking.

The reasons for Blinken's reticence to offer a full-throated endorsement of American domination are obvious. In addition to the human and financial costs of the Global War on Terror stated earlier, since the advent of the GWOT Americans have pushed the U.S. state and society in increasingly militarist and authoritarian directions. Since 2001, Americans have transferred at least $1.6 billion in military equipment to local law enforcement agencies, militarizing the police; have been guilty of manifold human rights violations, from CIA-led torture to domestic "government practices that amount to racial profiling" of Muslims and people of Middle Eastern and South Asian descent; have expanded the government's surveillance and data collection capabilities, violating citizens' civil liberties in the process; have empowered and enriched the "big five" defense contractors (Boeing, General Dynamics, Lockheed Martin, Northrop Grumman, and Raytheon); have centralized power in the executive branch and around the person of the president, establishing an "autocratic presidency"; and have further entrenched the national security state through the creation of new institutions such as the Department of Homeland Security, the Directorate of National Intelligence, the National Counterterrorism Center, and the Justice Department's National Security Division.[86] The costs of recent U.S. wars have been enormous, and no observer, no matter how much they might be in favor of U.S. global "leadership," can deny them.

The GWOT's manifold and manifest failures have engendered a strange situation. On one hand, a number of foreign policy elites clearly feel guilty for the disasters that they caused. To take a prominent example, in May 2022, George W. Bush, the individual who bears the most personal responsibility for the war on terror, was giving a speech on the Russia–Ukraine War when he criticized "the decision of one man to launch a wholly unjustified and brutal invasion of Iraq. I mean—of Ukraine. Iraq, too."[87] On the other hand, most officials remain unwilling to apologize for their commitment to imperial hegemony and its antidemocratic and violent consequences. This, in turn, has led a sense of tragic necessity to permeate their remarks. In congressional testimony given in 2013, for instance, Keith Alexander, then director of the National Security Agency (NSA), justified the NSA's unconstitutional surveillance capabilities in the following manner: "We're holding this hornets' nest [of surveillance programs] for the good of the nation. We would love to put it down, we would like to cast it aside, but if we do it is our fear that there will be a gap—and the potential for another 9/11—and we would not have done our duty."[88] Similarly, in a 2013 speech given at the National Defense University to address his administration's expansive use of drone strikes, Barack Obama admitted "that U.S. strikes have resulted in civilian casualties" before quickly adding that he "weigh[ed] these heartbreaking tragedies against the alternatives" and concluded that the latter were worse. Ultimately, for Obama, "doing nothing is not an option."[89] In these ways, both Alexander and Obama portrayed surveillance and drone technology, which they considered problematic, as tragic necessities. Because there is no alternative to "doing something," all one *can* do is feel bad.

U.S. officials feel guilty about the consequences of their foreign and security policies because the American Empire was supposed to be a liberal one whose embrace of reason, rationality, and law would ensure that it governed the world humanely and, to some degree, democratically. But as the political scientist Patrick Porter has aptly pointed out, world ordering is an inherently violent and illiberal project.[90] It is for this reason that liberal imperialists, similar to their forebears in the British and French empires, have embraced the idea that, as the political theorist Jeanne Morefield puts it, "tragedy produces liberal character."[91] Put another way, the feelings of guilt that liberals experience when they make "tragic" decisions in a "barbarous" world is the very thing that, liberals implicitly claim, *makes them liberal.* The argument goes as follows: If liberals didn't act, they wouldn't be liberal; and if they didn't feel guilty about the consequences of their actions, they also wouldn't be liberal. This is the logic that results in the apologetic and guilt-ridden affect central to imperialist realism.

This notion of tragic guilt permeates American popular culture. Christopher Nolan's 2023 mega-hit *Oppenheimer*, which grossed around $330,000,000 at the domestic box office, provides a salient example of this trend.[92] In a scene that occurs after the United States dropped its first atomic bomb on Hiroshima, the eponymous protagonist (played by Irish actor Cillian Murphy) gives a speech before an auditorium packed with scientists and their families. Until this moment, Oppenheimer pursued the bomb with unquestioning fervor. But the physicist's speech is anything but triumphant: the sound design, camerawork, and acting make clear beyond the shadow of a doubt that the sheer destruction caused by the bomb has led Oppenheimer to second-guess, and feel guilty about, his life's work. Yet after this scene, though he rails against the creation of the hydrogen bomb, the filmic Oppenheimer never again questions his role in the Manhattan Project. In effect, Oppenheimer moves on; in time, the bombs dropped on Hiroshima and Nagasaki become remembered as tragic necessities that prevented thousands of American soldiers from dying on the Japanese archipelago. This is a precise example of imperialist realism: a feeling of guilt almost immediately followed by a tragic acceptance, all underpinned by the idea that no other world is possible.

Portrayals of tragic guilt show up not only in prestige films such as *Oppenheimer* but also in more popcorn fare. Take, for instance, 2016's *Captain America: Civil War*, the thirteenth film in the

Marvel Cinematic Universe (MCU) franchise, which has grossed more than $30 billion worldwide, making it the most successful film franchise of all time.[93] *Civil War* was a huge hit, earning about $408,000,000 at the domestic box office.[94] It's also among the MCU's best reviewed films, enjoying a 90 percent critics' rating on Rotten Tomatoes.[95] The film's primary story concerns the titular "civil war" between the superheroes themselves. To make a long story short, the MCU's superheroes are split over whether they should be required to operate under the auspices of the United Nations. On one side stands Iron Man (played by Robert Downey, Jr.), who insists superheroes should be subject to some form of democratic control. On the other is Captain America (played by Chris Evans), who maintains that superheroes should not be held in thrall to any politician or bureaucrat.

In essence, *Captain America: Civil War* pits those who favor the democratic regulation of military force against those who don't. And, predictably in our age of imperialist realism, the film is very much on the latter's side. *Civil War*'s main antagonist is Helmut Zemo (played by the German actor Daniel Brühl). Zemo's primary goal, he informs Captain America, is "to see an empire fall." For this reason, he's created an army of super soldiers to destroy the Avengers, the superhero team to which Iron Man and Captain America belong. Though he is forbidden from doing so, Captain America decides to go after Zemo, ignoring the laws meant to constrain him in service of what he considers the greater good. This puts him at odds with Iron Man, who tries to prevent the captain from seizing Zemo. After several brutal fights, the movie ends with the Avengers fractured; some superheroes are willing to work with Iron Man and the United Nations, while others go on the lam with Captain America. Crucially, Iron Man allows Captain America to break his like-minded colleagues out of the prison to which they were confined after one of the film's battles. In this way, *Captain America: Civil War* embraces the tragic affect of imperialist realism. It would be great, the film suggests, if we lived in a world where all superheroes could be subject to democratic control without this causing significant harm. But unfortunately, Iron Man—and *Civil War*—concludes that we don't live in that world, and for this reason, justice requires that rogues such as Captain America be given free rein to do what they want absent government interference. Captain America thus acts like the United States does in real life—both the superhero and the country exist in a permanent state of exception, in which they determine what is right and what is wrong. Neither Captain America nor the United States can imagine a world in which they aren't free to crush their enemies whenever they desire. Such is the nature of imperialist realism.

The Eternal Present and Moving Beyond Imperialist Realism

The most important effect of imperialist realism is that it encourages U.S. foreign policymakers and ordinary Americans alike to conclude that there is no alternative to American Empire—that genuine, structural transformation is impossible and should therefore not be pursued. Imperialist realism strangles the American imagination, preventing us from thinking beyond an empire that has not only caused significant damage at home and abroad but also has reached the limits of its power.[96] Ironically for citizens of a nation that in the last decades has fought several "history wars," Americans tend to live in an eternal present in which they believe themselves to be, to quote the historian William Appleman Williams, "beyond history."[97]

The United States' arming of Ukraine after Russia's February 2022 invasion provides a salient example of this phenomenon. As policymakers and analysts debated whether the United States should send more and more weapons to Ukraine, they almost never referenced the actual history of U.S. intervention overseas. Instead, they usually framed the problem of arming Ukraine as an immediate one, effectively beyond history. One would think that the historical effects of U.S. interventions would have been at least mentioned when determining whether to ship matériel to Ukraine. But a historical discussion was either nowhere to be found or, at best, quickly skirted over—even by leftists. At the time of writing, the Russia–Ukraine War grinds on, with between 60,000 and 100,000 Ukrainian soldiers killed and a high of 250,000 Russian soldiers killed, to say nothing of the millions of Ukrainians displaced.[98] Russia, in fact, seems likely to achieve sovereignty over significant portions of eastern Ukraine. Much like it has in the past, American martial aid has prolonged the suffering of local peoples without achieving any significant political goal. Imperialist realism made this outcome likely because departing from past practice and *not* intervening was almost unthinkable.

The question, of course, is how to move beyond imperialist realism. The first step, attempted in this essay, is to identify and articulate its primary features. With this accomplished, we can hopefully begin developing an alternative way of apprehending the world that does not rest on the assumption that the U.S. Empire is a permanent feature of the geopolitical landscape. Though thinking beyond empire from within the empire is a challenging task, it is possible. Indeed, in the last several decades, there have been several glimmers of hope. The alter-globalization movement of the 1990s, Occupy Wall Street in the early 2010s, the rise of "millennial socialism" in the mid 2010s, and the recent campus protests against the Israeli military's annihilation of Gaza all indicate that anti-imperial politics remain extant in the United States. Furthermore, the Trump Administration has enacted a number of changes to the U.S. approach to the world that have shattered liberal shibboleths, which at the very least demonstrate that transformation is possible, even if in this instance the changes mostly are not productive.

World peace requires us to move beyond the imperialist realism that assumes the U.S. Empire will always exist. If we are able to imagine post-imperial utopias, perhaps we can initiate a process that, over time, will help create a more just and equal international order, in which all the nations of the world have some say in what happens on the global stage. This project may fail—it may even be likely to fail—but it must at least be tried.

Endnotes

1 U.S. Office of Management and Budget, "Statement of Administration Policy: H.R. 4016—Department of Defense Appropriations Act, 2026 (Rep. Calvert, R-CA)," July 15, 2025, White House, https://www.whitehouse.gov/wp-content/uploads/2025/07/SAP-HR4016.pdf.

2 David Vine, Patterson Deppen, and Leah Bolger, *Drawdown: Improving U.S. and Global Security Through Military Base Closures Abroad*, Quincy Brief No. 16 (Washington, D.C.: Quincy Institute for Responsible Statecraft, September 20, 2021), https://quincyinst.org/research/drawdown-improving-u-s-and-global-security-through-military-base-closures-abroad/#.

3 Richard Wike, Jacob Poushter, Laura Silver, and Janell Fetterolf, *U.S. Image Declines in Many Nations Amid Low Confidence in Trump* (Washington, D.C.: Pew Research Center, June 2025), 15, https://www.pewresearch.org/global/2025/06/11/us-image-declines-in-many-nations-amid-low-confidence-in-trump/

4 "The Art of the Flyover," National Football League, accessed July 23, 2025, https://www.nfl.com/photos/the-art-of-the-flyover-0ap3000000934319.

5 U.S. Department of Defense, Office of Local Defense Community Cooperation, *Defense Spending by State: Fiscal Year 2023* (Washington, D.C.: U.S. Department of Defense, 2024), 17, 121, https://oldcc.gov/defense-spending-state-fiscal-year-2023.

6 William Appleman Williams, "Empire as a Way of Life," *The Nation* 231, no. 4, August 2–9, 1980, 104–107, 110–119; William Appleman Williams, *Empire as a Way of Life: An Essay on the Causes and Character of America's Present Predicament Along with a Few Thoughts About an Alternative* (New York: Oxford University Press, 1980).

7 Williams, "Empire as a Way of Life," 104.

8 "Google Ngram Viewer," accessed May 1, 2025. This shift was anticipated as early as 2004, when an official in the George W. Bush Administration, widely believed to be Senior Advisor Karl Rove, told the *New York Times Magazine* that the United States was "an empire now, and when we act, we create our own reality." Ron Suskind, "Faith, Certainty and the Presidency of George W. Bush," *New York Times Magazine*, October 17,

2004, https://www.nytimes.com/2004/10/17/magazine/faith-certainty-and-the-presidency-of-george-w-bush.html. Unfortunately, I could not locate a poll in which Americans were directly asked whether their nation was an empire, but the evidence cited is suggestive.

9 Dina Smeltz, "American Support for Active U.S. Global Role Not What It Used to Be," Chicago Council on Global Affairs, August 22, 2024, https://globalaffairs.org/research/public-opinion-survey/american-support-active-us-global-role-not-what-it-used-be.

10 Ibid.

11 Jeffrey M. Jones, "Steady 66% Want Leading or Major World Role for U.S.," Gallup, March 6, 2025, https://news.gallup.com/poll/657725/steady-leading-major-world-role.aspx.

12 Dina Smeltz and Craig Kafura, "Americans Grow Less Enthusiastic about Active U.S. Engagement Abroad," Chicago Council on Global Affairs, October 12, 2023, https://globalaffairs.org/research/public-opinion-survey/americans-grow-less-enthusiastic-about-active-us-engagement-abroad.

13 The concept of imperialist realism repurposes critic Mark Fisher's idea of capitalist realism, which he defined as "the widespread sense that not only is capitalism the only viable political and economic system, but also that it is now impossible even to *imagine* a coherent alternative to it." Mark Fisher, *Capitalist Realism: Is There No Alternative?* (Winchester, UK: Zer0 Books, 2009), 2.

14 George S. Patton, "The Invasion Speech to the Third Army," in Terry Brighton, *Patton, Montgomery, & Rommel: Masters of Battle* (New York: Random House, 2008), 261.

15 Megan Brenan, "Majority in U.S. Still Say Gov't Should Ensure Healthcare," Gallup, January 23, 2023, https://news.gallup.com/poll/468401/majority-say-gov-ensure-healthcare.aspx; Jeffrey M. Jones, "More in U.S. See Health Coverage as Government Responsibility," Gallup, December 9, 2024, https://news.gallup.com/poll/654101/health-coverage-government-responsibility.aspx.

16 Raymond Williams, *Marxism and Literature* (Oxford: Oxford University Press, 1977), 133–34.

17 The features of imperialist realism discussed in this essay do not exhaust the concept's content but serve only as a starting point for further investigation.

18 There is a large literature on the "militarism" of the United States. The most important work on this subject remains Michael S. Sherry, *In the Shadow of War: The United States since the 1930s* (New Haven, CT: Yale University Press, 1995). See also Andrew J. Bacevich, *The New American Militarism: How Americans Are Seduced by War* (New York: Oxford University Press, 2005).

19 Stephen Wertheim, *Tomorrow, the World: The Birth of U.S. Global Supremacy* (Cambridge, MA: Harvard University Press, 2020).

20 Walter Lippmann, *Public Opinion* (New York: The Macmillan Company, 1943 [1922]); Walter Lippmann, *The Phantom Public* (New Brunswick, NJ: Transaction Publishers, 2011 [1925]).

21 John Dewey, "Public Opinion," review of *Public Opinion* by Walter Lippmann, *The New Republic* 30, no. 387, May 3, 1922, 286–288; John Dewey, "Practical Democracy," review of *The Phantom Public* by Walter Lippmann, *The New Republic* 45, no. 574, December 2, 1925, 52–54; John Dewey, *The Public and Its Problems* (New York: Henry Holt and Company, 1927).

22 Daniel Bessner, *Democracy in Exile: Hans Speier and the Rise of the Defense Intellectual* (Ithaca, NY: Cornell University Press, 2018), 76–79.

23 Bessner, *Democracy in Exile*, chapter 3.

24 Wertheim, *Tomorrow, the World*, chapter 2.

25 Bessner, *Democracy in Exile*, chapters 2, 3, and 5; Anders Stephanson, *American Imperatives: The Cold War and Other Matters* (New York: Verso, 2025), chapter 2.

26 Gallup Organization, Gallup Poll # 1941-0255: World War II/ Employment, 1941 [Dataset], Roper #31087238, Version 3, Gallup Organization [producer], Cornell University, Ithaca, NY: Roper Center for Public Opinion Research [distributor], https://ropercenter.cornell.edu/ipoll/study/31087238. Trends had been moving in a pro-intervention direction, at least when it came to the European war. In November 1941, 45 percent of Americans agreed that "the government has correctly recognized that Hitler is a threat to the United States, and in general it has followed the best course in doing all it can to help defeat

Hitler." Furthermore, 82 percent disagreed with the idea that "the war in the rest of the world is not likely to affect the United States, and there is no need for such a large defense program." Nevertheless, at this point in time, 11 percent of Americans still agreed with the statement that "the government has brought us much closer to the war in Europe than is necessary" and that "the best thing now is to stop doing anything that might bring us closer to the war." National Opinion Research Center (NORC), NORC Survey: Attitude Toward War in Europe, 1941 [Dataset], Roper #31094951, Version 3. National Opinion Research Center (NORC) [producer], Cornell University, Ithaca, NY: Roper Center for Public Opinion Research [distributor], https://ropercenter.cornell.edu/ipoll/study/31094951.

27 Gallup Organization, Gallup Poll # 1947-0396: Politics/Russia-US Relations, 1947 [Dataset], Roper #31087379, Version 4. Gallup Organization [producer], Cornell University, Ithaca, NY: Roper Center for Public Opinion Research [distributor], https://ropercenter.cornell.edu/ipoll/study/31087379 .

28 "About Declarations of War by Congress," U.S. Senate, accessed July 23, 2025, https://www.senate.gov/about/powers-procedures/declarations-of-war.htm; Monica Duffy Toft and Sidita Kushi, *Dying by the Sword: The Militarization of U.S. Foreign Policy* (New York: Oxford University Press, 2023), 14; Sidita Kushi and Monica Duffy Toft, "Introducing the Military Intervention Project: A New Dataset on U.S. Military Interventions, 1776–2019," *Journal of Conflict Resolution* 67, no. 4 (April 2023), 767.

29 Bessner, *Democracy in Exile*; David Allen, *Every Citizen a Statesman: The Dream of a Democratic Foreign Policy in the American Century* (Cambridge, MA: Harvard University Press, 2023).

30 Martin Gilens and Benjamin I. Page, "Testing Theories of American Politics: Elites, Interest Groups, and Average Citizens," *Perspectives on Politics* 12, no. 3 (September 2014), 564.

31 NORC at the University of Chicago, *Civic Cynicism in the United States: A Typology of Americans* (Chicago: NORC at the University of Chicago, November 2024), 1, https://www.norc.org/content/dam/norc-org/pdf2024/lsu-report.pdf.

32 "Terrorism," Gallup, accessed July 23, 2025, https://news.gallup.com/poll/4909/terrorism-united-states.aspx.

33 George W. Bush, "Address Before a Joint Session of the Congress on the State of the Union" (speech, Washington, D.C., January 29, 2002), in John T. Woolley and Gerhard Peters, ed., *The American Presidency Project* (Santa Barbara, CA, 1999–2025), https://www.presidency.ucsb.edu/documents/address-before-joint-session-the-congress-the-state-the-union-22.

34 "Summary of Findings," Costs of War Project, Thomas J. Watson Jr. School of International and Public Affairs, Brown University, accessed July 23, 2025, https://watson.brown.edu/costsofwar/papers/summary; U.S. Department of Defense, "Casualty Status as of 10 a.m. EST Jan. 30, 2025 [Operation Iraqi Freedom, Operation New Dawn, Operation Enduring Freedom, Operation Inherent Resolve, Operation Freedom's Sentinel]," accessed July 23, 2025, https://www.defense.gov/casualty.pdf.

35 John Sapienza and Yuliya Geikhman, "15 Best-Selling Call of Duty Games," *Screenrant*, September 17, 2024, https://screenrant.com/call-of-duty-best-selling-games/.

36 Eddie Makuch, "Best-Selling Games of Each Year Since 1998 in the U.S.," *Gamespot*, January 23, 2025, https://www.gamespot.com/gallery/best-selling-games-of-each-of-the-past-25-years-in-the-us/2900-5031/.

37 *Call of Duty: Black Ops Cold War* (Activision, 2020), Sony PlayStation 4; Sapienza and Geikhman, "15 Best-Selling Call of Duty Games"; Michael Caruso, "How Many Call of Duty Games Are There? Full List (2003–2025)," *Esports Insider*, April 23, 2025, https://esportsinsider.com/how-many-call-of-duty-games-are-there.

38 On the "Perseus" myth, see John Earl Haynes and Harvey Klehr, "The Atomic Spy Who Never Was: 'Perseus' and KGB/SVR Atomic Espionage Disinformation," *International Journal of Intelligence and Counterintelligence* 35, no. 3 (Fall 2022), 397–428.

39 Scott Selisker, *Human Programming: Brainwashing, Automatons, and American Unfreedom* (Minneapolis: University of Minnesota Press, 2016).

40 Ibid., 66.

41 On the duality between the "free" world and the "slave" world, see Stephanson, *American Imperatives*, *passim*; Peter Slezkine, "Free World

Leadership and the Limits of Liberalism," in *Cold War Liberalism: Power in a Time of Emergency*, ed. Daniel Bessner and Michael Brenes (New York: Cambridge University Press, 2026).

42 Selisker, *Human Programming*, chapter 2.

43 Madeleine K. Albright, interview by Matt Lauer, *The Today Show*, NBC-TV, Columbus, OH, February 19, 1998, https://1997-2001.state.gov/statements/1998/980219a.html.

44 See Hans J. Morgenthau, *Politics among Nations: The Struggle for Power and Peace* (New York: Alfred A. Knopf, 1948), 17–18; Kenneth N. Waltz, *Man, the State, and War* (New York: Columbia University Press, 1959), chapter 2.

45 In this way, the game's message mirrors its form—players of first-person shooters can win only by killing people.

46 Activision had long collaborated with military officials. Most infamously, in 2012, Oliver North, the disgraced lieutenant colonel who helped orchestrate the Iran–Contra scandal, consulted for, and appeared in, *Call of Duty: Black Ops II*. See Stephen Totilo, "*Call of Duty* Creators Say Oliver North Helped Make Their Game More Authentic," *Kotaku*, May 24, 2012, https://kotaku.com/call-of-duty-creators-say-oliver-north-helped-make-thei-5913092.

47 On the unipolar moment, see Charles Krauthammer, "The Unipolar Moment," *Foreign Affairs* 70, no. 1 (Winter 1990–1991), 23–33; Christopher J. Griffin, "Dilemmas of Dominance: American Strategy from George H.W. Bush to Barack Obama," in *The New Makers of Modern Strategy: From the Ancient World to the Digital Age*, ed. Hal Brands (Princeton, NJ: Princeton University Press, 2023), 869–894.

48 Here, I counted only references to U.S. "interests." See George W. Bush, *The National Security Strategy of the United States of America* (Washington, D.C.: White House, March 2006), https://history.defense.gov/Portals/70/Documents/nss/nss2006.pdf; Joseph R. Biden, Jr., *National Security Strategy* (Washington, D.C.: White House, October 2022), https://bidenwhitehouse.archives.gov/wp-content/uploads/2022/10/Biden-Harris-Administrations-National-Security-Strategy-10.2022.pdf.

49 Bush, *National Security Strategy*, 15.

50 Joseph R. Biden, Jr., "Remarks by President Biden on Afghanistan" (speech, Washington, D.C., August 16, 2021), Biden White House, https://bidenwhitehouse.archives.gov/briefing-room/speeches-remarks/2021/08/16/remarks-by-president-biden-on-afghanistan/.

51 Joseph R. Biden, Jr., "Remarks by President Biden on the End of the War in Afghanistan" (speech, Washington, D.C., August 31, 2021), Biden White House, https://bidenwhitehouse.archives.gov/briefing-room/speeches-remarks/2021/08/31/remarks-by-president-biden-on-the-end-of-the-war-in-afghanistan/.

52 U.S. Office of Management and Budget, "Statement of Administration Policy: H.R. 4016," 1.

53 Biden, *National Security Strategy*, 8.

54 Antony J. Blinken and Lloyd Austin, "Secretary Antony J. Blinken and Secretary Lloyd Austin Remarks to Traveling Press" (remarks, Poland, April 25, 2022), U.S. Department of State [2021–2025], https://2021-2025.state.gov/secretary-antony-j-blinken-and-secretary-lloyd-austin-remarks-to-traveling-press/.

55 Antony J. Blinken and Ursula von der Leyen, "Secretary Blinken and European Commission President Ursula von der Leyen Before Their Meeting" (remarks, Belgium, March 4, 2022), U.S. Department of State [2021–2025], https://2021-2025.state.gov/secretary-antony-j-blinken-and-european-commission-president-ursula-von-der-leyen-before-their-meeting-2/.

56 Antony J. Blinken, "Secretary Antony J. Blinken At the 'Call for Action: Urgent Humanitarian Response for Gaza' Conference" (remarks, Jordan, June 11, 2024), U.S. Department of State [2021–2025], https://2021-2025.state.gov/secretary-antony-j-blinken-at-the-call-for-action-urgent-humanitarian-response-for-gaza-conference/.

57 On officials' supposed desire for independent Palestinian statehood, see Joseph R. Biden, Jr. and Anthony Albanese, "Remarks by President Biden and Prime Minister Anthony Albanese of Australia in Joint Press Conference" (remarks, Washington, D.C., October 25, 2023), Biden White House, https://bidenwhitehouse.archives.gov/briefing-room/speeches-remarks/2023/10/25/remarks-by-president-biden-and-prime-

minister-anthony-albanese-of-australia-in-joint-press-conference/; Matthew Miller, Office of the Spokesperson, U.S. Department of State, "Secretary Blinken's Meeting with Palestinian Authority President Abbas," February 7, 2024, U.S. Department of State [2021–2025], https://2021-2025.state.gov/secretary-blinkens-meeting-with-palestinian-authority-president-abbas-4/.

58 Ali Harb, "'Empty Words': Advocates Say Biden's Gaza Ceasefire Nod at DNC Falls Short," *Al Jazeera*, August 20, 2024, https://www.aljazeera.com/news/2024/8/20/empty-words-advocates-say-bidens-gaza-ceasefire-nod-at-dnc-falls-short; Ali Harb, "Trump's Role in Gaza Ceasefire Fuels Arab American Anger with Biden," *Al Jazeera*, January 17, 2025, https://www.aljazeera.com/news/2025/1/17/trumps-role-in-gaza-ceasefire-fuels-arab-american-anger-with-biden.

59 Jacob Magid, "Biden Officials Vent Frustrations in Dealing with Netanyahu, Decry Missed Chance of Saudi Deal," *The Times of Israel*, April 28, 2025, https://www.timesofisrael.com/top-biden-aide-israel-missed-opportunity-for-saudi-deal-hopefully-it-wont-do-so-again/.

60 On Israeli war crimes, see United Nations General Assembly, United Nations Human Rights Council, *Report of the Independent International Commission of Inquiry on the Occupied Palestinian Territory, including East Jerusalem, and Israel*, A/HRC/59/26 (May 6, 2025), https://docs.un.org/en/A/HRC/59/26.

61 The question as to why members of the foreign policy establishment ignore recent mistakes is outside the scope of this essay. Potential reasons include self-identification with the imperial project, the desire to retain their jobs, and a belief that this is the best of all possible worlds.

62 Joseph R. Biden, Jr., "Remarks by President Biden on the United States' Response to Hamas's Terrorist Attacks Against Israel and Russia's Ongoing Brutal War Against Ukraine" (speech, Washington, D.C., October 20, 2023), Biden White House, https://bidenwhitehouse.archives.gov/briefing-room/speeches-remarks/2023/10/20/remarks-by-president-biden-on-the-unites-states-response-to-hamass-terrorist-attacks-against-israel-and-russias-ongoing-brutal-war-against-ukraine/.

63 Walter Russell Mead and Antony Blinken, "Dialogues on American Foreign Policy and World Affairs: A Conversation with Former Deputy

Secretary of State Antony Blinken" (conversation, Washington, D.C., July 9, 2020), Hudson Institute, https://www.hudson.org/foreign-policy/transcript-dialogues-on-american-foreign-policy-and-world-affairs-a-conversation-with-former-deputy-secretary-of-state-antony-blinken.

64 Ashley Parker and Michael Scherer, "'I Run the Country and the World': Donald Trump Believes He's Invincible. But the Cracks Are Beginning to Show," April 28, 2025, https://www.theatlantic.com/magazine/archive/2025/06/trump-second-term-comeback/682573/.

65 Biden, *National Security Strategy*, 2.

66 Joseph R. Biden, Jr., "Remarks by President Biden at United States Coast Guard Academy's 140th Commencement Exercises" (speech, Connecticut, May 19, 2021), Biden White House, https://bidenwhitehouse.archives.gov/briefing-room/statements-releases/2021/05/19/remarks-by-president-biden-at-united-states-coast-guard-academys-140th-commencement-exercises/.

67 Donald J. Trump, "Remarks on Foreign Policy" (speech, Washington, D.C., April 27, 2016), in John T. Woolley and Gerhard Peters, ed., *The American Presidency Project* (Santa Barbara, CA, 1999–2025), https://www.presidency.ucsb.edu/documents/remarks-foreign-policy.

68 John Winthrop, "Christian Charity, A Model Hereof," in *As a City on a Hill: The Story of America's Most Famous Lay Sermon*, by Daniel T. Rodgers (Princeton, NJ: Princeton University Press, 2018), 307.

69 Ivo H. Daalder and James M. Lindsay, *The Empty Throne: America's Abdication of Global Leadership* (New York: PublicAffairs, 2018).

70 Ibid., 3.

71 Ibid.

72 Ibid., 4.

73 Ibid.

74 Lindsey A. O'Rourke, *Covert Regime Change: America's Secret Cold War* (Ithaca, NY: Cornell University Press, 2018), 3, 12.

75 Paul Thomas Chamberlin, *The Cold War's Killing Fields: Rethinking the Long Peace* (New York: HarperCollins, 2018), 19.

76 Kushi and Toft, "Introducing the Military Intervention Project," 767.

77 Daalder and Lindsay, *The Empty Throne*, 2.

78 *The Lord of the Rings: The Rings of Power*, season 1, episode 1, "A Shadow of the Past," directed by J.A. Bayona, written by John D. Payne, Patrick McKay, and J.R.R. Tolkien, aired September 1, 2022, Amazon Prime Video (streaming).

79 Eliana Dockterman, "The Secretive, Extravagant, Bighearted World of *The Rings of Power*, the Most Expensive Show Ever Made," *Time*, August 15, 2022, https://time.com/6205837/the-rings-of-power-amazon-most-expensive/.

80 Ted Dickens, "The Easy Way Out!" *The National Insider* 12, no. 25 (June 16, 1968), 3–4.

81 Don Feder, "A Ringing Affirmation of a Moral Universe," *Jewish World Review*, December 31, 2001, http://www.jewishworldreview.com/cols/feder123101.asp.

82 "Game of Thrones—Statistics & Facts," Statista, March 26, 2025, https://www.statista.com/topics/4187/game-of-thrones/.

83 George R.R. Martin, the author of the book series *A Song of Ice and Fire*, upon which *Game of Thrones* is based, has stated that his books were in part meant to provide a more quotidian and realistic fantasy series when compared to Tolkien's *Lord of the Rings*. As Martin told *Rolling Stone*, in his opinion "*Lord of the Rings* had a very medieval philosophy: that if the king was a good man, the land would prosper. We look at real history and it's not that simple. … Tolkien doesn't ask the question: What was Aragorn's tax policy?" Nevertheless, even as Martin criticized Tolkien for writing about "a war for the fate of civilization and the future of humanity" when "the vast majority of wars throughout history are not like that," he wound up reproducing Tolkien's Manichaean assumptions, suggesting that certain fantasy worlds require an existential enemy to function. George R.R. Martin, "The Man Behind the Thrones: The *Rolling Stone* Interview," interview by Mikal Gilmore, *Rolling Stone* iss. 1208 (May 8, 2014), 42.

84 George W. Bush, "President Holds Prime Time News Conference" (remarks, Washington, D.C., October 11, 2001), George W. Bush White House, https://georgewbush-whitehouse.archives.gov/news/releases/2001/10/20011011-7.html.

85 Mead and Blinken, "A Conversation with Former Deputy Secretary of State Antony Blinken."

86 "Social & Political Costs," Costs of War Project, Thomas J. Watson Jr. School of International and Public Affairs, Brown University, accessed July 24, 2025, https://watson.brown.edu/costsofwar/costs/social; "Human Rights and Civil Liberties," Costs of War Project, Thomas J. Watson Jr. School of International and Public Affairs, Brown University, accessed July 24, 2025, https://watson.brown.edu/costsofwar/costs/social/rights; William D. Hartung, *Profits of War: Corporate Beneficiaries of the Post-9/11 Pentagon Spending Surge*, 20 Years of War: A Costs of War Research Series (Providence, RI: Watson Institute of International and Public Affairs and Center for International Policy, September 13, 2021), 4, https://watson.brown.edu/costsofwar/files/cow/imce/papers/2021/Profits%20of%20War_Hartung_Costs%20of%20War_Sept%2013%2C%202021.pdf; Richard W. Waterman, *Constitutional Ambiguity and the Interpretation of Presidential Power* (Albany: State University of New York Press, 2025), 229.

87 Jody Rosen, "When George W. Bush Confused Russia's War in Ukraine with Iraq," *New York Times Magazine*, June 8, 2022, https://www.nytimes.com/2022/06/08/magazine/george-w-bush-russia-war-iraq.html.

88 Paul Lewis, "NSA Chief Keith Alexander Blames Diplomats for Surveillance Requests," *The Guardian*, October 31, 2013, https://www.theguardian.com/world/2013/nov/01/nsa-keith-alexander-blames-diplomats-surveillance-foreign-leaders.

89 Barack Obama, "Remarks by the President at the National Defense University" (speech, Washington, D.C., May 23, 2013), Obama White House, https://obamawhitehouse.archives.gov/the-press-office/2013/05/23/remarks-president-national-defense-university.

90 Patrick Porter, *The False Promise of Liberal Order: Nostalgia, Delusion and the Rise of Trump* (Cambridge: Polity, 2020), 21.

91 Jeanne Morefield, *Empires Without Imperialism: Anglo-American Decline and the Politics of Deflection* (New York: Oxford University Press, 2014), 202.

92 *Oppenheimer*, directed by Christopher Nolan (Universal Pictures, 2023), 180 minutes; "Oppenheimer (2023) [Box Office Gross]," Box Office Mojo, accessed July 25, 2025, https://www.boxofficemojo.com/title/tt15398776/.

93 *Captain America: Civil War*, directed by Anthony Russo and Joe Russo (Walt Disney Studios Motion Pictures, 2016), 147 minutes, Disney+ (streaming); Katharina Buchholz, "The World's Biggest Movie Franchises," Statista, July 29, 2024, https://www.statista.com/chart/32732/most-successful-movie-franchises-by-worldwide-box-office-gross/.

94 "Captain America: Civil War [Box Office Gross]," Box Office Mojo, accessed July 25, 2025, https://www.boxofficemojo.com/release/rl3210970625/.

95 "All 36 Marvel MCU Movies Ranked (*Thunderbolts, Ant-Man*)," Rotten Tomatoes, accessed July 25, 2025, https://editorial.rottentomatoes.com/guide/all-marvel-cinematic-universe-movies-ranked/.

96 See "Empire Burlesque," this volume.

97 Andrew Hartman, *A War for the Soul of America: A History of the Culture Wars*, 2nd ed. (Chicago: University of Chicago Press, 2019), chapter 9; Williams, "Empire as a Way of Life," 104.

98 Seth G. Jones and Riley McCabe, *Russia's Battlefield Woes in Ukraine*, CSIS Briefs (Washington, D.C.: Center for Strategic and International Studies, June 2025), 11, 2, https://www.csis.org/analysis/russias-battlefield-woes-ukraine; "Ukraine Emergency," United Nations Refugee Agency, accessed July 25, 2025, https://www.unrefugees.org/emergencies/ukraine/.

THE PRINCIPLES OF A DEMOCRATIC SOCIALIST FOREIGN POLICY

As the insurgent left wing of the Democratic Party captures headlines and wins votes, many of its supporters are coalescing around a growing set of policy priorities: universal health care, higher taxes on the rich, the abolition of Immigration and Customs Enforcement. But when it comes to matters of war and peace and to America's place in the world, the Left is either silent or confused.

In the 2016 Democratic presidential primary campaign, Bernie Sanders did not make foreign policy a focus. Alexandria Ocasio-Cortez recently dismissed questions about the Israel–Palestine conflict by claiming she was "not the expert on geopolitics on this issue."[1] And as other candidates across the United States scramble to get votes from self-declared socialists by, say, supporting single-payer health care, few feel the need to appeal to the Left on foreign policy.

To be fair, there are good reasons leftists haven't grappled much with foreign policy. For one, there are few decision-makers they can learn from: since the early days of the Cold War, a bipartisan commitment to militarism and American hegemony has dominated foreign policymaking; those who depart from the consensus view have largely been kept out of the State Department, the Pentagon, and other parts of the government. At the same time, the Left itself lacks institutions dedicated to developing foreign policy ideas. While Republicans and moderate Democrats have a host of think tanks pushing interventionism, no corporation or billionaire has yet decided to fund a left-wing foreign policy think tank to which politicians could turn for advice.

But if the left wing of the Democratic Party wants to be taken seriously, it must speak convincingly about security and diplomacy. Without core, identifiable beliefs about foreign affairs, left-wing politicians will either embarrass themselves or repeat some version of the tired conventional wisdom. Moreover, there is an opportunity here: just as many Americans are fed up with the economic status quo, so too are they fed up with business as usual in foreign policy.

A foreign policy for the Left won't emerge overnight. A conversation is just starting to take place, and it will continue as more socialists win power and shape American politics. Though a concrete agenda remains a ways off, there are five broad principles that merge the Left's commitments to egalitarianism and popular sovereignty with a sober analysis of the limits of American power.

Democracy

Left-wing politics is, at its heart, about giving power to ordinary people. Foreign policy, especially recently, has been about the opposite. Since the 1940s, unelected officials ensconced in bodies such as the National Security Council have been the primary makers of foreign policy. This trend has worsened since the September 11 attacks, as Congress has relinquished its oversight role and granted officials in the executive branch and the military carte blanche. Foreign policy elites have been anything but wise and have promoted several of the worst foreign policy blunders in American history, including the wars in Vietnam and Iraq.

The Left should aim to bring democracy into foreign policy. This means taking some of the power away from the executive and, especially, White House institutions, such as the National Security Council, and returning it to Congress. In particular, socialist politicians should push to reassert Congress' long-abdicated role in declaring war, encourage more active oversight of the military, and create bodies that make national security information available to the public so that Americans know exactly what their country is doing abroad.

Accountability

The American foreign policy establishment is notoriously forgiving—of itself. Rarely are policymakers held to account when they offer bad advice, such as supporting a disastrous war in Iraq or helping organize torture or assassinations. This amnesia has plagued Democrats and Republicans alike.

This unaccountability cannot continue. A system that does not punish poor foreign policymaking is a system doomed to repeat its mistakes. Politicians on the left should make this a core tenet of their approach to foreign policy by promising that when they are elected, they will hold decision-makers and advisers professionally accountable.

But professional accountability is not enough. The Left should demand that those who violated domestic or international law see justice, even if that means prosecuting them. It will enable the Left to demonstrate to both the American people and the international community that it is serious about the rule of law.

Anti-militarism

The United States controls roughly 750 military bases in dozens of countries around the world. This is far more than any other power. The United States also spends more on its military than China, Russia, Saudi Arabia, India, France, Britain, and Japan combined. American Special Operations forces were deployed to 149 countries as of last year. Reducing this military footprint, and thus lessening the havoc the United States wreaks abroad, must be a priority for the Left.

This reduction should be framed as both a foreign policy goal and an issue of domestic justice. It is unconscionable that the United States spends so much on its military while inequality grows and social programs are underfunded. Cutting military spending will also address another priority of the Left: corruption. As William Hartung at the Center for International Policy has argued, almost half the military budget goes to private corporations that squander our tax dollars "on useless overhead, fat executive salaries, and startling (yet commonplace) cost overruns on weapons systems and other military hardware that, in the end, won't even perform as promised."[2] A less militaristic United States is a more just United States.

Threat Deflation

We can bring our troops home and cut the military budget because the United States doesn't face any serious external challengers. North Korea, Iran, the Islamic State, Russia, and China can't challenge American sovereignty in the ways Nazi Germany or the Soviet Union once did. While there are serious global threats, none is existential and none is unmanageable. But for too long politicians have inflated international threats to justify military adventurism, boost military spending, increase domestic surveillance, and campaign on a politics of fear.

The Left should change that. Candidates and policymakers alike should educate the public about the United States' relative safety. Such education will encourage a military drawdown, engender a more honest domestic politics, and protect Americans' civil liberties.

Internationalism

None of this means that the United States should retreat from the world. Rather, America should engage with other countries through peaceful diplomacy. An important first step would be to embrace international treaties and institutions endorsed by most nations, such as the Paris Agreement on climate change and the International Criminal Court. Moreover, policymakers should urge disarmament talks with all major powers and reinstate the Iran nuclear deal.

The Left should also commit itself to reducing global economic inequality by reordering the hierarchical relationships that benefit rich countries over poor ones. For example, the Left should not allow American-led corporations to use underpaid and abused workers to produce inexpensive products. Policymakers should also prevent the wealthy from avoiding taxation by working with foreign countries to shutter tax havens.

Finally, the Left should take human rights seriously. In particular, left-wing foreign policymakers should pressure allies such as Saudi Arabia and Israel to stop committing human rights abuses by withholding arms transfers and other forms of assistance.

What's Next?

A democratic socialist left is shaping the conversation in American politics right now. This makes it necessary for left-wing politicians to think beyond bread-and-butter issues and to develop new ways of approaching the United States' world role. An explicit program may not yet exist, but the five principles discussed above can serve as the base upon which future leaders can build a left-wing foreign policy that ushers in a more just and peaceful era.

Endnotes

1 Sydney Ember, "From New York to the Heartland: Ocasio-Cortez Debuts on National Campaign Stage," *New York Times*, July 20, 2018, https://www.nytimes.com/2018/07/20/us/politics/ocasio-cortez-bernie-sanders.html.

2 William D. Hartung, "The Scandal of Pentagon Spending: Your Tax Dollars Support Troops of Defense Contractor CEOs," *TomDispatch*, October 10, 2017, https://tomdispatch.com/william-hartung-how-the-military-industrial-complex-preys-on-the-troops/.

EMPIRE BURLESQUE

In February 1941, as Adolf Hitler's armies prepared to invade the Soviet Union, the Republican oligarch and publisher Henry R. Luce laid out a vision for global domination in an article titled "The American Century."[1] World War II, he argued, was the result of the United States' immature refusal to accept the mantle of world leadership after the British Empire had begun to deteriorate in the wake of World War I. American foolishness, the millionaire claimed, had provided space for Nazi Germany's rise. The only way to rectify this mistake and prevent future conflict was for the United States to join the Allied effort and

> accept wholeheartedly our duty and our opportunity as the most powerful and vital nation in the world and … exert upon the world the full impact of our influence, for such purposes as we see fit and by such means as we see fit.[2]

Just as the United States had conquered the American West, the nation would subdue, civilize, and remake international relations.

Ten months after Luce published his essay, the Japanese attacked Pearl Harbor, and the United States, which had already been aiding the Allies, officially entered the war. Over the next four years, a broad swath of the foreign policy elite arrived at Luce's conclusion: the only way to guarantee the world's safety was for the United

States to dominate it. By war's end, Americans had accepted this righteous duty, of becoming, in Luce's words, "the powerhouse ... lifting the life of mankind from the level of the beasts to what the Psalmist called a little lower than the angels."[3] The American Century had arrived.

In the decades that followed, the United States implemented a grand strategy that the historian Stephen Wertheim has fittingly termed "armed primacy."[4] According to the strategy's noble advocates, human flourishing, international order, and the future of liberal democratic capitalism depended on the nation's spreading its tentacles across the world. Whereas the United States had been wary of embroiling itself in extra-hemispheric affairs before the twentieth century, Old Glory could now increasingly be seen flying across the globe. To facilitate their crusade, Americans constructed what the historian Daniel Immerwahr has dubbed a "pointillist empire."[5] While most empires traditionally relied on the seizure and occupation of vast territories, the United States built military bases around the world to project its power. From these outposts, it launched wars that killed millions, protected a capitalist system that benefited the wealthy, and threatened any power—democratic or otherwise—that had the temerity to disagree with it.

As Luce desired, by the end of the twentieth century, the United States, a nation founded after one of the first modern anti-colonial revolutions, had become a world-spanning empire. The "city on a hill" had evolved into a fortified metropolis.

But in the past six years, two transformational events have begun to reshape the United States' place in the world. First, Donald Trump's election suggested to domestic and foreign audiences alike that the country might not be forever beholden to the idea that global "leadership" is a vital American interest. Instead of proclaiming the inviolability of the vaunted "liberal international order," Trump approached international relations as any corrupt businessman would: he tried to get the most while giving the least. He thus withdrew from several international organizations and agreements—including the World Health Organization, the Paris climate agreement, the Iran nuclear deal, the Intermediate-Range

Nuclear Forces Treaty, and the Open Skies Treaty—and initiated trade wars intended to boost American business. Taken with his bellicose rhetoric, these actions demonstrated that the world could no longer assume that the United States was committed to defending the geopolitical status quo.

Second, China's emergence as an economic and military powerhouse has decisively ended the "unipolar moment" of the nineties and aughts.[6] The country only recently referred to as a "rising tiger" (Orientalism never dies) now boasts, according to some measures, the largest military and economy on Earth.[7] The Asian Infrastructure Investment Bank and New Development Bank offer alternatives to the World Bank, International Monetary Fund, and other Western-dominated institutions, which, to put it mildly, aren't exactly beloved in the Global South.

For the first time since the collapse of the Soviet Union, the United States confronts a nation whose model—a blend of state capitalism and Communist Party discipline—presents a genuine challenge to liberal democratic capitalism, which seems increasingly incapable of addressing the many crises that beset it. China's rise, and the glimmers of the alternative world that might accompany it, make clear that Luce's American Century is in its final days. It's not obvious, however, what comes next. Are we doomed to witness the return of great power rivalry, in which the United States and China vie for influence? Or will the decline of U.S. power produce novel forms of international collaboration?

In these waning days of the American Century, Washington's foreign policy establishment—the think tanks that define the limits of the possible—has splintered into two warring camps. Defending the status quo are the liberal internationalists, who insist that the United States should retain its position of global armed primacy. Against them stand the restrainers, who urge a fundamental rethinking of the American approach to foreign policy, away from militarism and toward peaceful forms of international engagement. The outcome of this debate will determine whether the United States remains committed to an atavistic foreign policy ill-suited to the twenty-first century or whether the nation will take seriously the disasters of the past decades, abandon the hubris that has caused so much suffering worldwide, and, finally, embrace a grand strategy of restraint.

***

The principles of liberal internationalism were first articulated by Woodrow Wilson as World War I limped along in April 1917. The American military, the president told a joint session of Congress, was a force that could be used to make the world "safe for democracy."[8] (The United States would decide, of course, which countries counted as democracies.) Wilson's doctrine was informed by two main ideas: first, the Progressive Era fantasy that modern technologies and techniques—especially those borrowed from the social sciences—could enable the rational management of foreign affairs, and second, the notion that "a partnership of democratic nations" was the surest way to establish "a steadfast concert for peace."[9] Wilson's two Democratic successors, Franklin Delano Roosevelt and Harry S. Truman, institutionalized their forebear's approach, and since the forties, every president save Trump has embraced some form of liberal internationalism. Even George W. Bush put together a "coalition of the willing" to invade Iraq and insisted that his wars were being waged to spread democracy.[10]

Given liberal internationalism's unquestioned dominance in the halls of power, it's not surprising that its dogma still has the support of Washington's most influential think tanks, which have never been known to bite the hand that feeds them. Members of the Council on Foreign Relations, the Brookings Institution, and the Center for a New American Security consider U.S. hegemony to be an essential condition for global peace and American prosperity. According to these stalwart backers of U.S. supremacy, the fact that a major war between great powers has not broken out since World War II indicates that U.S. hegemony has been, on balance, a force for good.

This is not to say that liberal internationalists are living in the past. They appreciate that, unlike during World War II or the Cold War, most countries agree on the rules of the game. Neither China, nor even Iran and Venezuela, reject the Western international order in the way that Nazi Germany and the Soviet Union did. While states may break rules to advance their interests, few countries are genuine pariahs; in fact, Russia and North Korea might be the only ones. In the modern era, even adversaries interact extensively. During the Cold War, the United States and Soviet Union barely traded with each other. Now, China is one of the United States' largest trading partners.

This raises a question for liberal internationalists: How should the United States compete in this new world and contain "threats" to the established order? Unfortunately, most have converged on an answer from the past: whether they call it "democratic multilateralism," "the strategy of reinvigorating the free world," or "a fully developed democracy strategy," liberal internationalists hope to establish a coalition of democracies akin to the one that existed during the Cold War, although this time centered on democracies (or, at least, non-autocracies) in the Global South.[11] While claiming to reject the framing of a "new Cold War" with China that has permeated U.S. media, liberal internationalists promote what is effectively a Cold War-era strategy with a few more non-white countries added to the mix.

Like their Cold War predecessors, liberal internationalists believe that their struggle for democracy—and against China, which they regard as the major threat to U.S. power—will last indefinitely. As Michael Brown, Eric Chewning, and Pavneet Singh asserted in a recent Brookings Institution report, the United States must prepare for a "superpower marathon"—"an economic and technology race" with China that is unlikely to reach a "definitive conclusion."[12] American society, the liberal internationalists avow, will have to remain on a war footing for the foreseeable future. Peace is unthinkable.

The Chinese military, which employs more active personnel than any other nation, is of particular concern to liberal internationalists. To combat the threat of Chinese coercion in East Asia, they endorse a strategy in which the United States retains tens of thousands of troops in Japan and South Korea. This aggressive posture, they argue, will convince Chinese leaders that any anti-American actions they take will fail. And, ironically for those who have spent the past few years lambasting Russia for interfering in the 2016 presidential election, liberal internationalists also want to wage an information war against China, smuggling unflattering or damaging information into the country in an attempt to foment anti-communist dissent.

When it comes to the economy, liberal internationalists are bedeviled by the questions of whether, and if so, how much to confront China—a country that has repeatedly stolen U.S. intellectual property and rejects liberal capitalist ideals of the free market. On one hand, they worry that China could wield its economic power to force other countries to abide by its wishes. On the other, they believe that free exchange is vital to the United States' economic health. Liberal internationalists thus recommend that the nation adopt an approach whereby it pressures China economically, but within the bounds of international rules, norms, and laws. In this way, they hope to combat China without discrediting liberalism writ large. As this suggests, liberal internationalists are well aware of the beating that American prestige has taken in recent years, especially after the wars in Afghanistan and Iraq and the 2008 financial crisis. If the United States is to dominate, it has to abide by rules that in the past it was all too happy to break.

In effect, liberal internationalists want to have it both ways, to challenge China without risking a shooting war or economic decoupling. The problem, however, is that international relations are not nearly as manageable as liberal internationalists assume. The Russian invasion of Ukraine—which was at least partially impelled by NATO expansion into Eastern Europe—is a clear example of how behavior meant to deter war might very well incite it. Yet these basic facts are difficult for liberal internationalists to admit. For them, the American Century can be restored only by facing China head-on.

***

Restrainers, by contrast, understand that the American Century is over. They maintain that the expansive use of the U.S. military has benefited neither the United States nor the world, and that charting a positive course in the twenty-first century requires taking a root-and-branch approach to the principles that have guided U.S. foreign policy since World War II. Restrainers want to reduce the U.S. presence abroad, shrink the defense budget, restore Congress' constitutional authority to declare war, and ensure that ordinary Americans actually have a say in what their country does abroad.

The origins of restraint can be traced to George Washington's September 1796 farewell address, in which the president warned against "entangl[ing] our peace and prosperity in the toils of European ambition, rivalship, interest, humor, or caprice."[13] Twenty-five years later, on July 4, 1821, the secretary of state, John Quincy Adams, likewise insisted that a defining characteristic of the United States was that it had "abstained from interference in the concerns of others … She goes not abroad in search of monsters to destroy."[14] Restraint remained popular for much of the nineteenth and early twentieth centuries; during World War I, for instance, Wilson received substantial criticisms from those who argued that the United States should avoid undertaking messianic projects to remake the world. Of course, the history of U.S. foreign policy is far from one of restraint. From its beginnings, the United States expanded westward, displacing and killing Indigenous peoples and eventually seizing a number of populated colonies in the Pacific and Caribbean.

Nevertheless, if restraint did not always apply in practice, the strategy attracted many adherents. Things changed during World War II when restraint became associated with anti-Semitic "America Firsters," politically marginal libertarians and pacifists, and discredited "isolationists." In the Democratic Party, the former vice president Henry Wallace and other progressive restrainers were sidelined, as were Senator Robert A. Taft and other Republican anti-interventionists. Although restraint continued to percolate in social movements such as the Vietnam War resistance of the sixties and in think tanks such as the Cato Institute and the Institute for Policy Studies, it remained a negligible position until the foreign policy failures in Afghanistan, Iraq, and Libya.

In the wake of these blunders, interest in restraint has been reignited, as evidenced by the fact that two think tanks—Defense Priorities and the Quincy Institute, where I serve as an unpaid nonresident fellow—were recently founded with the goal of advocating for its fundamental principles. Gil Barndollar of Defense Priorities has usefully summarized the restrainers' limited set of foreign policy goals: helping to realize "the security of the U.S. itself, free passage in the global commons, the security of U.S. treaty allies, and preventing the emergence of a Eurasian hegemon."[15] Because the major problems of the twenty-first century cannot be solved by U.S. military force but instead require multilateral cooperation with nations that have adopted different political systems, there is no reason for the United States to promote democracy abroad or act as the global police force.

Accordingly, restrainers do not consider China an existential threat. When it comes to East Asia, their goal is to prevent war in the region so as to facilitate collaboration on global issues such as climate change and pandemics. This objective, they maintain, can be achieved without American hegemony.

Restrainers thus promote a "defensive, denial-oriented approach" focused on using the U.S. military to prevent China from controlling East Asia's air and seas.[16] They also want to help regional partners develop the ability to resist China's influence and power and argue that the United States should place its forces far from the Chinese coast, in clearly defensive positions. A similarly hands-off approach applies to Taiwan and human rights. If China wants to seize Taiwan, restrainers assert, then the United States should not fight World War III to prevent it from doing so. If China wants to oppress its population, there's not much that the United States can or should do about it.

The fundamental disagreement between the two schools of thought is this: liberal internationalists believe that the United States can manage and predict foreign affairs. Restrainers do not. For those of us in the latter camp, the withering away of the American Century cannot be reversed; it can only be accommodated.

***

The question of which strategy the United States should pursue is essentially a matter of historical interpretation. Was U.S. domination during the American Century good for the United States? Was it good for the world?

When one takes a long, hard look at U.S. foreign policy after 1945, it's clear that the United States caused an enormous amount of suffering that a more restrained approach would have avoided. Some of these American-led fiascoes are infamous: the wars in Korea, Vietnam, Afghanistan, and Iraq resulted in the death, displacement, and deracination of millions of people. Then there are the many lesser-known instances of the United States helping to install its preferred leaders abroad. During the Cold War alone, the nation imposed regime changes in Iran, Guatemala, Congo, British Guiana, Chile, South Vietnam, Bolivia, Brazil, and Panama.[17]

As this record suggests, the Cold War was hardly "the long peace" that many liberal internationalists valorize.[18] It was, rather, incredibly violent. The historian Paul Thomas Chamberlin estimates that more than 20 million people died in Cold War-era conflicts, the equivalent of more than 1,200 deaths a day for 45 years.[19] And U.S. intervention didn't end with the Cold War. Including the conflicts in Afghanistan, Iraq, and Libya, the United States militarily intervened abroad 112 times between 1990 and 2019, according to the Military Intervention Project at Tufts University.[20] And as Brown University's Costs of War Project has determined, by 2019 the Global War on Terror had been used to justify operations in almost half the world's countries.[21]

Such interventions obviously violated the principle of sovereignty—the very basis of international relations. But more importantly, they produced awful outcomes. As the political scientist Lindsey O'Rourke has underlined, countries targeted for regime change by the United States were more likely to experience civil wars, mass killings, human rights abuses, and democratic backsliding than those that were ignored.[22]

When it comes to the benefits that ordinary Americans received from their empire, it's similarly difficult to defend the historical record. It's true that in the three decades after World War II, armed primacy ensured favorable trade conditions that allowed Americans to consume more than any other group in world history (causing incredible environmental damage in the process). But as the New Deal gave way to neoliberalism, the benefits of supremacy attenuated. Since the late seventies, Americans have been suffering the negative consequences of empire—a militarized political culture, racism and xenophobia, police forces armed to the teeth with military-grade weaponry, a bloated defense budget, and endless wars—without receiving much in return, save for the psychic wages of living in the imperial metropole.

The more one considers the American Century, in fact, the more our tenure as global hegemon resembles a historical aberration. Geopolitical circumstances are unlikely to allow another country to become as powerful as the United States has been for much of the past seven decades. In 1945, when the nation first emerged triumphant on the world stage, its might was staggering. The United States produced half the world's manufactured goods, was the source of a third of the world's exports, served as the global creditor, enjoyed a nuclear monopoly, and controlled an unprecedented military colossus. Its closest competitor was a crippled Soviet Union struggling to recover from the loss of more than 20 million citizens and the devastation of significant amounts of its territory.

The United States' power was similarly astounding after the Soviet Union's collapse in the early nineties, especially when one aggregates its strength with that of its Western allies. In 1992, the G7 countries—Canada, France, Germany, Italy, Japan, the United Kingdom, and the United States—controlled 68 percent of global

GDP and maintained sophisticated militaries that, the Gulf War seemed to demonstrate, could achieve their objectives quickly, cheaply, and with minimal loss of Western life.[23]

But this is no longer the case. By 2020, the G7's GDP had dwindled to a little under 31 percent of the global total, and it is expected to fall to about 29 percent by 2024.[24] This trend will likely continue. And if the past 30 years of American war have demonstrated anything, it's that sophisticated militaries do not always achieve their intended political objectives. The United States and its allies aren't what they once were. Hegemony was an anomaly, an accident of history unlikely to be repeated, at least in the foreseeable future.

***

There are also more fundamental, even ontological, problems with the liberal internationalist approach. Liberal internationalism is a product of the fin de siècle, when Progressive thinkers, activists, and policymakers across the political spectrum believed that rationality could achieve mastery over human affairs. But the dream proved to be just that. No nation, no matter how powerful, has the capacity to control international relations—an arena defined by radical uncertainty—in the ways that Woodrow Wilson and other Progressives had hoped. The world is not a chessboard.

Furthermore, liberal internationalists' democracy-first strategy assumes a Manichaean model of geopolitics that is both inconsistent and counterproductive. For all their crowing about democracy, liberal internationalists have been just fine collaborating with dictatorships, from Saudi Arabia to Egypt, when it has served perceived U.S. interests. This will probably remain true, making any kind of democracy-first strategy a primarily discursive one. Nonetheless, discursively centering democracy could have drastic repercussions. Dividing the world into "good" democracies and "bad" authoritarian regimes narrows the space for engagement with many countries not currently aligned with the United States.

Decision-makers who view autocracies as inevitable opponents are less likely to take their interests seriously and may even misread their intentions. This happened repeatedly in the fifties and sixties, when U.S. officials insisted that the very nature of the Soviet system made it impossible to reach détente. In fact, détente was only achieved in the seventies, after decision-makers had concluded that the Soviet Union was best treated as a normal nation with normal interests, regardless of its political structure. Once Americans adopted this approach, it became clear that the Soviets, like them, preferred superpower stability to nuclear war.

Because it's difficult to know precisely what a government such as China's is up to, liberal internationalists tend to flatten the complexities that shape its behavior and assume that China will expand to the limits of its power. This idea owes much to the classical realist school of foreign policy, which, following the émigré political scientist Hans Morgenthau, maintains that nations have an *animus dominandi*, a will to dominate.[25] (The United States, unsurprisingly, is assumed to act according to more noble motivations.) For this reason, some liberal internationalists claim, China will fill any power vacuum it can.

But is this an accurate description of China—or, indeed, of any modern nation? Classical realism was born of the traumas of the thirties, when two great powers, Nazi Germany and imperial Japan, considered the conquest of foreign territory vital to their futures. The experience of German and Japanese expansion profoundly shaped the work of midcentury thinkers such as Morgenthau, who insisted that the search for *Lebensraum* reflected more general laws of international relations.

Unfortunately for those liberal internationalists indebted to classical realism, states make the decisions they do for many reasons, from regime type (Is a nation a democracy or an autocracy?) to individual psychology (Is a particular leader mentally well?) to culture (What behavior does a given nation valorize?). When it comes to trying to explain why China—or Russia or Iran or North Korea—acts as it does, it's not particularly useful to ignore everything that makes the country unique in favor of emphasizing immutable factors.

The historicist approach of restrainers is a far better way to analyze international relations. Restrainers focus on what China has done, not on what it might do; for them, China is a state that exists in the world, with its own interests and concerns, not an abstraction embodying transhistorical laws (which themselves reflect American anxieties).

And when examining what China has done, the evidence is clear: while the nation obviously wants to be a major power in East Asia, and while it hopes to one day conquer Taiwan, there's little to suggest that, in the short term at least, it aims to replace the United States as the regional, let alone global, hegemon. Neither China's increased military budget (which pales in comparison to the United States' $800 billion) nor its foreign development aid (which is not linked to a recipient country's politics) indicates that it desires domination. In fact, Chinese leaders, who tolerate the presence of tens of thousands of troops stationed near their borders, appear willing to allow the United States to remain a major player in Asia, something Americans would never countenance in the Western Hemisphere.

Ironically, liberal internationalists are imposing their own goals for hegemony onto China. Their commitment to armed primacy—a commitment that has led to war after war—threatens to increase tensions with a country that Americans must cooperate with to solve the real problems of the twenty-first century: climate change, pandemics, and inequality. When compared with these existential threats, the liberal internationalist obsession with primacy is a relic of a bygone era. For the sake of the world, we must move beyond it.

***

At the present moment, however, a majority of Americans side with the liberal internationalists, especially when forced to compare U.S. leadership with Chinese leadership: in a Pew poll taken in early

2020, "91% of Americans say it is better for the U.S. to be the world's leading power than China," up from 88 percent in 2018.[26]

Nonetheless, there's a growing generational divide over the future of U.S. foreign policy. A 2018 report by the Chicago Council on Global Affairs and the Charles Koch Institute, for instance, revealed that only 44 percent of millennials believed that it's "very important" for the United States to maintain "superior military power worldwide," compared with 64 percent of boomers.[27] In a Pew poll from 2019, meanwhile, "nearly half of adults younger than 30 (48%) [said] it would be acceptable if another country becomes as militarily powerful [as the United States], compared with 28% of adults ages 50 and older."[28]

The fact that younger Americans are waking up to the manifold and manifest failures of liberal internationalism presents the United States with an enormous opportunity: it can abandon an irresponsible and hubristic liberal internationalism for restraint. This will, admittedly, be a difficult task. Americans have ruled the world for so long that they see it as their right and duty to do so (especially since most don't have to fight their nation's wars). Members of Congress, meanwhile, get quite a bit of money, and their districts even get a few jobs, from defense contractors. Both retired generals and pointy-headed intellectuals rely on the defense industry for employment. And restraint is still a minority position in the major political parties.

It's an open question whether U.S. foreign policy can transform in a way that fully reflects an understanding of the drawbacks of empire and the benefits of a less violent approach to the world. But policymakers must plan for a future beyond the American Century, and reckon with the fact that attempts to relive the glories of an inglorious past will not only be met with frustration but could even lead to war.

The American Century did not achieve the lofty goals that oligarchs such as Henry Luce set out for it. But it did demonstrate that attempts to rule the world through force will fail. The task for the next 100 years will be to create not an American Century but a Global Century, in which U.S. power is not only restrained but reduced, and in which every nation is dedicated to solving the problems that threaten us all. As the title of a best-selling book from 1946 declared, before the Cold War precluded any attempts at genuine international cooperation, we will have either "one world or none."[29]

Endnotes

1 Henry R. Luce, "The American Century," *Life* 10, no. 7 (February 17, 1941), 61–65.

2 Ibid., 63.

3 Ibid., 65.

4 Stephen Wertheim, *Tomorrow, the World: The Birth of U.S. Global Supremacy* (Cambridge, MA: Harvard University Press, 2020), 4.

5 Daniel Immerwahr, *How to Hide an Empire: A History of the Greater United States* (New York: Farrar, Straus and Giroux, 2019), 18.

6 On the unipolar moment, see Charles Krauthammer, "The Unipolar Moment," *Foreign Affairs* 70, no. 1 (Winter 1990–1991), 23–33; Christopher J. Griffin, "Dilemmas of Dominance: American Strategy from George H.W. Bush to Barack Obama," in *The New Makers of Modern Strategy: From the Ancient World to the Digital Age*, ed. Hal Brands (Princeton, NJ: Princeton University Press, 2023), 869–894.

7 On China as a "rising tiger," see *China's Indigenous Innovation Trade and Investment Policies: How Great a Threat? Hearing before the Subcommittee on Terrorism, Nonproliferation, and Trade of the Committee on Foreign Affairs*, 112th Cong., 1st sess., 87, (2021) (statement of Gerald E. Connolly, Representative, Virginia), https://www.congress.gov/112/chrg/CHRG-112hhrg65057/CHRG-112hhrg65057.pdf. On China having the world's largest military in terms of active military personnel, see "Active Military Manpower (2022)," Global Firepower, archived November 9, 2022, at the Wayback Machine, https://www.globalfirepower.com/active-military-manpower.php. On China having the world's largest economy in terms of purchasing power parity, see "Gross Domestic Product 2022, PPP," World Bank, accessed August 4,

2025, https://databankfiles.worldbank.org/public/ddpext_download/GDP_PPP.pdf.

8 Woodrow Wilson, "Address to a Joint Session of Congress Requesting a Declaration of War Against Germany" (speech, Washington, D.C., April 2, 1917), in John T. Woolley and Gerhard Peters, ed., *The American Presidency Project* (Santa Barbara, CA, 1999–2025), https://www.presidency.ucsb.edu/documents/address-joint-session-congress-requesting-declaration-war-against-germany.

9 Ibid.

10 George W. Bush and Václav Havel, "President Bush, President Havel Discuss Iraq, NATO" (remarks, Czech Republic, November 20, 2002), George W. Bush White House, https://georgewbush-whitehouse.archives.gov/news/releases/2002/11/20021120-1.html; George W. Bush, "President Meets with Cabinet" (remarks, Washington, D.C., March 20, 2023), George W. Bush White House, https://georgewbush-whitehouse.archives.gov/infocus/iraq/news/20030320-5.html; George W. Bush, "President Bush Discusses Freedom in Iraq and Middle East" (speech, Washington, D.C., November 6, 2003), George W. Bush White House, https://georgewbush-whitehouse.archives.gov/news/releases/2003/11/20031106-2.html.

11 Bruce Jones and Adam Twardowski, *Bolstering Democracies in a Changing International Order: The Case for Democratic Multilateralism*, Brookings Blueprints for American Renewal & Prosperity Project (Washington, D.C.: Brookings Institution, January 25, 2021), https://www.brookings.edu/articles/bolstering-democracies-in-a-changing-international-order-the-case-for-democratic-multilateralism/; Thomas Wright, *Advancing Multilateralism in a Populist Age* (Washington, D.C.: Brookings Institution, February 2021), 8, https://www.brookings.edu/wp-content/uploads/2021/02/FP_20210204_multilateralism_wright_v2.pdf; Patrick W. Quirk, David O. Shullman, and Johanna Kao, *Democracy First: How the U.S. Can Prevail in the Political Systems Competition with the CCP*, Global China: Assessing China's Growing Role in the World (Washington, D.C.: Brookings Institution, September 2020), 2, https://www.brookings.edu/wp-content/uploads/2020/09/FP_20200914_democracy_assistance_quirk_shullman_kao.pdf.

12 Michael Brown, Eric Chewning, and Pavneet Singh, *Preparing the United States for the Superpower Marathon with China*, Global China: Assessing China's Growing Role in the World (Washington, D.C.: Brookings Institution, April 2020), 1, 6, https://www.brookings.edu/wp-content/uploads/2020/04/FP_20200427_superpower_marathon_brown_chewning_singh.pdf.

13 George Washington, "Farewell Address" (letter, Philadelphia, September 17, 1796 [published on September 19]), in John T. Woolley and Gerhard Peters, ed., *The American Presidency Project* (Santa Barbara, CA, 1999–2025), https://www.presidency.ucsb.edu/documents/farewell-address.

14 John Quincy Adams, *An Address, Delivered at the Request of the Committee of Arrangements for Celebrating the Anniversary of Independence, at the City of Washington on the Fourth of July 1821, upon the Occasion of Reading the Declaration of Independence* (Cambridge, MA: Hilliard and Metcalf, 1821), 31–32, https://www.google.com/books/edition/An_Address_Delivered_at_the_Request_of_t/QjM5AQAAMAAJ?hl=en&gbpv=0.

15 Gil Barndollar, *Global Posture Review 2021: An Opportunity for Realism and Realignment* (Washington, D.C.: Defense Priorities, July 12, 2021), 2, https://www.defensepriorities.org/wp-content/uploads/2024/03/DEFP_Global_Posture_Review_2021.pdf.

16 Michael D. Swaine, Jessica J. Lee, and Rachel Esplin Odell, "China & East Asia," in *A New Direction: A Foreign Policy Playbook on Military Restraint for the Biden Team*, QI Papers (Washington, D.C.: Quincy Institute for Responsible Statecraft, December 3, 2020), 6, https://quincyinst.org/research/a-new-direction-a-foreign-policy-playbook-on-military-restraint-for-the-biden-team/#.

17 Lindsey A. O'Rourke, *Covert Regime Change: America's Secret Cold War* (Ithaca, NY: Cornell University Press, 2018), 3.

18 John Lewis Gaddis, *The Long Peace: Inquiries into the History of the Cold War* (New York: Oxford University Press, 1987).

19 Paul Thomas Chamberlin, *The Cold War's Killing Fields: Rethinking the Long Peace* (New York: HarperCollins, 2018), 19.

20 Sidita Kushi and Monica Duffy Toft, "Introducing the Military Intervention Project: A New Dataset on U.S. Military Interventions, 1776–2019," *Journal of Conflict Resolution* 67, no. 4 (April 2023), 767.

21 Stephanie Savell and 5W Infographics, "This Map Shows Where in the World the U.S. Military Is Combatting Terrorism," *Smithsonian Magazine*, January 2019, https://www.smithsonianmag.com/history/map-shows-places-world-where-us-military-operates-180970997/.

22 O'Rourke, *Covert Regime Change*, 12.

23 Barry P. Bosworth, "Not-So-Great Expectations: The G-7's Waning Role in Global Economic Governance," Brookings Institution, May 24, 2016, https://www.brookings.edu/articles/not-so-great-expectations-the-g-7s-waning-role-in-global-economic-governance/; H.R. McMaster, *Crack in the Foundation: Defense Transformation and the Underlying Assumption of Dominant Knowledge in Future War* (Carlisle Barracks, PA: Center for Strategic Leadership, U.S. Army War College, Student Issue Paper, Volume S03-03, November 2003), https://media.defense.gov/2023/May/02/2003213354/-1/-1/0/3177.PDF; Samuel Moyn, *Humane: How the United States Abandoned Peace and Reinvented War* (New York: Farrar, Straus and Giroux, 2021), 225–226.

24 "G7 Countries' Share of the World's Gross Domestic Product (GDP) from 2000 to 2024, by Country," Statista, accessed July 27, 2025, https://www.statista.com/statistics/1370614/g7-country-gdp-share-world/.

25 Morgenthau translates the term as "the desire for power." See Hans J. Morgenthau, *Scientific Man versus Power Politics* (Chicago: University of Chicago Press, 1965 [1946]), 192.

26 Kat Devlin, Laura Silver, and Christine Huang, *U.S. Views of China Increasingly Negative Amid Coronavirus Outbreak* (Washington, D.C.: Pew Research Center, April 2020), 17, https://www.pewresearch.org/global/wp-content/uploads/sites/2/2020/04/PG_2020.04.21_U.S.-Views-China_FINAL.pdf; Kat Devlin, "Americans Leery of China as Trump Prepares to Meet Xi at G20," Pew Research Center, November 30, 2018, https://www.pewresearch.org/short-reads/2018/11/30/americans-leery-of-china-as-trump-prepares-to-meet-xi-at-g20/.

27 Trevor Thrall, Dina Smeltz, Erik Goepner, Will Ruger, and Craig Kafura, *The Clash of Generations? Intergenerational Change and American Foreign Policy Views* (Chicago: Chicago Council on Global Affairs and

Charles Koch Institute, June 2018), 13, https://globalaffairs.org/sites/default/files/2021-01/report_clash-of-generations_180625.pdf.

28 *In a Politically Polarized Era, Sharp Divides in Both Partisan Coalitions* (Washington, D.C.: Pew Research Center, December 2019), 14, https://www.pewresearch.org/politics/wp-content/uploads/sites/4/2019/12/PP_2019.12.17_Political-Values_FINAL.pdf.

29 Dexter Masters and Katharine Way, eds., *One World or None: A Report to the Public on the Full Meaning of the Atomic Bomb* (New York: Whittlesey House, McGraw-Hill Book Company, 1946).

PART II

PORTRAITS

BARACK OBAMA AND THE PROCESS PRESIDENCY

If journalism is history's first draft, administration memoirs are its second.

Freed from the daily scrum that comes with being a high-ranking leader, officials use memoirs to justify their choices and, they hope, rewrite history from their points of view. Memoirs are thus not especially interesting for what they reveal about the goings-on of a particular administration—the truth won't come out until the documents do—but for what they say about how a person hopes to be remembered.

And given the sheer number of memoirs released since they left office, the Obamanauts are anxious about how they'll be remembered. You can read Alyssa Mastromonaco's *Who Thought This Was a Good Idea?*; Pete Souza's *Obama: An Intimate Portrait*; Pat Cunnane's *West Winging It*; Dan Pfeiffer's *Yes We (Still) Can*; Ben Rhodes's *The World as It Is*; Valerie Jarrett's *Finding My Voice*; Samantha Power's *The Education of an Idealist*; or Susan Rice's *Tough Love.*[1] In various ways, these books retell stories from the Obama White House as they attempt to explain how an administration meant to augur a new type of post-partisan politics paved the way for Donald Trump.

But in the final analysis, these books are a sideshow—what everyone really wants to know is what the Big Kahuna himself thinks about things. Finally, after four years of waiting, we can start to answer that question by reading Barack Obama's 768-page doorstop, *A Promised Land*, the first of a planned two-volume memoir for which the president, in a joint deal with his wife, Michelle, received a $65 million advance, far eclipsing Bill Clinton's record-setting $15 million payday for his 2004 autobiography *My Life*.[2]

For socialists, *A Promised Land* is undeniably frustrating. The book adopts a circular form: Obama claims that his horizon is the left-wing position, details how any particular goal was impossible to achieve, and argues that his compromise solution was therefore a small but necessary victory on the road to progress.

As this suggests, Obama, who never lacked for confidence, is satisfied with his accomplishments in office. He's certain that he did his "very best," especially because he followed the *process*.[3] And it is the process that provides the lodestar for Obama's presidency.

> With a sound process — one in which I was able to empty out my ego and really listen, following the facts and logic as best I could and considering them alongside my goals and my principles — I realized I could make tough decisions and still sleep easy at night, knowing at a minimum that no one in my position, given the same information, could have made the decision any better.[4]

For Obama, process is politics; he is the ultimate subject of the "end of history." For him, and for the Obamanauts who served under him, the fundamental questions of modernity—How do we organize a society? What does democracy mean? What is the best system of political economy? Should the United States "lead" the world?—have been asked and answered. And this is why

Obama's was a process presidency—he believed that his project was a restorationist one, in which his primary duty as president was to restore faith in an American system damaged by the failures of George W. Bush. Even the election of Donald J. Trump, whose victory was propelled by ordinary people disgusted with that very system, cannot compel him to ask fundamental questions about the polity he led for eight years.

This inability suggests that Obama's presidency, initially identified as an example of liberalism's efflorescence, actually signaled its decline. Liberals such as Obama can no longer provide satisfactory solutions to the problems that bedevil Americans. After his two terms, the United States remains highly unequal, U.S. troops are still mired in Afghanistan, and little has been done to arrest climate change. No amount of "process" will solve these problems—what is required is the political will to transform the system from which they emerged.

And it is precisely this will that Obama not only lacked but also considered somewhat ridiculous.

***

Obama believes in America. "The pride in being American, the notion that America was the greatest country on earth," he affirms in no uncertain terms, "was always a given" to him.[5] There are personal reasons for his attachment to the United States. As the child of a white American woman and a Black Kenyan man and who spent his childhood in Hawaii and Indonesia, Obama long felt "unsure of where [he] belonged."[6] It was only when he identified himself with the United States, essentially equating his own success with his nation's, that he finally "locate[d] a community and purpose for [his] life."[7]

But how could a Black man, well-versed in the crimes committed by Americans at home and abroad—in fact, he moved to Indonesia a year after a U.S.-assisted genocide killed at least half a million people there—so fully identify with the United

States? The answer is surprisingly simple: for Obama, "the *idea* of America, the *promise* of America," was always more important than American realities.[8]

Nowhere is this truer than in the realm of foreign policy. Similar to many liberal internationalists, Obama understands that recent U.S. history is littered with mistakes that had disastrous effects on people's lives. When recounting the history of the post–World War II period, for example, he admits that Americans "bent global institutions to serve Cold War imperatives or ignored them altogether; we meddled in the affairs of other countries, sometimes with disastrous results; our actions often contradicted the ideals of democracy, self-determination, and human rights we professed to embody."[9] Nonetheless, and in contradiction with the story he just told, he affirms that the United States simultaneously embraced a "willingness to act on behalf of a common good."[10]

Obama doesn't even attempt to square this circle. For him, the idea of America always triumphs over its reality. At least Trump admitted that the United States, like all great powers, was home to "a lot of killers."[11]

And it is perhaps for this reason that Obama, who ran a campaign in which he promised to transform the United States, failed to seize the historical moment and change a system that had engendered two catastrophic foreign interventions and the worst economic depression since the 1930s. Certain that the arc of American history bends toward justice, he was satisfied with pursuing ameliorative programs that preserved the structures that had failed so many.

***

It's therefore unsurprising that, by the end of Obama's time in office, the United States' foreign policy remained relatively unchanged. Though he successfully withdrew troops from Iraq, the nation retained thousands of troops in Afghanistan; led a disastrous intervention in Libya; sold weapons and provided intelligence to Saudi Arabia to support its intervention in Yemen; gave support to

Syrian rebels and sent special operations forces to the country; and failed to attenuate tensions with China and Russia.

Most important, the structure of U.S. Empire endured: the nation still maintained hundreds of foreign military bases, still spent hundreds of billions of dollars on its military, and still had hundreds of thousands of troops deployed abroad. For all of Obama's talk about "hope and change," he was far more interested in the former than the latter.

When Obama first burst onto the national scene, it didn't necessarily look like he would be a politician of the status quo. The first prominent speech of his career was delivered in 2002 in the run-up to the Iraq War. The then-state-senator criticized the "dumb" and "rash" invasion being planned by "weekend warriors" such as Richard Perle and Paul Wolfowitz, presciently predicting "that even a successful war against Iraq will require a U.S. occupation of undetermined length, at undetermined cost, with undetermined consequences."[12]

But even in this early speech, the seeds that would germinate into Obama's static foreign policy were present. He made clear, for instance, that he endorsed wars "in defense of our freedom" (a vague phrase if ever there was one) and that, though he believed that Iraq was a dumb war of choice, Afghanistan and the war on terror were righteous wars of necessity.[13]

Even when he ran for president on an anti–Iraq War platform, Obama took pains to illustrate his embrace of the foreign policy status quo. He refused to sign a pledge that committed him to reducing the defense budget, and he publicly stated that he was willing to violate other nations' sovereignty if it meant that the United States would capture Osama bin Laden.

Nevertheless, Obama did differ from 2008 primary contenders such as Hillary Clinton in one crucial respect: he vigorously endorsed diplomacy. During one primary debate, he declared that, unlike his opponents, he was prepared to sit down and negotiate with Cuba's Fidel Castro, Iran's Mahmoud Ahmadinejad, and North Korea's Kim Jong Il. Though excoriated for this rather quotidian position—an example of the derangement of U.S. national security discourse in the years after the September 11 attacks—Obama held firm. Indeed, the president's greatest foreign policy accomplishments, the diplomatic opening to Cuba and the Iran nuclear deal, stemmed from this early willingness to engage with U.S. adversaries.

***

Besides his commitment to withdraw troops from Iraq, Obama's embrace of diplomacy was his most significant departure from the Bush Administration's foreign policy. In most other ways, he remained tied to the status quo of an increasingly delegitimized empire. This is why Obama's initial national security picks read like a who's who of the foreign policy establishment. He asked Robert M. Gates, "a Republican, a Cold War hawk, [and] a card-carrying member of the national security establishment" to remain on as secretary of defense; he appointed James L. Jones, a retired Marine Corps general who had previously led the European Command, to be his national security advisor; he installed Leon Panetta, Bill Clinton's chief of staff, as the director of the Central Intelligence Agency; and he asked Hillary Clinton to become his secretary of state.[14] All these people, Obama notes, "believed that American leadership"—i.e., U.S. hegemony—"was necessary to keep the world moving in a better direction."[15]

Obama defends these choices in terms of their supposed practicality. While explaining why he requested that Gates stay on as defense secretary, for example, he declares that "any wholesale turnover in the Defense Department seemed fraught with risk."[16] This is no doubt true. But if Obama was serious about "moving America's national security apparatus in a new direction," it's strange to appoint one of the most establishmentarian figures possible to one of the most important positions in his administration.[17]

He also claims that people such as Gates (and Jones and Panetta and Clinton) allowed him to oversee a more effective national security process, in which he was forced to "hear a broad range of perspectives" and "continually test even [his] deepest assumptions against people who had the stature and confidence to tell [him] when [he] was wrong."[18] (Obama, of course, appointed no anti-imperialists, or even heterodox foreign policy thinkers, to his national security team, despite the fact that they, too, would've tested his "deepest assumptions.")

Obama's choices were the correct ones for him. After becoming president, he quickly discovered that he "was a reformer, conservative in temperament if not in vision."[19] And predictably, the national security debates in the White House ran the gamut from A to B, with Obama proudly noting that "even the more liberal members of my team … had no qualms about the use of 'hard power' to go after terrorists and were scornful of leftist critics who made a living blaming the United States for every problem around the globe."[20] Within the first months of his presidency, it was obvious that no genuine strategic change in the American approach to the world was going to emanate from the Obama White House.

Partially for this reason, the antiestablishment energies that engendered Obama's election either went nowhere or migrated to the right wing, helping prepare the path for another Washington outsider to win the presidency in 2016.

***

So what did Obama do while in office? Ironically, given that he was elected on an anti–Iraq War platform, very little of *A Promised Land* is devoted to explaining the president's decision to remove most troops from that country. In Obama's telling, this choice was a no-brainer, and he rapidly approved a plan to withdraw the majority of troops within 19 months (though many Americans stayed in the country for years; today, a few thousand troops remain, as U.S. diplomats traipse around an embassy that cost $750 million).

Afghanistan presented a more significant problem. According to Obama, it was critical for the United States to prevent Hamid

Karzai's government from falling to the Taliban, as this was the only way to ensure that Afghanistan would stop serving as a "terrorist" safe haven. At the same time, Obama avows that he had little desire to transform the country into a functioning democracy, which he believed would take years, if it was ever accomplished.

Military leaders, however, disagreed, maintaining that if they had enough resources, they could accomplish the nation-building mission that George W. Bush had assigned them. Furthermore, many high-ranking officers didn't believe that a civilian who had never served in uniform knew how to conduct a war better than them.

The stage was thus set for a confrontation between the White House and the military.

When Obama entered office, the Joint Chiefs of Staff asked him to send an additional 30,000 troops to Afghanistan. Though he refused to deploy that high a number, in mid-February of 2009, he agreed to send 17,000 troops and 4,000 military trainers to the country.

One month later, Obama received a report on Afghanistan that argued in favor of adopting a policy centered on nation-building. While the president claims he didn't want to approve this plan, "the alternatives were worse. The stakes involved—the risks of a possible collapse of the Afghan government or the Taliban gaining footholds in major cities—were simply too high for us not to act."[21] As such, in late March, he announced the adoption of this new strategy.

Soon thereafter, General Stanley McChrystal, the commander of military forces in Afghanistan, advocated an even more expansive counterinsurgency program. In this, the general had the military's full support. Though Obama again affirms that he was reluctant to embrace McChrystal's strategy, he simultaneously argues that he just "couldn't ignore the unanimous recommendation of experienced generals."[22] To determine what to do, Obama retreated into the process, holding a series of National Security Council meetings to "methodically work through the details of McChrystal's proposal."[23]

The military wasn't having any of it. To circumvent Obama's process, David Petraeus (commander of Central Command), Mike

Mullen (chairman of the Joint Chiefs of Staff), and McChrystal all gave public statements endorsing the latter's strategy, which engendered a flurry of media coverage and impelled Republicans to come out in favor of the military's preferred approach.

This was a serious challenge to Obama, an obvious attempt by the military to undermine the will of the constitutionally mandated commander in chief. To his credit, Obama quickly nipped the mutiny in the bud, summoning Gates and Mullen to his office, dressing them down, and forcing them to promise that the military wouldn't undercut him in the future. (He later dismissed McChrystal for insulting members of his administration in an article printed in *Rolling Stone*.)

Though Obama disciplined the generals, their insouciance reveals that the military has become far too emboldened. As the president highlights, when he entered office, he learned that "basic policy decisions—about war and peace, but also about America's budget priorities, diplomatic goals, and the possible trade-offs between security and other values—had been steadily farmed out to the Pentagon and the CIA."[24] This is a serious problem for a civilian-run society and should become a major focus of criticism for the American left, especially given that, like Trump, Joe Biden decided to nominate a retired military officer as his secretary of defense.

Ironically, and tragically, the generals needn't have worried: in the end, Obama decided to send an additional 30,000 troops to Afghanistan. As usual, all the searching questions Obama asked himself during the process—e.g., "Does anyone think that spinning our wheels in Afghanistan for another ten years will impress our allies and strike fear in our enemies?"—didn't change the final decision to deploy more and more troops.[25] In the end, Obama trusted the experts, and as a matter of course, the foreign policy status quo endured.

Today, thousands of U.S. troops remain deployed in Afghanistan, and it was recently revealed by the *Intercept* that the CIA trained death squads that murdered at least 51 civilians, including children as young as eight years old.

***

Surprisingly, for someone who spent his youth on the peripheries of the American Empire in Hawaii and Indonesia, Obama displays a remarkably dismissive view of countries and leaders outside the North Atlantic. In particular, he suggests that it's ridiculous to imagine that the so-called BRICS (Brazil, Russia, India, China, and South Africa) are ready to exert significant influence on the global stage. Most insultingly (at least from Obama's perspective), he says that Luiz Inácio Lula da Silva, the Brazilian president who is perhaps the most successful center-left politician in modern history, has "the scruples of a Tammany Hall boss."[26]

If only Obama had the scruples of a Tammany Hall boss—then he might have rewarded the millions of workers who voted for him with some semblance of patronage to improve their lot in life.

In addition to criticizing Lula, Obama remarks that Vladimir Putin leads a regime that "resembled a criminal syndicate as much as it did a traditional government"; laments the "corruption and incompetence" of South Africa's African National Congress; and describes India as "a chaotic and impoverished place."[27] Without denying the elements of truth in these descriptions, it's not as if the United States doesn't have its own inequities and problems that, under Obama's framework, should prevent it from "leading" the world. The truth is that Obama simply thinks it's the United States' right and duty to enjoy its imperial privileges.

Indeed, Obama affirms that, for all their complaining, the world's countries actually desire U.S. hegemony. What struck him most, he avows, is that "at every international forum I attended ... even those who complained about America's role in the world still relied on us to keep the system afloat."[28] For Obama, the United States remains the indispensable nation, the only country willing "to act beyond narrow self-interest."[29] In contrast, he argues that the BRICS, and presumably other nations in the Global South, "abided by the established rules only insofar as their own interests were advanced … and they appeared happy to violate them when they thought they could get away with it."[30]

After all, it's not as if the United States has ever disregarded international law by overthrowing democratically elected foreign governments.

As this suggests, Obama devoted himself to "putting out fires that predated [his] presidency" and restoring confidence in a "damaged U.S. leadership."[31] If he failed to achieve these goals, he worried that the "older, darker forces [that] were gathering strength" and replacing "the hopeful tide of democratization, liberalization, and integration that had swept the globe after the end of the Cold War" would ultimately triumph.[32] Tragically, he couldn't see that the exact opposite was true: restoring the pre-Bush ancien régime only heightened the contradictions that engendered Bush's presidency in the first place—contradictions that later impelled Trump's victory. What was needed was a revolution that Obama refused to lead.

***

Though he barely mentions drones in *A Promised Land*, Obama does address the fact that, under his leadership, thousands of people in the Global South, especially young men, were murdered. Dispiritingly, if predictably, all he can do by way of explanation—and, one assumes, expiation—is offer his thoughts and prayers.

> I wanted somehow to save them — send them to school, give them a trade, drain them of the hate that had been filling their heads. And yet the world they were a part of, and the machinery I commanded, more often had me killing them instead.[33]

This statement is typical of *A Promised Land*. On the surface, it appears rather searching: Has any other president so openly articulated the tensions of being the head of the world's most powerful empire? But in actuality, this soliloquy ends precisely where policymaking should begin. Obama never seriously considers how he could alter the structures of exchange and distribution, the structures of the empire he leads, that "warped and stunted" the minds of the young men in Yemen, Afghanistan, Pakistan, Iraq, and Somalia he claims to care about.[34] Instead, his ultimate faith in the American idea allows him to do nothing but feel bad. While he "took no joy" in targeting "terrorists," in the end, "the work was necessary," and that was that.[35]

In fact, Obama didn't really disagree with Bush's anti-terrorism strategy. "Unlike some on the left," he affirms, he had "never engaged in wholesale condemnation of the Bush Administration's approach to counterterrorism (CT)."[36] His intent while in office was merely "to fix those aspects of our CT effort that needed fixing, rather than tearing it out root and branch to start over."[37] It's thus not especially surprising that Obama named John Brennan, a former member of the CIA who had served as acting director of Bush's National Counterterrorism Center, as his counterterrorism head. As with Gates, Jones, Panetta, and Clinton, this was about as establishment a pick as one could have possibly made.

Indeed, a little more than two years after assuming the presidency, Obama committed the military to a new regime change effort, this time in Libya. As usual, Obama avows that he "found the idea of waging a new war in a distant country with no strategic importance to the United States to be less than prudent."[38] And, as usual, he made the militarist choice anyway.

Obama provides humanitarian, multilateralist, and pragmatic explanations for his decision to topple the government of Muammar Gaddafi: Gaddafi was set to massacre innocents in Benghazi; the Arab League had voted to support an international intervention; and he had developed a plan that he believed would engender regime change "swiftly, with the support of allies, and with the parameters of our mission clearly spelled out."[39] Of course, we all know how the story ended: today, Libya is mired in chaos, home to incredible violence and suffering.

***

Obama ran for office claiming to be an Abraham Lincoln or a Franklin Delano Roosevelt. In actuality, he governed like a Bill Clinton, confining himself to the politics of earlier generations. His administration remained tied to Saudi Arabia, Bahrain, and other despotic governments; dismissed Putin's worries about NATO and European Union expansion; did almost nothing to democratize international governing organizations; violated Pakistan's sovereignty to assassinate bin Laden; and paid embarrassing obeisance to Israel. While Obama defends these and other positions by claiming that they were the only realistic options, for him, realism seems to mean doing nothing to upend the traditional U.S. approach to the world.

It's for this reason that it's impossible to believe Obama's assertion that he "was determined to shift a certain mindset that had gripped not just the Bush Administration but much of Washington—one that saw threats around every corner, took a perverse pride in acting unilaterally, and considered military action as an almost routine means of addressing foreign policy challenges."[40] Though the tone of foreign policy did genuinely change under Obama—unlike Bush, he was willing to express humility—this is cold comfort for those who continue to labor under the boot of American Empire. When it came down to it, the military bases remained; the budget remained; and the violence remained.

On a visit to India, Obama offered a comment about Prime Minister Manmohan Singh that reflected his own blinkered approach to governance: "Like me," Obama remarks, Singh:

> had come to believe that [slow, painstaking reform] was all any of us could expect from democracy ... Not revolutionary leaps or major cultural overhauls; not a fix for every social pathology or lasting answers for those in search of purpose and meaning in their lives. Just the observance of rules that allowed us to sort out or at least tolerate our differences, and

> government policies that raised living standards and improved education enough to temper humanity's baser impulses.[41]

According to Obama, the best a president could do was tinker at the margins.

But what Trump's election demonstrated was that tinkering was not, and will never be, enough. When a system fails its people, the people will demand something different. And this is precisely what Obama was congenitally unable to offer, to which the numerous districts that flipped from Obama to Trump in 2016 testify. Ordinary Americans know that the system isn't working for them, and when transformation is on the ballot, they will vote for it, whether it's Obama-style "hope and change" or Trump-style "America first."

Ultimately, Obama cannot admit his own failures. At one point in *A Promised Land*, he goes so far as to ask himself whether it was

> possible that abstract principles and high-minded ideals were and always would be nothing more than a pretense, a palliative, a way to beat back despair, but no match for the more primal urges that really moved us, so that no matter what we said or did, history was sure to run along its predetermined course, an endless cycle of fear, hunger and conflict, dominance and weakness?[42]

Obama seems to think that the answer to this question is "yes"; that there is little anyone can do to really change the world. This is a nihilistic approach to governance that denies the very real power of the president of the United States. It's also ahistorical, as the manifold revolutionary transformations that have occurred in the last century demonstrate.

In retrospect, it appears that Obama was the exact wrong president for the exact right time. Now we can only hope that a genuinely visionary leader, aligned with grassroots movements and dedicated to pushing politics in a more progressive direction, one day becomes president.

Unfortunately, if recent history has revealed anything, it is that we might be waiting quite a while.

Endnotes

1 Alyssa Mastromonaco with Lauren Oyler, *Who Thought This Was a Good Idea? And Other Questions You Should Have Answers to When You Work in the White House* (New York: Twelve, 2017); Pete Souza, *Obama: An Intimate Portrait* (New York: Little, Brown and Company, 2017); Pat Cunnane, *West Winging It: An Un-Presidential Memoir* (New York: Gallery Books, 2018); Dan Pfeiffer, *Yes We (Still) Can: Politics in the Age of Obama, Twitter, and Trump* (New York: Twelve, 2018); Ben Rhodes, *The World as It Is: A Memoir of the Obama White House* (New York: Random House, 2018); Valerie Jarrett, *Finding My Voice: When the Perfect Plan Crumbles, the Adventure Begins* (New York: Viking, 2019); Samantha Power, *The Education of an Idealist: A Memoir* (New York: Dey St., 2019); Susan Rice, *Tough Love: My Story of the Things Worth Fighting For* (New York: Simon and Schuster, 2019).

2 Jim Milliot and Rachel Deahl with additional reporting from Francis Hoch, "The Obamas' Book Deals Spark $65 Million Mystery," *Publishers Weekly*, March 3, 2017, https://www.publishersweekly.com/pw/by-topic/industry-news/book-deals/article/72949-the-obamas-book-deals-spark-65-million-mystery.html; Kenneth P. Vogel, "Tax Returns Show Clintons Got Rich Quick," *Politico*, April 4, 2008, https://www.politico.com/story/2008/04/tax-returns-show-clintons-got-rich-quick-009393.

3 Barack Obama, *A Promised Land* (New York: Crown, 2020), xiii.

4 Ibid., 294.

5 Ibid., 13.

6 Ibid., 9.

7 Ibid., xiv.

8 Ibid., 14.

9 Ibid., 329.

10 Ibid.

11 Alissa J. Rubin, "Allies Fear Trump Is Eroding America's Moral Authority," *New York Times*, March 10, 2017, https://www.nytimes.com/2017/03/10/world/europe/in-trumps-america-a-toned-down-voice-for-human-rights.html.

12 Barack Obama, "Transcript: Obama's Speech Against the Iraq War" (speech, Chicago, October 2, 2002), *NPR*, https://www.npr.

org/2009/01/20/99591469/transcript-obamas-speech-against-the-iraq-war.

13 Ibid.

14 Obama, *A Promised Land*, 215.

15 Ibid., 310.

16 Ibid., 215.

17 Ibid., 216.

18 Ibid., 217.

19 Ibid., 305.

20 Ibid., 310–311.

21 Ibid., 321.

22 Ibid., 433.

23 Ibid.

24 Ibid., 435.

25 Ibid., 438.

26 Ibid., 337.

27 Ibid., 337–338.

28 Ibid., 339.

29 Ibid.

30 Ibid.

31 Ibid., 345, 343.

32 Ibid., 346.

33 Ibid., 353.

34 Ibid.

35 Ibid., 354.

36 Ibid.

37 Ibid., 355.

38 Ibid., 655.

39 Ibid., 659.

40 Ibid., 447.

41 Ibid., 602.

42 Ibid., 366.

GEORGE SOROS AFTER THE OPEN SOCIETY

Late last month, the same day she got fired from ABC for her racist tweet about Obama adviser Valerie Jarrett, Roseanne Barr accused Chelsea Clinton of being married to George Soros's nephew. "Chelsea Soros Clinton," Barr tweeted, knowing that the combination of names was enough to provoke a reaction.[1] In the desultory exchange that followed, the youngest Clinton responded to Roseanne by praising Soros's philanthropic work with his Open Society Foundations.[2] To which Barr responded in the most depressing and expected way possible, repeating false claims earlier proffered by the likes of Glenn Beck and Dinesh D'Souza:

> Sorry to have tweeted incorrect info about you! Please forgive me! By the way, George Soros is a nazi who turned in his fellow Jews 2 be murdered in German concentration camps & stole their wealth-were you aware of that? But, we all make mistakes, right Chelsea?[3]

Barr's tweet was quickly retweeted by conservatives, including Donald Trump, Jr. This shouldn't have surprised anyone. On the radical right, Soros comes up almost as often as the Clintons, invoked by media personalities—Beck and D'Souza but also Alex

Jones, Ann Coulter, Mike Cernovich, and Sean Hannity—as a one-word answer to the question of liberal hegemony.[4] He is a verbal tic, a key that fits every hole. "Some names invoke an emotional outcry from the red-meat crowds," former Republican congressman Jack Kingston recently told the *Washington Post*, "and certainly he [Soros] is one of them on the right."[5] Right-wingers, Kingston continued, view Soros as a "sort of sinister [person who] plays in the shadows."[6] This version of Soros is often indistinguishable from the anti-Semitic caricature that has dogged the philanthropist for decades—and rich Jews like him for centuries. But in recent years the caricature has evolved into something that more closely resembles a James Bond villain. The elders of Zion had nothing on this new, all-powerful Trump-era Soros. Even to conservatives who reject the darkest fringes of the far-far right, *Breitbart*'s description of Soros as a "globalist billionaire" dedicated to making America a liberal wasteland is uncontroversial common sense.[7]

Over the last decade, the anti-Soros rhetoric on the right has migrated from message boards and fringe platforms such as InfoWars, to Twitter, and back to InfoWars, now a mainstream platform. But in spite of the obsession with Soros, there is surprisingly little interest in what he actually thinks—in anything that isn't a hagiographic account of his career in high finance or a murky tale about his philanthropic commitments. Unlike most members of the billionaire class who speak in platitudes and remain withdrawn from serious engagement with civic life—Bill Gates and Mark Zuckerberg come to mind—Soros is an intellectual. The person who emerges from his popular books and many articles is not an out-of-touch plutocrat but a provocative and consistent thinker unambiguously committed to pushing the world in a cosmopolitan direction in which racism, income inequality, American Empire, and the alienations of contemporary capitalism would be things of the past. Soros is as comfortable with Wittgenstein as he is with Warren Buffett, which makes him a sui generis figure in American life, someone whose likes we will not see again for quite a while. He is extremely perceptive about the limits of markets and US power in both domestic and international contexts. He is, in short, among the best the meritocracy has produced.

It is for this reason that Soros's failures are so telling; they are the failures not merely of one man, but of an entire class—and an entire way of understanding the world. From his earliest days as a banker in postwar London, Soros believed in a necessary connection between capitalism and cosmopolitanism. For him, as for most members of his cohort and the majority of the Democratic Party's leadership, a free society depends on free (if regulated) markets. But this assumed connection has proven to be a false one. The decades since the end of the Cold War have demonstrated that, absent a perceived existential enemy, capitalism tends to undermine the very culture of trust, compassion, and empathy upon which Soros's "open society" depends by concentrating wealth in the hands of the very few—one of whom is Soros.

Instead of the global capitalist utopia predicted in the halcyon 1990s by those who proclaimed an end to history, the United States is presently ruled by an oafish heir who enriches his family as he dismantles the "liberal international order" that was supposed to govern a peaceful, prosperous, and united world. While Soros recognized earlier than most the limits of hyper-capitalism, his class position made him unable to advocate the root and branch—read: anti- or post-capitalist—reforms necessary to bring about the world he desires. The system that allows George Soros to accrue the wealth that he has has proven to be a system in which cosmopolitanism will never find a stable home.

***

The highlights of Soros's biography are well known. Born to middle-class Jewish parents in Budapest in 1930 as György Schwartz, Soros—his father changed the family name in 1936 to avoid anti-Semitic discrimination—led a tranquil childhood until World War II, when after the Nazi invasion of Hungary he and his family were forced to assume Christian identities and live under false names.

Miraculously, Soros and his family survived the war, escaping the fate suffered by more than two-thirds of Hungary's Jews. Feeling stifled in newly communist Hungary, in 1947 Soros immigrated to the United Kingdom, where he matriculated at the London School of Economics and got to know the Austrian-born philosopher Karl Popper, who became his greatest interlocutor and central intellectual influence. In 1956, Soros moved to New York City to pursue a career in finance. After spending over a decade working in various Wall Street positions, in the late 1960s he founded the Quantum Fund, which became one of the most successful hedge funds of all time. As his fund accrued staggering profits, Soros personally emerged as a legendary trader; most famously, in November 1992, he earned $1.5 billion and "broke the Bank of England" by, in the words of the journalist Steve Schaefer, "betting the British pound and several other European currencies were priced too richly against the German deutsche mark."[8]

Today, Soros is one of the richest men in the world and, along with Gates and Zuckerberg, one of the United States' most politically influential philanthropists. But whereas Gates lists middlebrow authors such as Steven Pinker and John Brooks as his favorite thinkers, and Zuckerberg doesn't seem interested in much besides tax evasion and pablum, Soros has for decades pointed to academic philosophy as his source of inspiration. Throughout his career, he has committed himself to writing systematically about social, economic, and political ideas. In particular, he has highlighted Popper's 1945 classic two-volume *The Open Society and Its Enemies* as key to his worldview.[9]

Since 1987, Soros has published nine books (two of which he updated and rereleased), two essay collections, and a number of pieces in *The New York Review of Books*, *The New York Times*, and elsewhere. These texts make clear that, similar to many on the center-left who rose to prominence in the 1990s, Soros's defining intellectual feature is his internationalism, or, in the words of the alt-right, his "globalism." For Soros, the goal of contemporary human existence is to establish a world defined not by sovereign states but by a global community whose constituents understand that everyone shares an interest in freedom, equality, and prosperity. In his opinion, the creation of such a global open society is the only way to ensure that humanity overcomes the existential challenges of climate change and nuclear proliferation.

Soros's commitment to internationalism is as much personal as societal. He has described himself in terms that echo the archetypal wandering Jew, writing that he does "not belong to any community" and takes "pride in being in the minority, an outsider."[10] Unsurprisingly, this hasn't moderated the brutal onslaught of anti-Semitic attacks he has been subjected to throughout his life, especially since he began working in Eastern Europe in the 1980s. Despite this assault, Soros has not embraced ethno-nationalism or religion but has been straightforward in his derision of the particularities of national and ethnic identities. Unlike Gates, whose philanthropy focuses mostly on ameliorative projects such as eradicating malaria, Soros truly wants to transform national and international politics and society. Whether or not his vision can survive the blitzkrieg of the anti-Semitic, Islamophobic, and xenophobic right-wing nationalism ascendant in the United States and Europe remains to be seen. What is certain is that Soros will spend the remainder of his life attempting to make sure it does.

***

Soros's thought and philanthropic career are organized around the idea of the "open society," a term developed and popularized by Popper in *The Open Society and Its Enemies*. In Popper's schema, open societies guarantee and protect rational exchange, while closed societies force people to submit to authority, whether that authority is religious, political, or economic.[11]

Soros has attempted to open foreign societies he deemed closed by creating within them the infrastructure and culture upon which he believes the free exchange of ideas and capital must rest. He has also tried to combat two ideas hegemonic in the United States that he considers antithetical to the open society: the belief "that the common interest is best served by allowing everyone to look out for his or her own interests," which he terms market fundamentalism; and the conviction that U.S. interests are best served when the nation is a hyper-power.[12] And he has promoted a global open society by encouraging the reform of international institutions such as the World Bank and United Nations, which he considers atavistic, cumbersome, and incapable of solving the grave problems the world's peoples presently face.

Soros began his philanthropic activities in 1979, when he "determined after some reflection that I had enough money" and could therefore devote himself to making the world a better place.[13] To do so, he established the Open Society Fund, which quickly became a transnational network of foundations. Though he made some effort at funding academic scholarships for Black students in apartheid South Africa, Soros's primary concern was the communist bloc in Eastern Europe; by the end of the 1980s, he had opened foundation offices in Hungary, Poland, Czechoslovakia, Bulgaria, and the Soviet Union itself. Like Popper before him, Soros considered the countries of communist Eastern Europe to be the ultimate models of closed societies. If he were able to open these regimes, he could demonstrate to the world that money could—in some instances, at least—peacefully overcome oppression without necessitating military intervention or political subversion, the favored tools of the Cold War's leaders.

Soros set up his first foreign foundation in Hungary in 1984, and his efforts there serve as a model of his activities during this period. Over the course of the decade, he awarded scholarships to Hungarian intellectuals to bring them to the United States; provided Xerox machines to libraries and universities; and offered grants to theaters, libraries, intellectuals, artists, and experimental schools. In his 1990 book *Opening the Soviet System*, Soros wrote that he believed his foundation had helped "demolish the monopoly of dogma [in Hungary] by making an alternate source of financing available for [dissenting] cultural and social activities," which, in his estimation, played a critical role in producing the internal collapse of communism.[14]

Soros's use of the word *dogma* points to two critical elements of his thought: his fierce belief that ideas, more than economics, shape life, and his confidence in humanity's capacity for progress. For Soros, progress was in the final analysis an intellectual problem. Throughout his writings he repeatedly stands Marx on his head, returning him to the original Hegelian position. According to Soros, the dogmatic mode of thinking that characterized closed societies made it impossible for them to accommodate to the vicissitudes of history. Instead, "as actual conditions change," people in closed societies were forced to abide by an atavistic ideology that was increasingly unpersuasive.[15] When this dogma finally became too obviously disconnected from reality, Soros claimed, a revolution that overturned the closed society usually occurred. Closed societies were thus very different from open societies, which were dynamic and able to correct course whenever their dogmas strayed too far from reality. In some sense, then, Soros considered the Eastern Bloc's collapse overdetermined, though he still believed human action was necessary to bring about the final breakdown.

As he witnessed the Soviet empire's downfall between 1989 and 1991, Soros needed to answer a crucial strategic question: Now that the closed societies of Eastern Europe were opening, what was his foundation to do? On the eve of the Soviet Union's dissolution, Soros published a revised and expanded edition of *Opening the Soviet System*, retitled *Underwriting Democracy*, which revealed his new strategy: he would dedicate himself to building permanent institutions that would "sustain the ideas that motivated" anti-communist revolutions while modeling the practices of open society for the liberated peoples of Eastern Europe.[16] The most important of these was Central European University (CEU), which opened in Budapest in 1991. Funded by Soros, CEU was intended to serve as the wellspring for a new, transnational, European world—and the training grounds for a new, transnational, European elite.

In its first years, most of CEU's professors hailed from Western Europe or the United States and educated a mixed constituency of Western and Eastern European students, though Soros provided only the latter with full scholarships. In this way, the university attempted to construct an Eastern–European elite whose members were committed to open society and able to steer their countries in the liberal capitalist direction that Soros hoped they would go. At the same time, Soros continued to promote intra–European solidarity. For instance, in Hungary, the foundation supported "Western know-how programs" such as "media workshops" that trained Eastern Europeans in Western cultural and professional mores, and "East-East programs" that published materials created in other Eastern European countries in Hungarian.[17] While he never framed his project in this way, Soros was in effect attempting to solve the age-old "Jewish question" by building a pan–European society in which religion, ethnicity, and nationality were publicly inconsequential.

Despite the creativity and relentlessness of his philanthropic efforts, from the beginning Soros was anxious that his project would fail in the long term. "There is no easy transition from closed to open society," he wrote in 1990, eight years before Viktor Orbán would emerge and, eventually, prove him right.[18] "It is not enough to remove the constraints of a closed society; it is necessary to construct the institutions, laws, habits of thought, yes, even traditions of an open society."[19] How could Soros ensure that newly opened societies would remain free? Soros had come of age in the era of the Marshall Plan and experienced American largesse firsthand in postwar London. This was a critical experience that demonstrated to him that weakened and exhausted societies could not be rehabilitated without a substantial investment of foreign aid, which would alleviate extreme conditions and provide the minimum material base that would enable the right ideas about democracy and capitalism to flourish.

For this reason, in the late 1980s and early 1990s Soros repeatedly argued "that only the *deus ex machina* of Western assistance" could make the Eastern Bloc permanently democratic.[20] "People who have been living in a totalitarian system all their lives," he claimed, "lack the knowledge and experience necessary to bring [an open society] about. They need outside assistance to turn their aspirations into reality."[21] Soros insisted that the United States and Western Europe give the countries of Eastern Europe a substantial amount of pecuniary aid, provide them with access to the European Common Market, and promote cultural and educational ties between the west and the east "that befit a pluralistic society."[22] Once accomplished, Soros avowed, Western Europe must welcome Eastern Europe into the European community, which would prevent the continent's future repartitioning.

Soros's prescient pleas went unheeded. For the remainder of his life, he attributed the emergence of kleptocracy and hypernationalism in the former Eastern Bloc to the West's paucity of "vision and … political will" during this crucial moment.[23] "Democracies," he lamented in 1995, "suffer from a deficiency of values. They are notoriously unwilling to take any pain when their vital self-interests are not directly threatened."[24] For Soros, the West had failed in an epochal task and in so doing had revealed its shortsightedness and fecklessness.

But it was more than a lack of political will that constrained the West during this moment. In the era of "shock therapy," Western capital did flock to Eastern Europe—but this capital was invested mostly in private industry, as opposed to democratic institutions or grassroots community building, which helped the kleptocrats and anti-democrats seize and maintain power.[25] Soros had identified a key problem but was unable to appreciate how the very logic of capitalism, which stressed profit above all, would necessarily undermine his democratic project. He remained too wedded to the system he had conquered.

***

In the wake of the Cold War, Soros dedicated himself to exploring the international problems that prevented the realization of a global open society. After the 1997 Asian Financial Crisis, in which a currency collapse in Southeast Asia engendered a world economic downturn, Soros wrote three books—1998's *The Crisis of Global Capitalism*, 2000's *Open Society*, and 2002's *On Globalization*—that addressed the two major threats he believed beset open society: hyperglobalization and market fundamentalism, both of which had become hegemonic after communism's collapse.

Soros argued that the history of the post–Cold War world, as well as his personal experiences as one of international finance's most successful traders, demonstrated that unregulated global capitalism undermined open society in three distinct ways. First, because capital could move anywhere to avoid taxation, Western nations were deprived of the finances they needed to provide citizens with public goods. Second, because international lenders were not subject to much regulation, they often engaged in "unsound lending practices" that threatened financial stability.[26] Finally, because these realities increased domestic and international inequalities, Soros feared they would encourage people to commit unspecified "acts of desperation" that could damage the global system's viability.[27] Soros saw, far earlier than most of his fellow center-leftists, the problems at the heart of the financialized and deregulated New Economy of the 1990s and 2000s. More than any of his liberal peers, he recognized that embracing the most extreme forms of its capitalist ideology might lead the United States to promote policies and practices that undermined its democracy and threatened stability both at home and abroad.

In Soros's opinion, the only way to save capitalism from itself was to establish "some global system of political decision making" that heavily regulated international finance.[28] Yet as early as 1998, Soros acknowledged that the United States was the primary opponent of global institutions; by this point in time, Americans had refused to join the International Court of Justice, had declined to sign the Mine Ban Treaty, and had unilaterally imposed economic sanctions when and where they saw fit. Still, Soros hoped that, somehow, American policymakers would accept that, for their own best interests, they needed to lead a coalition of democracies dedicated to "promoting the development of open societies [and] strengthening international law and the institutions needed for a global open society."[29]

But Soros had no program for how to modify American elites' increasing hostility to forms of internationalism that did not serve their own military might or provide them with direct and visible economic benefits. This was a significant gap in Soros's thought, especially given his insistence on the primacy of ideas in engendering historical change. Instead of thinking through this problem, however, he simply declared that "change would have to begin with a change of attitudes, which would be gradually translated into a change of policies."[30] Soros's status as a member of the hyperelite and belief that, for all its hiccups, history was headed in the right direction made him unable to consider fully the ideological obstacles that stood in the way of his internationalism.

***

The George W. Bush Administration's militarist response to the September 11 attacks compelled Soros to shift his attention from economics to politics. After the invasions of Afghanistan and Iraq, he concluded that it was U.S. unilateralism and its attendant disregard for other countries that prevented the cooperation upon which a global open society must depend. For this reason, between 2001 and the 2004 presidential election, Soros dedicated himself to rebuffing—publicly, loudly, and repeatedly—the Bush Administration's arguments about the need for unrestrained American hegemony. Bush also inspired Soros to align himself explicitly with the Democratic Party, which he had never done so vociferously before.

Everything about the Bush Administration's ideology was anathema to Soros, who fulminated against the administration at the very moment self-described center-leftists such as Tom Friedman were genuflecting to power in a performatively masculine obeisance. As Soros declared in his 2004 *The Bubble of American*

Supremacy, Bush and his coterie embraced "a crude form of social Darwinism" that assumed that "life is a struggle for survival, and we must rely mainly on the use of force to survive."[31] Whereas "prior to September 11, the excesses of [this] false ideology were kept within bounds by the normal functioning of our democracy," after the attacks the Bush "[A]dministration deliberately fostered the fear that has gripped the country" to silence opposition and win support for a counterproductive policy of militaristic unilateralism.[32] To Soros, assertions such as "either you are with us, or you are with the terrorists" eerily echoed the rhetoric of the Nazis and Soviets, which he hoped to have left behind in Europe.[33] Soros worried—wisely—that Bush would lead the nation into "a permanent state of war" characterized by foreign intervention and domestic oppression.[34] The president was thus a threat not only to world peace but also to the very idea of open society.

But the Bush Administration's foreign policies forced Soros to confront an intellectual puzzle; while he believed that in most instances the creation of open societies could be accomplished through financial measures, he admitted that it sometimes necessitated military intervention, as in the examples of the Somali, Haitian, and Bosnian civil wars. How, then, could he square his liberal internationalism, which accommodated the possibility of violence and bloodshed, with his rejection of the Bush Administration's foreign policy? To do so, Soros developed the notion of "the people's sovereignty."[35] According to Soros:

> Sovereignty belongs to the people; the people are supposed to delegate it to the government through the electoral process. But not all governments are democratically elected and even democratic governments may abuse the authority thus entrusted to them. If the abuses of power are severe enough and the people are deprived of opportunities to correct them, outside interference is justified … By specifying that *sovereignty belongs to the people*, we can penetrate into the nation-state and protect the rights of the people.[36]

Soros therefore explicitly endorsed the "responsibility to protect," a legal doctrine popular among liberal jurists such as Samantha Power in the 1990s and 2000s.[37] But why didn't Saddam Hussein's oppression of Iraqis violate the people's sovereignty, as the Bush Administration argued in the run-up to the Iraq War? Like other liberal internationalists, Soros had arrived at an unstable and unsatisfactory, yet widely held, position: foreign intervention was justifiable when a member of the elite who had the world's best interests at heart said it was.

Nevertheless, for Soros the idea of the people's sovereignty was more than just a matter of convenience. It was proof of his remarkable, if unexamined and ultimately shallow, faith in ordinary people's political instincts. He was certain, for instance, that Bush's "extremist ideology" did not "correspon[d] to the beliefs and values of the majority of Americans," and he was "confident that [Bush would] be rejected" and that John Kerry would win the 2004 presidential election.[38] Bush's defeat, Soros hoped, would spur "a profound reconsideration of America's role in the world" that would lead citizens to reject unilateralism and embrace international cooperation.[39]

But Kerry did not win, which forced the philanthropist to question, for the first time, ordinary Americans' political acumen. After the 2004 election, Soros underwent something like a crisis of faith. Adopting the chauvinism common to many émigrés to the United States throughout its history, in his 2006 *The Age of Fallibility* Soros attributed Bush's reelection to the fact that the United States was "a 'feel-good' society unwilling to face unpleasant reality."[40] Americans, Soros avowed, would rather be "grievously misled by the Bush Administration" than confront the failures of Afghanistan, Iraq, and the war on terror head on.[41] Because they were influenced by market fundamentalism and its obsession with "success," Soros continued, Americans were eager to accept politicians' claims that the nation could win something as absurd as a war on terror.[42] Bush's victory convinced Soros that the United States would survive as an open society only if Americans began to acknowledge "that the truth matters"; otherwise, they would continue to support the war on terror and its concomitant horrors.[43] How Soros could change American minds, though, remained unclear.

***

The financial crisis of 2007–2008 encouraged Soros to refocus on economics. The collapse did not surprise the philanthropist, who considered it the predictable upshot of market fundamentalism. Rather, it was most important for convincing him that the world was about to witness, as he declared in his 2008 *The New Paradigm for Financial Markets*, "the end of a long period of relative stability based on the United States as the dominant power and the dollar as the main international reserve currency."[44] Anticipating American decline, Soros started to place his hopes for a global open society on the European Union (EU), despite his earlier anger at the union's members for failing to fully welcome Eastern Europe in the 1990s. Though he admitted that the EU had serious problems, it was nevertheless an organization in which nations voluntarily "agreed to a limited delegation of sovereignty" for the common European good.[45] It thus provided a regional model for a world order based on the principles of open society.

Soros's hopes in the EU, however, were quickly dashed by three crises that undercut the union's stability: the ever-deepening international recession, the Middle Eastern refugee crisis, and Vladimir Putin's revanchist assault on norms and international law. While Soros believed that Western nations could theoretically mitigate these crises, he concluded that, in a repetition of the failures of the post-Soviet period, they were unlikely to band together to do so. In the last 10 years, Soros has been disappointed by the fact that the West refused to forgive Greece's debt, failed to develop a common refugee policy, and would not consider augmenting Russian sanctions with the matériel and financial support Ukraine required to defend itself after Putin's 2014 annexation of Crimea. He was further disturbed that many nations in the EU, from the

United Kingdom to Poland, witnessed the reemergence of a right-wing ethno-nationalism thought lost to history. By January 2016, these various crises led Soros to affirm that "the EU is on the verge of collapse"; once Britain voted to leave the union the following June, he became convinced that "the disintegration of the EU [was] practically irreversible."[46] The EU did not serve as the model Soros hoped it would.

Soros experienced firsthand the racialized authoritarianism that in the last decade has threatened not only the EU but also democracy in Europe generally. Since 2010, the philanthropist has repeatedly sparred with Viktor Orbán, the nationalist, Euroskeptic, anti-Semitic, and anti-immigrant prime minister of Hungary. Recently, Soros accused Orbán of "trying to reestablish the kind of sham democracy that prevailed in the period between the First and Second World Wars in Admiral [Miklós] Horthy's Hungary" for the sole purpose of "perpetuat[ing] [himself] in power."[47] The prime minister, for his part, has alleged that Soros's foundations desire to undermine Hungary by making it easy for people who "come from a different [i.e., Islamic] way of life and a different culture" to settle there.[48] For Soros, Orbán's behavior recalls that of the fascists; for Orbán, Soros is a Jewish foreigner who cannot possibly comprehend the interests of real (Christian) Hungarians.

The battle between Soros and Orbán has heated up since March 2017, when Hungary's Ministry of Human Capacities informed Michael Ignatieff, the rector of Central European University—which Orbán derisively refers to as the "Soros University"—that CEU might be closed for awarding "foreign university degrees here in Hungary while not conducting teaching [i]n [its] country of origin, as prescribed by Hungarian regulations."[49] According to a press release published by the ministry in early April 2017, which reeks of anti-Semitism:

> The Soros university has enjoyed privileges unavailable to any other institution of higher education in Hungary. Even though its students are only required to attend a single

> course, the university has been able to issue them with two degrees—Hungarian and American. This may be good business for George Soros, but in the competition between universities it represents an unfair advantage.[50]

Though CEU was reaccredited for five more years last February, Orbán—who won a landslide reelection in April—has refused to end his standoff with the university. (He has also pledged to pass "Stop Soros" bills.)[51] A starker symbol of the failure of the open society in Hungary—Soros's nation of origin and where his foundation got off the ground—could hardly be imagined.

But while Orbán threatens Hungary's open society, it is Donald Trump who threatens the open society writ large. Even more than Orbán's attack on CEU, Trump's election demonstrated to Soros that "open societies are in crisis."[52] Trump is everything Soros is not: he came from wealth, he is racist, and he appears to have no major interests besides himself. The president stands, literally and figuratively, in opposition to open society and everything Soros holds dear.

Soros has correctly attributed Trump's victory to the deleterious effects that market fundamentalism and the Great Recession had on American society. In a December 2016 op-ed, Soros argued that Americans voted for Trump, "a con artist and would-be dictator," because "elected leaders failed to meet voters' legitimate expectations and aspirations and that this failure led electorates to become disenchanted with the prevailing versions of democracy and capitalism."[53] Specifically, instead of fairly distributing the wealth created by globalization, capitalism's "winners" failed to "compensate the losers," which led to a drastic increase in domestic inequality—and anger.[54] Though Soros believed that the United States' "Constitution and institutions … are strong enough to resist the excesses of the executive branch," he worried that Trump would form alliances with Putin, Orbán, and other authoritarians, which would make it near impossible to build a global open society.[55] In Hungary, the United States, and many of the parts of the world that have attracted Soros's attention and investment, it is clear that his project has stalled.

***

Despite Soros's tremendous efforts on behalf of ordinary people, in issue areas ranging from gun control to sex worker rights to education, he has never seriously grappled with the idea of the public. Strangely for someone whose project relies on changing people's minds, in his many books Soros never once discussed education. For Soros, the majority of the demos is little more than a phantasm, occasionally glimpsed but seldom engaged; it is the elites who truly matter. In this, Soros is a typical meritocrat, speaking in grand terms about making the world a better place, but always reliant on a supposedly cognitively superior elite.

Soros's disinterest in the public is difficult to square with his prescription for social change. Because he adheres to an ideas-driven philosophy of history, his ultimate solution to many social and political problems is to declare that people must experience a "change of heart."[56] In a 2010 lecture, for example, Soros proclaimed that capitalist democracy could be protected only if citizens followed "a rather simple rule: people should separate their role as market participants from their role as political participants. As market participants we ought to pursue our self-interest; as participants in the political process we ought to be guided by the public interest."[57] How, exactly, such a massive ideological shift might occur remains shrouded in mystery, as it did throughout Soros's career.

Soros's future path is unclear. On one hand, some of Soros's latest actions suggest he has moved in a left-wing direction, particularly in the area of criminal justice reform. He recently funded a super PAC to assist the campaign of Larry Krasner, the radical Philadelphia district attorney, and backed several California district attorney candidates similarly devoted to prosecutorial reform.[58] Possibly more than any other public figure, Soros recognizes the sheer injustice at the heart of the American carceral state. On the other hand, some of his behavior indicates that Soros remains committed to a traditional Democratic Party ill-equipped to address the problems that define our moment of crisis. During the 2015–2016 Democratic primary race, for instance, he gave millions of dollars to a super PAC that supported Hillary Clinton's campaign.[59] If Soros continues to fund truly progressive projects, he will make a substantial contribution to the open society; if he decides to defend banal Democrats, however, he will contribute to the ongoing degradation of our public life.

Throughout his career, Soros has made a number of wise and exciting interventions. From a democratic perspective, though, this single wealthy person's ability to shape public affairs is catastrophic. In one of his many insightful moments, Soros himself recognized that "the connection between capitalism and democracy is tenuous at best."[60] The problem for billionaires such as himself is what they do with this information. The open society envisions a world in which everyone recognizes each other's humanity and engages each other as equals. If most people are scraping for the last pieces of an ever-shrinking pie, however, it is difficult to imagine how we can build the world in which Soros—and, indeed, many of us—wants to live. Presently, Soros's cosmopolitan dreams remain exactly that. The question is why, and the answer might very well be that the open society is possible only in a world where no one—whether Soros or Gates or DeVos or Zuckerberg or Buffett or Musk or Bezos—is allowed to become as rich as he has.

Endnotes

1 John Koblin, "After Racist Tweet, Roseanne Barr's Show Is Canceled by ABC," *New York Times*, May 29, 2018, https://www.nytimes.com/2018/05/29/business/media/roseanne-barr-offensive-tweets.html.

2 Laurel Wamsley, "ABC Cancels 'Roseanne' After Racist Twitter Rant from Its Star," *NPR*, May 20, 2018, https://www.npr.org/sections/

thetwo-way/2018/05/29/615211939/abc-cancels-roseanne-after-abhorrent-twitter-rant-from-its-star.

3 Eugene Scott, "Roseanne Barr's Racist Twitter Remark Undercuts the Americans She Tried to Lift Up on Her Show," *Washington Post*, May 29, 2018, https://www.washingtonpost.com/news/the-fix/wp/2018/05/29/roseanne-barrs-racist-twitter-remark-undercuts-the-americans-she-tried-to-lift-up-on-her-show/. For Glenn Beck's anti-Soros remarks, see J.J. Goldberg, "So Glenn Beck Calls George Soros a Nazi Collaborator? Marty Peretz Said It First," November 15, 2010, *Forward*, <https://forward.com/opinion/133132/so-glenn-beck-calls-george-soros-a-nazi-collaborat/.> For Dinesh D'Souza's, see Eric Alterman, "Soros Slander Reveals Anti-Semitism at the Heart of the Far Right," *The Nation*, September 7, 2017, https://www.thenation.com/article/archive/soros-slander-reveals-anti-semitism-at-the-heart-of-the-far-right/.

4 For Alex Jones's anti-Soros remarks, see JTA, "Pro-Trump Radio Host: George Soros is Head of 'Jewish Mafia," *Times of Israel*, March 30, 2017, https://www.timesofisrael.com/pro-trump-radio-host-george-soros-is-head-of-jewish-mafia/. For Ann Coulter's and Mike Cernovich's, see Ryan W. Miller, "George Soros: How He Got His Billions, His Ties to the Clintons and the Conspiracy Theories Around Him," *USA Today*, October 24, 2018, https://www.usatoday.com/story/news/nation-now/2018/10/24/george-soros-billionaire-explosive-suspicious-package-hillary-clinton-barack-obama/1750885002/. For Sean Hannity's, see Adam Gabbatt, "Sean Hannity Targets Media Watchdog Amid Questions over Future at Fox News," May 25, 2017, https://www.theguardian.com/media/2017/may/25/sean-hannity-fox-news-media-matters-seth-rich.

5 Michael Kranish, "'I Must Be Doing Something Right': Billionaire George Soros Faces Renewed Attacks with Defiance," *Washington Post*, June 9, 2018, https://www.washingtonpost.com/politics/i-must-be-doing-something-right-billionaire-george-soros-faces-renewed-attacks-with-defiance/2018/06/09/3ba0e2b0-6825-11e8-9e38-24e693b3-8637_story.html.

6 Ibid.

7 John Binder, "Soros-Linked Group: Trump Is 'Racist' for Calling MS-13 Gang 'Animals,'" *Breitbart*, May 24, 2018, https://www.breitbart.com/

politics/2018/05/24/soros-linked-group-trump-is-racist-for-calling-ms-13-gang-animals/.

8 "Profile: George Soros," *Forbes*, accessed July 30, 2025, https://www.forbes.com/profile/george-soros/; Steve Schaefer, "Forbes Flashback: How George Soros Broke the British Pound and Why Hedge Funds Probably Can't Crack the Euro," *Forbes*, July 7, 2015, https://www.forbes.com/sites/steveschaefer/2015/07/07/forbes-flashback-georgesoros-british-pound-euro-ecb/.

9 Karl R. Popper, *The Open Society and Its Enemies: The Spell of Plato*, vol. I (London: George Routledge & Sons, 1945); Karl R. Popper, *The Open Society and Its Enemies: The High Tide of Prophecy: Hegel, Marx, and the Aftermath*, vol. II (London: George Routledge & Sons, 1945).

10 George Soros, *Opening the Soviet System* (London: Weidenfeld and Nicolson, 1990), 6.

11 The best explication of Popper's work, and one that informs my own, remains Malachi Haim Hacohen, *Karl Popper, the Formative Years, 1902–1945: Politics and Philosophy in Interwar Vienna* (New York: Cambridge University Press, 2000).

12 George Soros, *The Crisis of Global Capitalism: Open Society Endangered* (New York: PublicAffairs, 1998), xx.

13 George Soros, with Byron Wien and Krisztina Koenen, *Soros on Soros: Staying Ahead of the Curve* (New York: John Wiley & Sons, 1995), 112.

14 Soros, *Opening the Soviet System*, 25.

15 Ibid., 84.

16 George Soros, *Underwriting Democracy* (New York: Free Press, 1991), 129.

17 Ibid., 136.

18 Soros, *Opening the Soviet System*, 115.

19 Ibid.

20 Ibid., 2.

21 Ibid., 118.

22 Ibid., 129.

23 Soros, *Soros on Soros*, 161.

24 Ibid., 204.

25 On "shock therapy," see Jeffrey Sachs, *Understanding "Shock Therapy,"* Occasional Paper (London, UK: Social Market Foundation, 1994),

https://www.earth.columbia.edu/sitefiles/file/about/director/documents/SMF7.pdf.

26 Soros, *The Crisis of Global Capitalism*, 122.

27 George Soros, *Open Society: Reforming Global Capitalism* (New York: PublicAffairs, 2000), xix.

28 Soros, *The Crisis of Global Capitalism*, xxix.

29 Soros, *Open* Society, x.

30 Soros, *The Crisis of Global Capitalism*, 210.

31 George Soros, *The Bubble of American Supremacy: Correcting the Misuse of American Power* (New York: PublicAffairs, 2004), xi.

32 Soros, *The Bubble of American Supremacy*, xi, 9.

33 Ibid., ix.

34 Ibid., 26.

35 Ibid., 143, 102–103.

36 Ibid., 102–103.

37 Ibid., 103–109.

38 Ibid., 15–16, 189.

39 Ibid., 188.

40 George Soros, *The Age of Fallibility: The Consequences of the War on Terror* (New York: PublicAffairs, 2006), xxiii.

41 Ibid.

42 Ibid., 90.

43 Ibid., 91.

44 George Soros, *The New Paradigm for Financial Markets: The Credit Crisis of 2008 and What It Means* (New York: PublicAffairs, 2008), 155.

45 Soros, *The Age of Fallibility*, 164.

46 George Soros, "'The EU Is on the Verge of Collapse'—An Interview," interview by Gregor Peter Schmitz, *New York Review of Books*, February 11, 2016, https://www.nybooks.com/articles/2016/02/11/europe-verge-collapse-interview/; George Soros, "Brexit and the Future of Europe," *Project Syndicate*, June 20, 2016, https://www.project-syndicate.org/commentary/brexit-eu-disintegration-inevitable-by-george-soros-2016-06.

47 Soros, "'The EU is on the Verge of Collapse.'"

48 Viktor Orbán, "Interview with Prime Minister Viktor Orbán on Commercial Station TV2's 'Facts—Evening' Television Programme,"

interview by Csaba Azurák, September 17, 2015, Website of the Hungarian Government, https://2015-2019.kormany.hu/en/the-prime-minister/the-prime-minister-s-speeches/interview-with-prime-minister-viktor-orban-on-commercial-station-tv2-s-facts-evening-television-programme.

49 "The Future of the 'Soros University' Depends on Intergovernmental Negotiations," March 31, 2017, Miniszterelnök, https://2015-2022.miniszterelnok.hu/the-future-of-the-soros-university-depends-on-intergovernmental-negotiations/; Ministry of Human Capacities, "Several Universities are Operating Unlawfully–Report Published on Higher Education Institutions Operating in Hungary," March 29, 2017, Website of the Hungarian Government, https://2015-2019.kormany.hu/en/ministry-of-human-resources/news/several-universities-are-operating-unlawfully-report-published-on-higher-education-institutions-operating-in-hungary.

50 Ministry of Human Capacities, "The CEU Is Misleading Public Opinion," April 4, 2017, Website of the Hungarian Government, https://2015-2019.kormany.hu/en/ministry-of-human-resources/news/the-ceu-is-misleading-public-opinion.

51 Shaun Walker, "Orbán: Election Victory Gives Us Mandate to Pass 'Stop Soros' Laws," *The Guardian*, April 10, 2018, https://www.theguardian.com/world/2018/apr/10/orban-election-victory-gives-us-mandate-to-pass-stop-soros-laws.

52 George Soros, "Open Society Needs Defending," *Project Syndicate*, December 28, 2016, https://www.project-syndicate.org/magazine/open-society-needs-defending-by-george-soros-2016-12.

53 Ibid.

54 Ibid.

55 Ibid.

56 See, e.g., George Soros, *On Globalization* (New York: PublicAffairs, 2002),177; Soros, *The Bubble of American Supremacy*, 121; Soros, *The Age of Fallibility*, xvii; George Soros, "A New Policy to Rescue Ukraine," *New York Review of Books*, January 7, 2015, https://www.nybooks.com/articles/2015/02/05/new-policy-rescue-ukraine/.

57 George Soros, "Capitalism versus Open Society," in *The Soros Lectures at the Central European University* (New York: PublicAffairs, 2010), 89–90.

58 Chris Brennan, "$1.45 Million Soros Investment in Philly DA's Race Draws Heat for Krasner, *Philadelphia Inquirer*, May 7, 2017, https://www.inquirer.com/philly/news/politics/Soros-145-million-investment-in-DAs-race-draws-heat-for-Krasner.html; Alexander Sammon, "After a Career Suing Cops, This Lawyer Wants to be Philly's Next District Attorney," *Mother Jones*, May 12, 2017, https://www.motherjones.com/politics/2017/05/larry-krasner-district-attorney-philadelphia-reformer/; Don Thompson, "Big-Money Soros Contributions Change Prosecutor Campaigns," *Associated Press*, May 15, 2018, https://apnews.com/general-news-0aa7d76876c24be7a8a9d4cab737342b; Don Thompson, "Soros-Backed California County Prosecutors Fail in 3 Races," *Associated Press*, June 7, 2018, https://apnews.com/general-news-46b1c59775d04d37b82c03a9294ae640. See also Scott Bland, "George Soros' Quiet Overhaul of the U.S. Justice System," *Politico*, August 30, 2016, https://www.politico.com/story/2016/08/george-soros-criminal-justice-reform-227519.

59 Soros was the largest donor to this super PAC. See "Priorities USA Action PAC Donors," Open Secrets, accessed August 1, 2025, https://www.opensecrets.org/political-action-committees-pacs//C00495861/donors/2016.

60 Soros, *The Crisis of Global Capitalism*, 111.

THE DISCONTENTS OF FRANCIS FUKUYAMA

The end of the Cold War was supposed to usher in a better world. After four decades of struggle, the great battle between liberalism and Bolshevism had ended in the former's decisive victory. Many in the West hoped that liberalism would now have free rein to shape events around the world. Utopia, at least of a liberal form, was finally within humanity's grasp.

No essay embodied this feeling more than "The End of History?" Published in 1989 in *The National Interest* and written by a then-unknown State Department official named Francis Fukuyama, the piece proffered a simple three-step argument.[1] First, Fukuyama claimed that throughout the world, people had decided that liberal democratic capitalism was superior to the authoritarian communism produced by Bolshevism and Maoism. Second, he argued that liberalism's triumph meant that "History"—understood as the struggle between rival ideologies—had ended. Finally, he concluded that, over time, many nations that hadn't yet become liberal capitalist democracies would inevitably do so, and that this would be good for humankind.

Today, many critics argue that Fukuyama was naive at best, foolish at worst. Nationalist authoritarianism, they note, reigns in countries such as Russia, China, Turkey, Poland, and Hungary, while Western democracies hardly resemble the tempered utopia that Fukuyama imagined. Inequality has run rampant; people are alienated and depressed; and liberal governments seem incapable of performing basic functions. A hegemonic liberalism has not been able to tame capitalist excesses, and as a result, many have come to question liberalism writ large.

To take the United States as a paradigmatic example, increasing stratification has sparked a severe backlash against the form of liberalism that seemed destined to rule when Fukuyama wrote "The End of History?" On the left, a new generation, spurred in part by the Bernie Sanders presidential campaigns, has embraced a politics that organizes itself under the banner of socialism. On the right, nationalist reaction is back with a vengeance, as Donald Trump's racist and xenophobic campaign and presidency impelled the resurgence of a right-wing radicalism that has not been seen since the 1990s, when white supremacists carried out spectacular acts such as the Oklahoma City bombing. Meanwhile, the so-called center is adrift, unable to address the many problems that bedevil liberal democratic capitalism. To add insult to injury, beyond formal politics, exhaustion and ennui define much of American life. Across social classes, people have given up on the very idea of a better future.

Elite liberals can sense that they are losing ground and are anxious to redeem a tradition that has plainly been unable to deliver on its great promises. Liberalism is in crisis, and for the first time since the Cold War's end, liberal thinkers feel the need to justify liberalism itself. From Mark Lilla's *The Once and Future Liberal* to Adam Gopnik's *A Thousand Small Sanities* to James Traub's *What Was Liberalism?*, writers have begun to man the intellectual barricades, defending and promoting liberalism as the best possible solution to the world's problems.[2] Fukuyama's recent *Liberalism and Its Discontents* is part of this liberal counter-offensive.[3] As a thinker, Fukuyama is the most distinguished of liberal apologists, and if anyone could make the positive case for liberalism, it's him. But *Liberalism and Its Discontents* is not especially illuminating, repeating tired criticisms of the Left and the Right that don't add much to scholarly analysis or political conversation. In essence, Fukuyama believes that embracing centrist liberalism was, and remains, the "mature" thing to do. While adolescents and fools endorse politics of radical change, adults accept that liberalism's limited reforms are the best humanity can hope for. Though Fukuyama is willing to acknowledge many of liberalism's limitations, he cannot envision a world beyond it.

The tragedy of our times is that he doesn't really need to, because the argument he proffered in "The End of History?" has proved correct. No ideology has arisen to challenge liberalism, whether in the United States or elsewhere. Fukuyama and the other defenders of liberalism thus don't actually have to be that persuasive. Liberalism reigns, and it looks set to do so into the foreseeable future. History, for the moment at least, remains at its end.

***

Though most remember "The End of History?" as triumphant in tone, it was also melancholic, often sounding almost like a breakup letter. There was good reason for this: for the first decade of his career, Fukuyama was in a long-distance relationship with the Soviet Union. It was the lodestar around which he organized his life. The Soviet Union provided Fukuyama with a calling—his professional specialty was Soviet behavior in the Third World—and it also gave him ideological perspective. Whatever the Soviet Union was, the United States (and Fukuyama) was not. The Soviet Union was the Joker to Fukuyama's Batman. When it went away, he lost far more than a worthy adversary; he lost the object against which he'd calibrated his own moral and political compass.

From the start of his career, Fukuyama was interested in questions of ideology. When he began writing in the late 1970s as an intern at the RAND Corporation, a materialist realism that focused primarily on power relations abounded, both in the academy and in Washington, D.C. Thinkers such as Kenneth Waltz and policymakers such as Henry Kissinger insisted that the Soviet Union was a "normal" nation with "normal" (read: power-focused) interests. Fukuyama disagreed with this consensus. Against his elders, the young analyst maintained that the Soviets were actually ideological enemies of the United States who desired to remake the world in their communist image. Where Kissinger understood geopolitics as a great game of power and interests, Fukuyama centered ideas. He thus spent the early years of his career analyzing Soviet efforts to create "ideological states" in places such as Afghanistan, Angola, Mozambique, and Nicaragua.[4] According to Fukuyama, ideology—not just power—needed to be taken seriously in international relations.

When Mikhail Gorbachev became the general secretary of the Soviet Communist Party in March 1985, Fukuyama started to notice that communism's traditional nostrums seemed to hold less sway in both the Soviet metropole and the larger world. Gorbachev, Fukuyama wrote, not only abandoned "the old ideological language of Marxism–Leninism and vanguard parties," he also focused his efforts on working with states such as India, which could hardly be described as communist.[5] Furthermore, Soviet developmental economists had begun to argue in favor of modernization efforts "that combine[d] socialist and market-oriented solutions," while Third World leaders themselves made it clear that they were primarily interested in development and were not especially concerned with the ideological precepts that helped them achieve it.[6] Faith in the communist project, Fukuyama concluded, had seriously diminished.

Despite these transformations, however, Fukuyama remained unable to abandon the Cold War; his attraction to it was that profound. Even as one part of Fukuyama understood that the U.S.–Soviet relationship was entering a new phase, another part of him refused to believe it. As late as 1988, in the last essay he published before "The End of History?," Fukuyama affirmed that even if "centrally planned economies and one-party dictatorships are in bad odor," the United States needed to make strategy "on the assumption that [it's] dealing with the same old Soviet Union."[7] Though Fukuyama couldn't help but notice that the passion was gone from the relationship, he wanted it to continue. And anyway, things could change. Maybe the old magic would return.

But by the time "The End of History?" appeared in *The National Interest* in the summer of 1989, Fukuyama—who had by then migrated from RAND to the State Department—had come to terms with the undeniable reality: the Cold War was over. In February, the Soviets had begun withdrawing their tanks and soldiers from Czechoslovakia. In April, the Polish trade union Solidarity had been legalized; that same month, Soviet troops had started leaving Hungary. In July, Gorbachev had declared that he would not prevent the ongoing reforms in Eastern Europe. While the final collapse of the Soviet Union was still two and a half years away, not even Fukuyama could deny the facts. The U.S.–Soviet struggle, a struggle that had defined his life and career, was at an end.

***

"The End of History?" was more than just a piece of commentary; it was a diagnosis, an announcement of victory, and a lament, an explication of where Fukuyama thought the world was, as well as an expression of how he felt about it. Fukuyama concluded that the U.S. triumph in the Cold War was an epochal achievement, even as he appreciated that the future would not be as romantic without his old Soviet rival. And that's why there's a question mark in the title. Though "The End of History?" makes it clear that, intellectually, Fukuyama knows the answer to his question, emotionally he finds it difficult to accept.

Fukuyama's argument in "The End of History?" was straightforward but profound. He claimed that the struggle between ideologies that had defined history in the nineteenth and twentieth centuries was, in effect, over—that there were no longer any "viable systematic alternatives to Western liberalism."[8] From the

Soviet Union, where Gorbachev had implemented glasnost and perestroika, to China, where Deng Xiaoping had liberalized the economy, communists had accepted liberalism's "democratizing and decentralizing principles."[9] These transformations, Fukuyama insisted, were not merely important; they were epochal. "What we may be witnessing," he ventured, "is not just the end of the Cold War, or the passing of a particular period of postwar history, but the end of history as such: that is, the end point of mankind's ideological evolution and the universalization of Western liberal democracy as the final form of human government."[10] Whether in a year, a generation, or a century, eventually everyone would become liberal.

In Fukuyama's telling, liberalism had proved itself superior to competing ideological alternatives because it was able to resolve all "fundamental 'contradictions' in human life," especially "that between capital and labor."[11] If inequality existed in liberal societies, he asserted, it was not because of their "underlying legal and social structure[s]" but because of "the historical legacy of premodern conditions."[12] Black Americans, for example, were poor not because of liberal democratic capitalism, but because of "the 'legacy of slavery and racism'"—atavisms that more liberalism would cure.[13] The same was true when it came to war. Following the philosopher Immanuel Kant, who claimed that "perpetual peace" could be achieved if every government embraced liberal precepts, Fukuyama avowed that at the end of history there would no longer be "ideological grounds for major conflict between nations."[14] War might thus become a thing of the past.

In these ways, "The End of History?" was triumphalist. But it was also suffused with an intense anxiety about what might come next. While Fukuyama is often considered one of late-twentieth-century liberalism's greatest advocates, he was always a bit skeptical of the ideology's ability to satiate the innate human desire for connection and meaning. In particular, Fukuyama envied communists, because communism provided its adherents with a profound sense of community, engendering feelings of global solidarity that encouraged leftist governments to aid and make sacrifices for one another, even when doing so wasn't in their avowed national interest. Unlike communism, Fukuyama explained in an essay from the mid-1980s, liberalism had little "explicit doctrine governing the duty to engage in international capitalist solidarity"—the latter, in fact, was almost a contradiction in terms, given liberal capitalism's individualistic ethos.[15] Where communist nations such as Cuba and the Soviet Union offered "fraternal assistance ... as a matter of principle," cooperation between liberal governments would "likely have to be arranged on an ad hoc basis, probably among states ... directly affected by a common threat."[16] Under communism, people believed in a grand project and cooperated to bring it about; under liberalism, neither collective action nor social goodwill was encouraged. Though Fukuyama, of course, thought Marxist–Leninist beliefs were silly at best and destructive at worst, he nevertheless envied the kinds of solidarities they engendered. Ironically, the only time liberalism could inspire similar associations and feelings was when it was engaged in an epic battle with an existential enemy. Without such an enemy, liberalism was a bit bloodless.

This pessimistic understanding of liberalism helps explain the melancholic notes in "The End of History?" History's end, Fukuyama predicted mournfully, "will be a very sad time," because "the worldwide ideological struggle that called forth daring, courage, imagination, and idealism, will be replaced by economic calculation, the endless solving of technical problems, environmental concerns, and the satisfaction of sophisticated consumer demands."[17] Liberalism may work better than communism, but it couldn't satisfy the human yearning for connection and meaning; as Fukuyama later wrote, the ideology ultimately had a "vacuum" at its center.[18] For this reason, he prophesied that in a liberal world shorn of momentous conflict, many people would not be all that happy. He wasn't wrong.

***

The strange blend of triumphalism and melancholy that characterized "The End of History?" did not exactly spur a rapturous response from Fukuyama's fellow conservatives. Gertrude Himmelfarb and Irving Kristol insisted that history was far too dynamic ever to end.[19] The philosopher Timothy Fuller accused Fukuyama of bad dialectics for positing "the victory of one prong of the opposition as if it were not ineluctably tied to the other."[20] Samuel P. Huntington maintained that human nature was too irrational to permit Fukuyama's predicted end—or as Huntington abrasively put it: "in history there may be total defeats, but there are no final solutions."[21] The Right wasn't yet ready to say goodbye to ideological conflict.

But where conservative eggheads rejected Fukuyama's thesis, significant parts of the public embraced it. As *The New York Times Magazine*'s James Atlas reported in October 1989, "The End of History?" had rapidly "become the hottest topic around," with one Washington, D.C., newsdealer informing *Atlas* that *The National Interest* was "'outselling everything, even the pornography.'"[22] Several months after the essay's release, Atlas observed, "you still can't pick up a magazine or a newspaper without stumbling across some reference to Fukuyama."[23] "The End of History?" nailed the zeitgeist, as the end of an era bred an era of ends, from Arthur C. Danto's "the end of art" to Bill McKibben's *The End of Nature*.[24] Fukuyama, in short, did what the best writers do: he gave a feeling a phrase.

Fukuyama became that rare thing: a celebrity intellectual. He left the State Department and embarked on a lucrative career as a thought leader. "The End of History?" and its 1992 book-length expansion, *The End of History and the Last Man* (notice the lack of a question mark), were smash hits—according to Google Scholar, these works have been cited tens of thousands of times.[25] In the more than three decades since "The End of History?" appeared, Fukuyama has written regularly for *Foreign Affairs*, *Commentary*, and *The American Interest* and has moved among several elite institutions, including RAND, Johns Hopkins, and Stanford, where he is currently a senior fellow at the Freeman Spogli Institute for International Studies. A more successful intellectual career could hardly be imagined.

As his career took off, Fukuyama ranged widely in his subject matter, writing about everything from biotechnology to identity politics. But throughout it all, he remained best known, and most respected, as a theorist of liberalism. And while he may have had his misgivings about the ideology back in 1989, three decades of eating from the celebrity trough, coupled with the appearance of some apparent anti-liberal challengers, have led him to become a vociferous defender of the creed.

Indeed, defense sits at the heart of *Liberalism and Its Discontents*, a manifesto designed to fend off the attacks of what Fukuyama terms the "progressives on the left" and the "populists on the right."[26] You've already heard others deliver arguments similar to the ones Fukuyama offers here, in venues from *The Atlantic* to MSNBC to *The New York Times*. The Left and the Right are intolerant. The Left is anti-capitalist; the Right is antidemocratic. Both are bad for liberalism. Et cetera, et cetera, et cetera.

Unfortunately, much of *Liberalism and Its Discontents* is defined by the false equivalence Fukuyama draws between the Left and the Right. In effect, he insists that anyone who rejects liberal centrism is slouching toward authoritarianism. But, as Fukuyama well knows, there is an enormous difference between the Left and the Right, especially in the United States. While the Right wants to overturn some of the institutions of liberal democracy, the Left has long since made its peace with them. No major leftist leader, from Bernie Sanders to Alexandria Ocasio-Cortez, or institution, from the Democratic Socialists of America to *Jacobin*, questions the legitimacy of liberal democracy as such or rejects core liberal precepts such as free speech, free elections, freedom of the press, or freedom of assembly. Joseph Stalin or *Pravda* they are not. The Left, if anything, argues that democratic socialism can be achieved only through democratic means. But for Fukuyama to make his case, he has to clear the decks by equating left and right, even when the two are clearly not equivalent. This approach isn't especially convincing.

More interesting than Fukuyama's predictable criticisms is his willingness to confront liberalism's "discontents" head-on. In particular, and unlike in "The End of History?," he recognizes that actually existing liberalism has produced an enormous amount of inequality. Yet Fukuyama doesn't blame liberalism itself for this reality but instead the radical neoliberals who rejected "state intervention ... as a matter of principle."[27] The solution to inequality is therefore obvious: de-radicalize contemporary liberalism and return it to its reformist and centrist roots. Specifically, Fukuyama urges neoliberals to accept "that markets themselves function only when they are strictly regulated by states"; that social welfare is necessary; and that "economic efficiency" is not the be-all and end-all of human life.[28] If minds change, he avows, society will too.

As this suggests, Fukuyama rejects the left-wing argument "that liberalism inevitably leads to neoliberalism and an exploitative form of capitalism."[29] He points out that for much of the late nineteenth and twentieth centuries, incomes in liberal societies rose as liberals themselves "put into place extensive social protections and labor rights."[30] In Fukuyama's view, liberalism and social progress historically go together. But is this true? On the one hand, the benefits that the working classes in the liberal West achieved were gained at the expense of the Global South, which was cannibalized for the metropole's enjoyment. On the other hand, as Fukuyama is aware, the era to which he refers was also a time when liberalism had to do battle with other grand ideologies and thus was forced to temper some of its worst tendencies. Strangely, Fukuyama doesn't consider that liberalism at the end of history might be disposed to its cruelest extremes. If the past 30 years demonstrate anything, it's that absent any genuine ideological threat, liberals will enact maximalist policies, from the broad deregulation of industry to the dismantling of the welfare state. Put another way, reforming liberalism might be an impossible project to realize at history's end.

***

For many people, Fukuyama's earlier prediction that the end of history would be "a very sad time" has turned out to be true.

In fact, in *Liberalism and Its Discontents*, Fukuyama sometimes acknowledges as much. For example, he notes that manifold liberal subjects feel "lonely and alienated in their individualism."[31] Yet at the same time, he affirms that "modern liberal states have dense networks of voluntary civil society organizations that provide community, social services, and advocacy to their members and to the political community more broadly."[32] What gives? Is the end of history sad or not?

Clearly, when it comes to exploring what it feels like to live at history's end, Fukuyama the analyst stands in tension with Fukuyama the liberal booster. The former appreciates that life under liberalism is often grim, defined by anomie, precarity, and despair; the latter can't believe that, and so he doesn't. Though Fukuyama can't ignore liberalism's numerous problems, he also can't bring himself to imagine that there might be an alternative. To him, accepting the inevitability of liberalism is identical with mature thinking. Liberalism, to paraphrase Winston Churchill, is the worst ideology, except for all the others. It's what we've got, so let's defend it and make it better.

Today, Fukuyama retains his commitment to the thesis he presented in "The End of History?" As he explained in *The Atlantic* in October 2022, neither China nor Russia nor Iran nor any other authoritarian state poses a real challenge to liberalism. Autocratic governments, he notes, make bad decisions—they invade Ukraine or enact a zero-COVID policy—and most people don't want to live under them. It's not a surprise that there are far more migrants to Europe or the United States than to Russia or China. "No authoritarian government," Fukuyama correctly affirms, "presents a society that is, in the long term, more attractive than liberal democracy."[33] History remains at its end.

It's difficult to say that Fukuyama is wrong. Liberalism faces no serious challengers to its domination, either from the Left or from the Right. But this leads us to a question. Why haven't liberalism's failures engendered a more robust ideological backlash? Even clearly anti-liberal rivals to the United States, such as China and

Russia, don't proffer alternative, universally applicable ideological systems to the world. Instead, both countries act like the nationalist authoritarian regimes they are, focusing primarily on improving their relative power positions within their respective regions. At the same time, while President Joseph Biden regularly invokes the notion of a Manichaean struggle between democracy and authoritarianism to justify the United States' foreign policy, the U.S. government, like its enemies, seems far more concerned with military and economic power than ideology. Perhaps there hasn't been a vigorous ideological response to liberalism because we're entering a post-ideological age defined more by power politics than by ideational struggle.

The decreasing importance of ideology becomes especially clear when one realizes that most countries, whether liberal democracies such as the United States, the United Kingdom, France, and Germany, or autocracies such as China, Russia, Iran, and Hungary, have one thing in common: they're all capitalist. Capital, it appears, doesn't really care what ideology a given state embraces.

So where does this leave us? Unfortunately, in much the same place that we found ourselves 25 years, 50 years, or 100 years ago—struggling for control over our lives. The only difference is that we now know, contra Fukuyama, that liberalism is incapable of making capitalism's wonders work for most of humanity. But this failure might provide us with an opportunity, at least at some point in the future. When capitalism's contradictions prove to be too great, it's possible that liberalism's hegemony will collapse, and we will be able to conceive of ideas presently unthinkable. And with new ideas, history might restart again.

Endnotes

1 Francis Fukuyama, "The End of History?" *The National Interest* no. 16 (Summer 1989), 3–18.

2 Mark Lilla, *The Once and Future Liberal: After Identity Politics* (New York: Harper, 2017); Adam Gopnik, *A Thousand Small Sanities: The*

Moral Adventure of Liberalism (New York: Basic Books, 2019); James Traub, *What Was Liberalism? The Past, Present, and Promise of a Noble Idea* (New York: Basic Books, 2019).

3 Francis Fukuyama, *Liberalism and Its Discontents* (New York: Farrar, Straus and Giroux, 2022).

4 On the concept of "ideological states," see Francis Fukuyama, *The New Marxist-Leninist States in the Third World* (Santa Monica, CA: RAND Corporation, P-7020, September 1984), 21.

5 Francis Fukuyama, "Patterns of Soviet Third World Policy," *Problems of Communism* 36, no. 5 (September–October 1987), 12.

6 Francis Fukuyama, "The Political Character of the Overseas Empire," in *The Future of the Soviet Empire*, ed. Henry S. Rowen and Charles Wolf, Jr. (New York: St. Martin's Press, 1987), 70.

7 Francis Fukuyama, "Discord or Cooperation in the Third World?" in *Coping with Gorbachev's Soviet Union*, Significant Issues Series 10, no. 9 (Washington, D.C.: Center for Strategic and International Studies, 1988), 25, 35.

8 Fukuyama, "The End of History?," 3.

9 Ibid., 13.

10 Ibid., 4.

11 Ibid., 8, 9.

12 Ibid., 9.

13 Ibid.

14 Immanuel Kant, *Zum ewigen Frieden: Ein philosophischer Entwurf* (Königsberg: Friedrich Nicolovius, 1795); Fukuyama, "The End of History?," 17.

15 Francis Fukuyama, "Soviet Experience with Cooperative Forces," in *Developing Cooperative Forces in the Third World: Report of a RAND Conference, March 14–15, 1985*, ed. Charles Wolf, Jr. and Katharine Watkins (RAND Corporation: Santa Monica, CA, N-2325-USDP, June 1985), 147.

16 Ibid.

17 Fukuyama, "The End of History?," 18.

18 Francis Fukuyama, "A Reply to My Critics," *The National Interest* no. 18 (Winter 1989/90), 28.

19 Gertrude Himmelfarb, "Responses to Fukuyama," *The National Interest* no. 16 (Summer 1989), 24–26; Irving Kristol, "Responses to Fukuyama," *The National Interest* no. 16 (Summer 1989), 26–28.

20 Timothy Fuller, "More Responses to Fukuyama," *The National Interest* no. 17 (Fall 1989), 93.

21 Samuel P. Huntington, "No Exit: The Errors of Endism," *The National Interest* no. 17 (Fall 1989), 10.

22 James Atlas, "What Is Fukuyama Saying? And to Whom Is He Saying It?," *New York Times Magazine*, October 22, 1989, https://www.nytimes.com/1989/10/22/magazine/what-is-fukuyama-saying-and-to-whom-is-he-saying-it.html.

23 Ibid.

24 Arthur C. Danto, "The End of Art," in *The Philosophical Disenfranchisement of Art* (New York: Columbia University Press, 2005 [1986; original essay from 1984]), 81–115; Bill McKibben, *The End of Nature* (New York: Random House, 1989).

25 Francis Fukuyama, *The End of History and the Last Man* (New York: Free Press, 1992).

26 Fukuyama, *Liberalism and Its Discontents*, ix.

27 Ibid., 22.

28 Ibid., 23, 36.

29 Ibid., 80.

30 Ibid.

31 Ibid., 45.

32 Ibid., 76.

33 Francis Fukuyama, "More Proof That This Really Is the End of History," *The Atlantic*, October 17, 2022, https://www.theatlantic.com/ideas/archive/2022/10/francis-fukuyama-still-end-history/671761/.

H.R. MCMASTER AND THE TRAGEDY OF AMERICAN EMPIRE

The February 2017 replacement of National Security Advisor (NSA) Michael Flynn with Lieutenant General Herbert Raymond McMaster was greeted by the American journalistic and foreign policy establishment with barely restrained glee. In place of the erratic, unsavory Flynn, Donald Trump had chosen "a battle-tested veteran … considered one of the military's most independent-minded officers," in the words of one report in *The New York Times*.[1] "McMaster," wrote Fred Kaplan in *Slate*, "is widely viewed as the Army's smartest officer"—someone who "has made a career of speaking truth to power."[2] McMaster was everything Flynn was not: calm, self-effacing, and, crucially, an intellectual. Here at long last was a true scholar-warrior, a man who rejected the bizarre conspiracy theories and apocalyptic obsessions that were guide and mantra for Flynn, Steve Bannon, Sebastian Gorka, and Trump's other unsavory foreign policy mediocrities. McMaster's many supporters in government, journalism, and the nonprofit sector hoped that the decorated veteran could, at last, rationalize Trump's foreign policy. With McMaster calling the shots, the American

Century—and the American Empire that undergirded it—could continue well into the future.

Until earlier this week, it seemed that the advocates of U.S. global dominance had good reason to be reassured. McMaster is a passionate champion of our foreign policy consensus: he believes that the American Empire is a force for good in the world and appears ready to do whatever he can to defend its international standing. And he is a talented manager able to synthesize large amounts of information into easily digestible lessons—a useful skill in an administration led by a Twitter-addicted reality TV star.

But as the furor over Deputy Attorney General Rod Rosenstein's complicity in the firing of former FBI Director James Comey has revealed, the regime, person, and policy "agenda" of Donald Trump have made it virtually impossible for even dedicated public servants to impose order on chaos. Instead of rationalizing the Trump Administration, people such as Rosenstein and McMaster have been sucked into its morass. On Tuesday night, McMaster found himself standing outside the White House, visibly uncomfortable and reading carefully drafted legalese that would be contradicted by the President a few hours later. McMaster had been forced into a position he has been unwilling to occupy throughout his long career: political operative. He is not particularly good at this job.

That McMaster has been swallowed up by an administration that he was perhaps uniquely suited to reform is an extraordinary irony. Now derided by the very same people who praised his appointment, McMaster is beginning to lose the credibility that got him the job. *Slate*'s Kaplan recently published an article titled "The Tarnishing of H.R. McMaster"; in *Politico*, Jack Shafer has claimed that McMaster is now "diminished when measured by his own standards"; the journalist Tom Ricks told Shafer that McMaster might very well have lost the trust of the military, which "may never welcome him back in."[3] Short of a spectacular reversal of fortune, McMaster's career, and perhaps even his place in history, has been irrevocably stained.

What does H.R. McMaster believe? I've spent the last couple of months reading everything he has published since 1991 that I could find; what emerges from these texts is somewhat paradoxical. On one hand, McMaster has been willing throughout his career to critique fellow officers for placing too much faith in military technology. On the other hand, McMaster's views about the United States' role in the world are highly traditional: he believes that the nation presently confronts existential challenges that, because they threaten the values of "civilized peoples," must be annihilated.[4] For all his supposed intellectual independence, McMaster clearly and unquestioningly embraces the premises that have supported the American Empire since 1945. The fact that such a perspicacious officer could endorse such an outdated vision of the world suggests that not only the Trump Administration, but also the entire culture of the American national security establishment, is broken.

***

H.R. McMaster first rose to power during the Gulf War, when in February 1991 a small armored unit he commanded destroyed astonishing numbers of Republican Guard armored forces in the Battle of 73 Easting. Over the course of two days, McMaster's unit demolished dozens of Iraqi vehicles, killed scores of enemy soldiers (and captured many more), and suffered no casualties. To many interested observers, the Battle of 73 Easting was a clear demonstration of the power of the post–Cold War American military, whose superior technology would enable the United States to do what it wanted in a unipolar world.

But McMaster learned a different lesson from the battle. For him it revealed that in addition to technology, one of the most critical combat resources was independence of mind. As his unit pressed the advance against disorganized Iraqi forces, McMaster refused to halt his attack at a previously agreed-upon location, which enabled his unit to annihilate the enemy. A number of his superiors bristled at his insubordination, but it didn't matter: McMaster had discovered that unorthodox behavior could lead to battlefield success.

News of McMaster's victory spread quickly throughout the military. As Alex Roland, a professor of military history at Duke University, put it, by the Gulf War's end McMaster was seen as a "war hero, the brilliant and daring young captain [who] dominat[ed] the famous Battle of 73 Easting."[5] But instead of continuing in a command position—the traditional means through which officers rose through the ranks—McMaster chose to pursue the study of military history at the University of North Carolina–Chapel Hill. "Promotion boards," in the words of one retired officer, "were not impressed with doctorates or teaching assignments," and McMaster must have known that taking time away from troop duties could jeopardize his career.[6] For him the risk was worth it.

McMaster's dissertation analyzed the Joint Chiefs of Staff's (JCS) failure to speak out against President Lyndon Johnson and Secretary of Defense Robert McNamara's tendentious remarks to the public and Congress regarding the course of the Vietnam War and the military's support for U.S. strategy. As with the choice to attend graduate school in the first place, McMaster's dissertation topic suggested that here was an unorthodox—perhaps even transgressive—officer. Within the Army, the JCS's Vietnam–era mistakes were taboo subjects; one of McMaster's PhD committee members even advised him not to focus on this topic for fear it would negatively affect his career. Nevertheless, McMaster believed that if the Army was to serve as a force for good in the world, it needed to learn from past mistakes—career goals be damned.

***

Dereliction of Duty (1997), the book that emerged from McMaster's dissertation, is the foundational text of his worldview. In it, McMaster laid out the argument he had intuited in the Iraqi desert: that technological might was not the key to military victory. This critique would animate him for the next 20 years.

Throughout *Dereliction of Duty*, McMaster took particular aim at McNamara's strategy of "graduated pressure," which was premised upon the assumption "that [the North Vietnamese] would respond 'rationally' to precisely controlled military stimuli."[7] McNamara believed that the United States could "communicate" with the North Vietnamese by methodically increasing military pressure.[8] But this strategy, McMaster argued, reflected the dangerous fantasies of "economists, managers, and systems analysts," whose lack of empathy prevented them from appreciating "that Hanoi's commitment to revolutionary war made losses that seemed unconscionable to American white-collar professionals" acceptable.[9] Though the U.S. military was able to employ weaponry far superior to the North Vietnamese's, it could not win the war at a tolerable cost. McMaster went so far as to claim that McNamara's love of technology perverted his thinking by encouraging him to confuse tactical with strategic success—that is, to confuse success in battle with success in war. McMaster's conclusion was that war was to some degree an intellectual problem, in which bad ideas resulted in bad strategy.[10]

After teaching history at West Point from 1994 to 1996, McMaster returned to troop duties. His next major work, *Crack in the Foundation* (2003), which was released by the U.S. Army War College's Center for Strategic Leadership eight months after the United States invaded Iraq, applied *Dereliction of Duty*'s lessons to the modern American military. The paper's message was simple:

> The intellectual foundation for building tomorrow's military force rests on the unfounded assumption that technologies emerging from the "information revolution" will lift the fog of war and permit U.S. forces to achieve a very high degree of certainty in future military operations.[11]

McMaster disparaged the so-called "Revolution in Military Affairs" (RMA), which after the Gulf War had captured the hearts and minds of many military officers and defense thinkers. According to RMA advocates, "American technological superiority … made possible a new way of waging war" that was predictable, efficient, humane, and cheap.[12] McMaster rejected this argument as naive, insisting that as long as war remained human—as long as it was informed by culture, politics, will, psychology, and emotion—no one would be able to forecast its course or confidently limit its destruction. War, McMaster affirmed, was not "an engineering or business management problem that will succumb to systems analysis, reasoned judgment, and the application of superior technology."[13] This was the misapprehension that had doomed the U.S. effort in Vietnam and, due to the advocacy of RMA's champions (such as Secretary of Defense Donald Rumsfeld, who is not named in the report), now threatened to doom U.S. efforts in Iraq and Afghanistan.

Soon after *Crack in the Foundation*'s publication, McMaster was provided with the opportunity to put his argument into practice. In 2004, he assumed command of the 3rd Armored Cavalry Regiment, which in 2005 was charged with carrying out counterinsurgency (COIN) operations in the small city of Tal Afar in northern Iraq. By this point in the war, anti-Western forces had coalesced into an insurgency, and Tal Afar was a critical node in the insurgency's strategic network. By the time McMaster left the city in 2006, however, he had established an exceptional degree of control over it—a testament to his tactical brilliance.

McMaster's theory of counterinsurgency was premised upon the notion that ordinary people desired security, respect, and municipal services above all else. If a foreign military force was able to provide these, it would be possible to reduce sectarian tensions by helping previously warring groups achieve political accommodation with one another. Eventually, U.S.-trained Indigenous police and government officials could assume responsibility for a pacified city or region, at which point the U.S. military could withdraw.

McMaster wrote in a 2008 article that before the innovations he introduced in Tal Afar, COIN had been grounded in the short-term strategy of "defeat[ing] networked enemy organizations through attacking leadership and reducing critical capabilities."[14] But post-McMaster, COIN had become a long-term strategy. Tal Afar had succeeded because soldiers took the time to develop relationships with ordinary Iraqis, learn the local political landscape, and establish the institutional capacity for self-government. For this reason, McMaster avowed that "until civilian departments within the U.S. government expand deployable capabilities in order to establish local governance and rule of law, develop police forces, improve basic services, build institutional capacity, and set conditions for economic growth and development," the military would have to be prepared to assume these political responsibilities abroad.[15]

Yet this approach, while an intellectual advance over RMA and the blind technologism that had dominated the U.S. military since the fall of the Soviet Union, proved hopelessly naive in the contemporary American context. McMaster's version of COIN explicitly relied on a large and yearslong commitment to a given region—an enormous financial, matériel, and human burden unlikely to be supported in a political climate increasingly hostile to prolonged foreign entanglements. But COIN wasn't simply a hard sell for a fatigued public at home: for it to work, the American national security establishment would have to reconceive its priorities and significantly increase funding for the State Department. Like other empires throughout history, the U.S. has made diplomacy less central to its foreign relations than it might otherwise be. McMaster's desire to militarize diplomacy—or civilianize war—was a clever response to budget realities, but a doomed one: soldiers are not diplomats, and the military does not have the capacity, knowledge, or experience to establish lasting political solutions without civilian aid. For all the success he and his regiment had in Tal Afar in 2005 and 2006, it didn't and couldn't last: in 2014, the city was seized by ISIS.

***

H.R. McMaster is one of the United States' most astute theorists of modern warfare. Unlike so many other military thinkers, he understands that history is complex, contingent, and irrational and that no amount of technological superiority can tame the real world's unpredictable dynamism. He also rightly feels an ethical responsibility to the people who live in countries the United States invaded. So how could he have gotten it so wrong? Why, in spite of his sophistication, did his solutions to the American disasters in Iraq and Afghanistan ultimately fail to produce even medium-term victory?

McMaster's intellectual reputation rests on the quality he displayed on the battlefield in 1991, in *Dereliction of Duty* in 1997, and in *Crack in the Foundation* in 2003: his commitment to thinking that goes against the grain and troubles colleagues and superiors. The cheers that greeted his appointment in February were predicated on exactly this notion: that McMaster was a tenured radical, an establishmentarian committed to discarding whatever elements of the establishment that needed discarding. Yet McMaster remains a prisoner of ideas formed over half a century ago. He has never once doubted the underlying premises that have guided American foreign policy since World War II. He is unwavering in his belief that the U.S. must continue to serve as the world's policeman and retain its permanent military mobilization. He has never considered whether the imperial projects undertaken in Iraq and Afghanistan were illegitimate from the start and destined to fail. He has never questioned how Americans' obsession with security might affect democracy at home. McMaster would have been an adequate, perhaps even excellent, leader if American imperialism had proven to be an unalloyed good. Recent history, though, has demonstrated that ours is a moment that requires a new, post-imperialist understanding of the U.S.'s role in the world. This is something that McMaster is unlikely to provide.

Like so many of his less perceptive peers, McMaster has embraced the flawed assumptions that have been used to justify any number of unwise recent American entanglements. To McMaster, ISIS, Iran, and other Islamic enemies of the United States are equivalent to the Nazis and Soviets, and he insists that the contemporary geopolitical environment is defined—as it was during World War II and the Cold War—by an existential struggle between good and evil. As he said in a 2010 speech:

> We are engaged, as previous generations were engaged, against enemies that pose a great threat to all civilized peoples. As those generations defeated Nazi fascism, Japanese imperialism, and communist totalitarianism, we will defeat these enemies that cynically use a perverted interpretation of religion to incite hatred and violence.[16]

At the end of this speech, McMaster approvingly quoted President Barack Obama for affirming that "'evil does exist in the world.'"[17] "The righteous use of violence," McMaster wrote in a 2014 book review, was a critical means to defeat barbaric enemies like ISIS and Iran.[18]

McMaster spent a large portion of the last 12 years deployed in Iraq and Afghanistan, where he often witnessed the brutality of ISIS and the Taliban firsthand. These experiences no doubt led him to see in these enemies echoes of previous groups that committed horrific crimes against humanity. But McMaster's experiences have distorted his analysis of the real threat these organizations pose to U.S. national security. Unlike the Nazis or Soviets, neither ISIS nor the Taliban (nor associated states such as Iran) have the institutional or matériel capacity to overwhelm any Western power, let alone the United States. Even if these groups are able to carry out the occasional terrorist attack in the United States or Europe, they are simply not existential threats to the West. In an era in which the United States confronts state and non-state actors who express allegiance to ideologies that will not be eradicated anytime soon, McMaster's logic of absolute war, in which an enemy is not considered defeated until he is annihilated, is in reality a logic of permanent war.

The logic of absolute war has proven disastrous since its inception. Dwight Eisenhower, so often invoked in the contemporary foreign policy context as a sage and sane leader, was convinced that the

Soviet Union could not be negotiated with, only defeated. This belief may have prevented the Cold War from ending decades earlier than it did: when Eisenhower participated in the 1955 Geneva Summit, he refused to negotiate with the Soviet Union in good faith, forestalling any chance of an early U.S.–Soviet détente. When McMaster publicly paints Iran or Syria as evil in only slightly more shaded terms than George W. Bush did in his infamous "axis of evil" state of the union, he too forestalls any hope of diplomatic engagement with key rivals.[19] Whatever one might think of Iran, it is not Nazi Germany; it is a nation the United States must deal with in the coming years.

The human cost of the logic of absolute war has of course been more disastrous than the diplomatic one. The overthrow of democratically elected governments in Iran, Guatemala, and Chile; the bombing of Laos and Cambodia; the support for brutal dictators such as Egypt's Hosni Mubarak; the deployment of drones that have killed scores of innocents; and the dropping of the mother of all bombs on Afghanistan—all these have been undertaken in service of fighting a Manichaean war between good and evil. The "righteous" struggle against "enemies that pose a great threat to all civilized peoples" has unquestionably increased human suffering and done a great deal to engender anti-American fervor throughout the world.

In all his writings, McMaster has never considered *why*, exactly, our adversaries might detest us. America's opponents, he has written, "hate us not for anything we have done, but for who we are."[20] He has repeatedly insisted that soldiers must study history, like he did, yet he has evaded the well-documented story of how generations of Western colonialists seized raw materials from the Middle East and installed or supported leaders who oppressed their populations. McMaster has been most interested in the past for the instrumental purpose of improving America's war-fighting capabilities, which has led him to ignore major historical questions seemingly unrelated to this subject. His history is a circumscribed one, rooted in the belief that U.S. hegemony necessarily makes the world a better place.[21]

This was untrue in the past, and it is manifestly untrue today. In the Middle East alone, U.S. interventions have engendered a humanitarian disaster in Iraq, the rise of ISIS, military dictatorship in Egypt, and civil war in Syria. The time has come for leaders such as McMaster to rethink the United States' world role.

Some critics might argue that, though regrettable, the United States cannot be held responsible for brutally engaging in what the political scientist Hans Morgenthau referred to as the eternal struggle for power.[22] Yet there is more at stake than geopolitics; the logic of absolute war harms American democracy. Americans' fears of terrorism, which were impelled and sustained by the logic of absolute war, have encouraged warrantless wiretapping, illegal detention and torture, and increased government secrecy, all of which surrender the very values for which we are supposedly fighting. Moreover, the enormous cost of America's national defense effort—which, according to the Congressional Budget Office, consumes approximately one-sixth of all federal spending—has diverted resources from social programs that might restore Americans' lost sense of community.[23] If Americans persist in believing that everything must be done to defeat ISIS, Iran, and similar groups, there is little doubt that our democracy will continue to suffer.

Though he may have begun his career as an institutional critic, the constraints of America's bipartisan imperial vision left McMaster with little space for truly independent thought. One of the starkest examples of McMaster's limited perspective was displayed in a 2013 essay, in which he and two coauthors commended the U.S. Army for "provid[ing] advice and assistance to the Saudi Arabian National Guard's military schools, brigades, and headquarters for the past 39 years."[24] McMaster's praise of U.S. assistance to Saudi Arabia—a vicious dictatorship responsible for reprehensible human rights abuses—is as stark an example of willful moral blindness (and intellectual incoherence) as is possible. When someone lauds Saudi Arabia, it is hard to take his or her claims about U.S. moral superiority vis-à-vis ISIS or Iran seriously. In fact, the only people who seem to get away with such contradictions are members of the American foreign policy elite.

***

After the United States bombed a Syrian airfield in April, McMaster gave an interview to Fox News in which he offered a series of muddled remarks concerning American strategy in the Middle East. When asked whether the United States intended to defeat ISIS or focus on ousting Syrian leader Bashar al-Assad, McMaster responded "that there has to be a degree of simultaneous activity as well as sequencing of the defeat of ISIS first."[25] McMaster's inarticulateness reflected the strategic confusion of American policy in the Middle East, which has been compounded by the strategic confusion of an administration led by a doddering 70- year-old ill-suited for the position in which he finds himself.

For his part, McMaster remains fixated on ISIS. In a 2016 book review, he described the group's "control over territory, resources and populations [as] not only a present-day international security problem, but also a multi-generational threat to all civilized peoples."[26] He also insisted that Americans must understand

> ISIS not as the disease itself, but as a symptom of a disease [whose eradication] will require not only military operations, but also a long-term, multinational effort combining political, social, diplomatic, intelligence, communications, law-enforcement and economic projects aimed at both denying ISIS its safe haven and support base, and at healing and strengthening fragmented societies so that ISIS or its next manifestation is unable to regenerate.[27]

It seems that McMaster hopes the United States will, finally, fully commit itself to a Middle Eastern occupation. But one wonders why he would consider this a realistic possibility. The Trump era has not seen an increased appetite on the part of American voters for another war in the greater Middle East, and it has always been difficult to imagine how McMaster could have convinced the president to again invade a sovereign nation, or persuaded the American people to occupy Iraq or Syria as they once occupied Germany and Japan. This is even more true after McMaster's embarrassing public performance this week.

Any perceptive observer of the Trump Administration could have predicted that H.R. McMaster's impact as national security advisor would have been limited—not only because of the competing power centers in the White House or the pervasive influence of Steve Bannon, but also because the overarching quality of the Trump regime is chaos. Even the most careful manager would have been unable to execute serious, long-term plans in an administration dominated by stops, starts, and profound uncertainty.

One of the most depressing aspects of the Trump Administration is that, despite Trump's repeated critiques of recent American military interventions, the project of American Empire will likely remain unchallenged and undiminished. During the presidential campaign, a number of critics on the left and right argued that Trump's isolationist rhetoric should be taken seriously—that his disinterest in foreign adventurism and nation-building were genuine. This was probably always a fantasy, but after the bombing of Syria, it became provably false. The president's world tour is unlikely to mitigate the fact that under Trump, U.S. foreign policy is more of the same, only amateurishly executed.

Even if McMaster is pushed out (and reports in various news outlets suggest that Bannon wants him gone and that Trump himself is unhappy with his performance—apparently the lieutenant general talks too much in meetings), the core of his worldview will still dominate U.S. foreign policy thinking: ISIS and Iran will continue to be viewed as evil, the United States will continue to dedicate itself to never-ending war, and decision makers will continue to feel that they have the right to do most of what they want on the world stage. We cannot know whether a bit more independence of thought might have pushed McMaster to contest United States foreign policy or the very notion of American Empire. What we do know is that for all his iconoclasm and perspicacity, McMaster was never a true reformer, but rather an extraordinarily accomplished product of a corroded system.

Endnotes

1 Peter Baker and Michael R. Gordon, "Trump Chooses H.R. McMaster as National Security Advisor," *New York Times*, February 20, 2017, https://www.nytimes.com/2017/02/20/us/politics/mcmaster-national-security-adviser-trump.html.

2 Fred Kaplan, "Trump Just Hired the Army's Smartest Officer," *Slate*, February 20, 2017, https://slate.com/news-and-politics/2017/02/new-national-security-adviser-h-r-mcmaster-is-the-armys-smartest-officer.html.

3 Fred Kaplan, "The Tarnishing of H.R. McMaster," *Slate*, May 16, 2017, https://slate.com/news-and-politics/2017/05/h-r-mcmasters-reputation-is-being-destroyed-by-trumps-deceit.html; Jack Shafer, "H.R. McMaster Takes a Dive," *Politico*, May 17, 2017, https://www.politico.com/magazine/story/2017/05/17/hr-mcmaster-trump-leak-russian-classified-intel-215149/.

4 H.R. McMaster, "Remaining True to Our Values—Reflections on Military Ethics in Trying Times," *Journal of Military Ethics* 9, no. 3 (September 2010), 184.

5 Alex Roland, email message to author, March 12, 2017.

6 Email message to author, March 15, 2017.

7 H.R. McMaster, *Dereliction of Duty: Lyndon Johnson, Robert McNamara, the Joint Chiefs of Staff, and the Lies That Led to Vietnam* (New York: HarperCollins, 1997), 62, 162.

8 Ibid., 62.

9 Ibid., 163.

10 Though the historiography of the Vietnam War remains outside the scope of this essay, a number of prominent scholars disagree with several of McMaster's claims. In particular, Harvard historian Fredrik Logevall

argues in his *Choosing War* that, contra McMaster, McNamara was not at all blinded by a hubristic faith in the power of technology and was, in fact, privately rather skeptical about the United States' ability to eventually win the war, even as he championed escalation. According to Logevall, McNamara understood all too well the obstacles in the way of victory, as did, for that matter, President Lyndon Johnson. Fredrik Logevall, *Choosing War: The Lost Chance for Peace and the Escalation of War in Vietnam* (Berkeley: University of California Press, 1999).

11 H.R. McMaster, *Crack in the Foundation: Defense Transformation and the Underlying Assumption of Dominant Knowledge in Future War* (Carlisle Barracks, PA: Center for Strategic Leadership, U.S. Army War College, Student Issue Paper, Volume S03-03, November 2003), 1, https://media.defense.gov/2023/May/02/2003213354/-1/-1/0/3177.PDF.

12 Ibid., 13.

13 Ibid., 76.

14 H.R. McMaster, "Learning from Contemporary Conflicts to Prepare for Future War," *Orbis* 52, no. 4 (Fall 2008), 574.

15 Ibid., 567.

16 McMaster, "Remaining True to Our Values," 184.

17 Ibid., 193.

18 H.R. McMaster, review of *Modern War: A Very Short Introduction*, by Richard English, *Survival* 56, no. 2 (April–May 2014), 222.

19 George W. Bush, "Address Before a Joint Session of the Congress on the State of the Union" (speech, Washington, D.C., January 29, 2002), in John T. Woolley and Gerhard Peters, ed., *The American Presidency Project* (Santa Barbara, CA, 1999–2025), https://www.presidency.ucsb.edu/documents/address-before-joint-session-the-congress-the-statethe-union-22.

20 H.R. McMaster, "The Battle of 73 Easting," in *Leaders in War: West Point Remembers the 1991 Gulf War*, ed. Frederick W. Kagan and Chris Kubik (New York: Frank Cass, 2005), 117.

21 A defender of McMaster might note that before becoming national security advisor, constitutionally, McMaster had no right to interrogate civilian policy. He could not critique colonialism and empire, because to do so would have been to question the basic premises of U.S. foreign

relations, which are supposed to be determined by civilian leaders. Whatever one thinks of these claims, they are highly problematic in practice. The reason a president should be reticent about appointing a military officer NSA (or secretary of defense, a position now held by former general James Mattis) is that the position requires its holder to criticize U.S. grand strategy and the assumptions that sustain it. For all of McMaster's military insight, his previous career has not prepared him for his present responsibilities.

22 Hans J. Morgenthau, *Politics among Nations: The Struggle for Power and Peace* (New York: Alfred A. Knopf, 1948).

23 "Defense and National Security," Congressional Budget Office, accessed October 26, 2025, https://www.cbo.gov/topics/defense-and-national-security.

24 Chris McKinney, Mark Elfendahl, and H.R. McMaster, "Why the U.S. Army Needs Armor: The Case for a Balanced Force," *Foreign Affairs* 92, no. 3 (May/June 2013), 132.

25 Colin Wilhelm, "McMaster: U.S. Eager for Regime Change in Syria," *Politico*, April 9, 2017, https://www.politico.com/story/2017/04/hr-mcmaster-syria-regime-change-237038.

26 H.R. McMaster, review of *ISIS: Inside the Army of Terror*, by Michael Weiss and Hassan Hassan, *Survival* 58, no. 2 (April–May 2016), 214.

27 Ibid.

ROBERT M. GATES AND AMERICA'S FOREVER FOREIGN POLICY

Robert M. Gates was born in 1943 in Wichita, Kansas, and joined the Central Intelligence Agency 23 years later. He became a lieutenant in the U.S. Air Force in 1967; served for nine years on the National Security Council; and served as deputy national security adviser, as deputy director and director of central intelligence, and as secretary of defense under George W. Bush and Barack Obama, the only defense secretary in history to serve consecutively under two presidents. To describe Gates as part of the foreign policy establishment that emerged after World War II is to understate the case. His very person embodies that establishment.

In the years since he left the Department of Defense in 2011, Gates has written a memoir (*Duty*) and a work of "leadership studies" passionlessly titled *A Passion for Leadership*.[1] His latest book, *Exercise of Power: American Failures, Successes, and a New Path Forward in the Post–Cold War World*, was published in June 2020, as American failures—from the COVID-19 pandemic response to the plague of police violence against civilians to the never-ending disaster in Afghanistan—accumulated and any different path forward allegedly rested on the election of a senescent 77-year-old institutionalist.[2] Unlike its more straightforward predecessors, *Exercise of Power* is a curious and circuitous text, full of withering assessments of recent U.S. foreign policy catastrophes even as it remains fatally encumbered by Gates's own position as both longtime insider and true believer. It is a book of, and for, its era—a moment when American elites are chastened by the nation's many self-inflicted crises but unwilling or unable to come to terms with the implications of their failures.

"How did our country go so quickly from unique global power," Gates asks, "to a country that is widely perceived as no longer willing to bear the costs or accept the responsibility of global leadership—or even capable of governing itself effectively?"[3] His answer is simple, and partially correct: post–Cold War presidents and members of Congress alike have failed "to understand the complexity of American power, both in its expansiveness *and* in its limitations."[4] During the Cold War, Gates writes, U.S. leaders appreciated the importance of "the arsenal of nonmilitary assets"—diplomacy, economic sanctions, development assistance, propaganda—to exercising power.[5] But once the Soviet Union collapsed, many of those same leaders, high on their own supply of unilateral hubris and unburdened by existential anxieties about inadvertently sparking World War III—began to view the military as the tool to transform the world. For this reason, they foolishly proffered military solutions to nonmilitary problems.

Gates considers it crucial for American leaders to reform their ways. But for all his perspicacity, he cannot depart from the shibboleths about the U.S. Empire—or what he euphemistically terms "American leadership"—that have guided and defined his life, a life coterminous with this empire's greatest expansion.[6] Like many members of the foreign policy establishment, Gates cannot imagine nor countenance a world in which the United States abandons some of its power (and some of its sovereignty) to address the actual problems of the twenty-first century. Instead, Gates's world is filled with monsters that only American power can destroy.

Nothing can shake Gates's conviction that global peace and prosperity rest on the United States remaining the prime military, political, economic, and cultural power. To read Gates is thus to confront an elegist unaware that he's mourning. The imperial project to which Gates dedicated his life has failed, but in his dotage he remains unable to imagine another one. And he's not alone: Joe Biden's appointment of Tony Blinken as secretary of state and Lloyd Austin as secretary of defense suggests that the most recent geriatric to become president agrees with the former secretary. It is for this reason that *Exercise of Power* is worth taking seriously: it may very well provide a blueprint for the Biden Administration's foreign policy. As history has shown time and again, the failure of a bad idea does not strip it of its power.

***

For the politicians, intellectuals, bureaucrats, and generals who constructed the so-called American Century, it was crucial that U.S. "leadership" wouldn't be exclusively enforced with violence. While decision-makers always intended U.S. primacy to rest on the strength of the military and the dollar, they also hoped that it could become at least somewhat consensual. As such, midcentury policymakers created institutions such as the United Nations (to provide countries with a forum to express their opinions), the International Monetary Fund (to encourage financial stability and growth), the World Bank (to reconstruct Western Europe), and the U.S. Agency for International Development (to provide foreign aid). Though the United States committed manifold crimes during the Cold War—overthrowing foreign governments, initiating deadly wars, funding dictators—American elites nonetheless maintained that legitimate world leadership rested on providing for the global commons. For this reason, they were sometimes, if not always, reluctant to wantonly deploy armed force.

After the Cold War, however, decision-makers began to insist that the U.S. "victory" definitively revealed two things: first, that liberal democratic capitalism was the only viable system of political economy, and second, that the United States was the engine of world history. Secretary of State Madeleine Albright crystallized the beliefs of the national security establishment when she declared in a 1998 interview on *The Today Show* that America was "the indispensable nation. We stand tall and we see further than other countries into the future."[7] When coupled with the post–Gulf War "Revolution in Military Affairs"—the idea that technological developments had made war both easier to win and more humane—these exceptionalist convictions encouraged politicians and defense officials alike to regularly intervene abroad.

In the late 1980s and throughout the 1990s, the United States provided the majority of force for interventions in Panama (to topple Manual Noriega); Iraq (to force the nation's withdrawal from Kuwait); Somalia (to assist local aid workers); Bosnia (to support anti-Serb forces on the ground); Haiti (to reinstall Jean-Bertrand Aristide as president); Kosovo (to halt Slobodan Milosevic's ethnic cleansing campaign); and Sudan (to attack al-Qaeda). After the September 11 attacks, the nation pushed the Taliban, Saddam Hussein, and Muammar Gaddafi out of power. It goes without saying that many of these interventions ended in disaster. To take only the most recent examples: the United States remains stuck in Afghanistan, Iraq remains unstable, and Libya remains mired in violence and has even witnessed the return of slave markets.

Gates appreciates that post–Cold War U.S. foreign policy was, to put it mildly, catastrophic, even as he insists that the United States should continue to dominate the world. Why? Because no amount of history or reason can overcome his—and by extension the foreign policy establishment's—pseudo-religious commitment to American exceptionalism. This leads to often incongruous arguments, as when Gates notes that his nation regularly "worked with despotic (often murderous) governments" as he simultaneously maintains that "America must lead" because it's the only country able "to ensure that authoritarianism, twice defeated in the twentieth century, does not prevail in the twenty-first."[8]

Like most members of the so-called foreign policy blob, Gates at once acknowledges criticism of this position without taking such criticism especially seriously. That his critics are the people he's supposed to serve doesn't, in his mind, strengthen the opposition's case. "Most Americans," he admits, "have long wanted to just mind our own business and be left alone."[9] But according to Gates and, for that matter, nearly everyone involved with American foreign policy at a high level, this is a wrongheaded view that policymakers must ignore and overcome. To the extent that he supports educating the public about foreign policy, Gates envisions a top-down affair in which presidents "develop a foreign policy that [they] can persuade the public to support and then patiently, repeatedly, educat[e] the citizenry as to why that policy is necessary and deserving of support."[10] A democratic exchange this is not.

But as *Exercise of Power* itself repeatedly demonstrates, presidents—and the experts who provide them with intellectual ballast—have themselves failed to institute wise foreign policies. The worst foreign policy disasters of the post–1945 period—Korea, Iran, Guatemala, Vietnam, Chile, Afghanistan, Iraq, Libya—were supported by "the best and the brightest" ensconced in Washington, D.C. Clearly, the only way to prevent further destruction is for U.S. foreign policy to become more, not less, democratic by developing mechanisms to incorporate meaningfully the will of ordinary Americans into the foreign policymaking process. Gates, of course, isn't interested in such reforms, and his faith in U.S. righteousness and belief in the wisdom of his cohort prevent him from questioning the fundamental idea that has served as his life's lodestone and from which all U.S. foreign policy tragedies have sprung: "that our long-term self-interest demands that we continue to accept the burden of global leadership."[11]

***

If *Exercise of Power* has one overriding concern, it's the ascent of China. Gates does not discount the crises that the twenty-first century has already wrought—climate change, global inequality, pandemics, and other transnational challenges—but like leaders in both the Democratic and Republican parties, he insists that the People's Republic of China is the predominant geopolitical problem of our era. Gates avows that a so-called new Cold War will erupt between the United States and China, if it hasn't already. Like the old Cold War, the new one will not be a battle between geopolitical rivals with divergent but legitimate interests, but a Manichaean struggle between democracy and totalitarianism, a mostly useless term popularized after World War II to describe the ideologically opposite but (supposedly) similar statist regimes of Nazi Germany and the Soviet Union and thus manufacture consent for the nascent Cold War. Though Gates doesn't believe that a hot war will erupt between the United States and China—he continually, and vaguely, refers to U.S.–PRC "competition"—he presents this competition as essentially permanent.[12]

This dualistic framing of international relations has an ignoble history. Manichaean wars (or, if you like, Manichaean "competitions") have tended to be endless and to serve few people but the defense contractors, lobbyists, and think-tank analysts who profit from them. And in retrospect, it appears that Americans have tended to project their own peculiar, millenarian, universalist beliefs—beliefs that emerge from the Puritan substrate that permeates American politics—onto foreign powers that did not share them. Beginning with the doctrine of containment laid out by the State Department's George Kennan in his famous "Long Telegram" of February 1946, and continuing into the Cold War and post–Cold War eras, American elites have insisted that their perceived enemies—first the Bolsheviks, and now the Chinese—shared their longing to dominate the world.[13] Ironically, however, neither the Soviet Union nor the People's Republic of China ever expressed any sincere desire—or, more important, took any sincere actions—to rule the globe as the United States has done. Today, for example, China has only one overseas military base in Djibouti, compared to the United States' 750. These are simply not analogous.

There is little doubt that China desires to be the most powerful player in East Asia and will do everything it can to protect its access to foreign markets and raw materials. But these aspirations and goals are a far cry from the truly global, extra-hemispheric hegemony sought and achieved by the United States after World War II. Gates, though, elides the differences and therefore considers any of China's attempts to affirm its regional authority, or to improve its international bargaining power (by, for example, creating institutions such as the Asian Infrastructure Investment Bank), as direct attacks on U.S. interests. As American foreign policymakers have done for decades, Gates presents the entire world as a vital U.S. interest—an intellectual framework perfectly suited to encouraging long, fruitless wars such as the new Cold War for which he so desperately yearns.

Ironically, for an avowed American exceptionalist, Gates worries that the nature of "Chinese authoritarian state capitalism" provides the country with significant advantages in a geopolitical competition with the United States.[14] Unlike his own country, which is hampered by its free-market ideology, China "can direct both its massive state-owned enterprises and its banks to allocate large sums of money and people to specific initiatives and leverage its economic power both to promise great benefits for working with China or to bring great pressure on governments that oppose or try to thwart its policies."[15] Gates inquires as to whether "a democracy, unable to compel its companies to invest abroad, [can] compete ... with authoritarian state capitalism?"[16]

In asking this question, Gates unwittingly attaches himself to a transatlantic tradition dating back to the 1930s. During that decade, the rise of fascism compelled a generation of thinkers, from Kennan to Hans Speier, to worry about the so-called "totalitarian advantage" enjoyed by autocratic regimes. According to these intellectuals, the dictatorial and centralized nature of "totalitarian" states made them better able to mobilize and disburse resources than cumbersome and bureaucratic democracies. As such, over the course of the mid-twentieth century, intellectuals became increasingly anxious that democracies would lose any wars fought against authoritarians unless they undertook drastic measures.

Whereas midcentury elites, informed by New Deal–era politics, focused on building state and parastate institutions—the National Security Council, the Central Intelligence Agency, the Department of Defense, the U.S. Agency for International Development, the RAND Corporation, and so on—to mitigate this perceived disadvantage, Gates, who came of age during neoliberalism's ascendance in the 1970s and 1980s, when many of the aforementioned institutions were augmented with private actors such as the Heritage Foundation and Chemonics, highlights the importance of the private sector. For example, he praises President Donald Trump's International Development Finance Corporation, which was created in 2018 "to finance private development projects" and thus "counter China's investments in other countries by providing financially sound alternatives to state-led projects."[17] Ever a product of his times, Gates maintains that the primary way the U.S. government will overcome China's attempt to develop the Global South is by tightening the already-close relationship between capital and the national security state, regardless of the damage that such connections have historically wrought in Latin America, Africa, and elsewhere. As always, Gates remains in thrall to the failed policies of the past.

The first Cold War diverted money from welfare to weapons; encouraged domestic oppression; destroyed the American left; brought the world to the brink of nuclear war; and, most important, resulted in the deaths and deracination of tens of millions of people throughout the globe. It was a low point in human history that should have highlighted to elite and ordinary Americans alike the dangers of maximalist, Manichaean thinking. There is no reason to believe that a new Cold War would be any less of a tragedy. That Gates, a prominent and much-admired dean of the foreign policy establishment, is committed to such reckless and atavistic thinking—and the reckless and atavistic policy that flows from it—tells us much about what we are likely to see in a Biden

Administration. The Cold War is over, but for many of our foreign policymakers, it never ended.

***

For all his emphasis on nonmilitary tools and "soft power," Gates offers no meaningful departure from the militarist consensus that has long defined U.S. foreign policy. Because we can't possibly know the character of future war, Gates argues that "our military forces must be trained and equipped to have the greatest possible versatility across the broadest possible spectrum of conflict."[18] The military should be able "to defeat the most technologically advanced nation-states as well as nonstate actors (such as ISIL, al-Qaeda, and the Taliban) and still provide security assistance and training in underdeveloped countries."[19] As these statements reveal, when national security elites have access to a military hammer, all international challenges begin to look like nails, especially in a country where the State Department's budget is hundreds of billions of dollars less than the Defense Department's. It almost goes without saying that the permanent—and wildly expansive—mobilization that Gates calls for is a recipe for permanent war.

One of the many problems with permanent mobilization is that the U.S. military is ultimately controlled by one person: the president. To borrow a phrase coined by the political scientist Harold M. Barger, the American presidency is an "impossible" one—nobody can fulfill its evermore complicated and expanding duties.[20] As Gates himself notes, the president "sit[s] at the bottom of a funnel, at the wide top of which are more than 3 million men and women in and out of uniform in a dozen or more departments and agencies engaged in helping to formulate American foreign and national security policies or in implementing them."[21] Additionally, the United States has "interests" in every world region, each of which has its own complex history. No individual can possibly know what's going on in their own bureaucracy, let alone throughout the world, and make the responsible "life-and-death decisions" the

American president is supposed to.[22] Gates seems to believe that this system could function if the office were occupied by someone intelligent, as opposed to a dotard like Trump. But this is wishful thinking, as Barack Obama's disastrous Libyan intervention, as well as his other bad choices, make clear. It is simply impossible for any single individual to effectively and morally wield so much power.

***

The majority of *Exercise of Power* is dedicated to drawing lessons from the recent history of U.S. foreign policy. Despite his blinkered worldview, Gates gets a number of things right. Most important, he implores policymakers to ask themselves the following questions before they deploy military force:

> Are core U.S. national interests or those of our allies threatened? What other countries are willing and able to help us? What is the legal basis for intervening? Are our objectives realistic? Is the intervention time-limited? What is the potential cost in lives and treasure? What is the level of support in Congress and among the public? What are possible unintended consequences? What can go wrong?[23]

Inspired by earlier military thinkers such as Secretary of Defense Caspar Weinberger and Chairman of the Joint Chiefs of Staff Colin Powell, Gates correctly insists that "the bar for use of our military for purposes short of protecting our vital interests and those of our allies should be a high one."[24] The question, however, is who gets to define what "vital interests" are; as post–1945 U.S. history has demonstrated, the elites who manipulate the levers of power usually define these interests quite capaciously, especially when their career advancement depends on maintaining the American Empire. Put another way, as long as U.S. foreign policymaking remains highly undemocratic, then Gates's prescription will do little to stem the tide of endless war.

Gates also rightly reserves particular ire for "nation-building," the process of using military and nonmilitary power to engender social, political, economic, and cultural transformation in foreign countries. He argues that recent experiences in Haiti, Somalia, Afghanistan, and Iraq suggest that nation-building usually "involve[s] a serious mismatch between responsibilities and resources."[25] First, soldiers, who are the ones tasked with nation-building on the ground, are generally not trained to do so and thus often fail at their job. Second, it is extremely difficult to coordinate the manifold agencies involved in nation-building, a situation that impels counterproductive bureaucratic turf wars. Finally, nation-building requires altering a society's entire way of life, which is a generations-long project virtually impossible to achieve absent a lengthy, expansive, and brutal military occupation.

Ultimately, Gates blames the failures of nation-building—especially in Afghanistan and Iraq—on the fact that "America's singular power in every dimension after the end of the Cold War … obscured for our leaders the reality of very real limitations to that power. It tempted [Bill] Clinton, [George W.] Bush, and even Obama to think we could change other countries, despite history and culture, and make them more like us."[26] (According to the political scientists Sidita Kushi and Monica Duffy Toft of Tufts University's Military Intervention Project, "over 25% of all U.S. military interventions [since 1776—a total of almost 400] occurr[ed] during the post–Cold War era.")[27] As such, Gates implicitly if unknowingly argues that the interventions in Afghanistan and Iraq were not only responses to the September 11 attacks, but were also manifestations of the "end of history" discourse that permeated elite culture in the 1990s and 2000s. In this framing, September 11 was merely the proximate excuse that U.S. leaders needed to enact long-held plans to transform the world—an argument bolstered by the fact that it was Clinton who, in 1998, signed the Iraq Liberation Act, which declared that it was U.S. policy to topple Saddam Hussein.

Though Gates is right to be skeptical of nation-building, his skepticism emerges from a racialized solipsism that fails to consider the historical, structuring conditions of international relations. For example, he notes that despite the United States' use of military force and foreign aid to stabilize and develop Somalia, in the past three decades the Somalis have remained mired in conflict. According to Gates, no matter what the United States does, nothing in that "dysfunctional country" will change "until the Somalis themselves figure out how to stop killing each other."[28]

Gates here blames Somalia's problems on its own people and offers no historical explanation for the country's present state. He doesn't, for instance, address the fact that the area that comprises present day Somalia was colonized by the British, French, Italians, and Egyptians. More important, he ignores that it was the United States that provided substantial financial support to Siad Barre, the dictator whose oppressive rule helped spark the civil war that engulfed Somalia in the 1990s. Ironically for a trained historian (Gates received a PhD in Russian and Soviet History from Georgetown University), he exists in an eternal now in which the structuring conditions of the past have little influence on the present.

Gates's disinterest in history is crucial because it forces his gaze away from the fundamental cause of many of the modern world's problems: the last five centuries of North Atlantic dominance, colonialism, and exploitation, all of which engendered the oppressive structures of exchange and interaction that make some countries very wealthy and most countries very poor. To make the world safer and more prosperous—not only for Americans but also for everyone—one has to transform these structures themselves. If the past 75 years of U.S. hegemony have demonstrated anything, it's that no single country can ever force global peace and prosperity. These will only be achieved when all nations—the great powers first among them—abandon elements of their sovereignty and develop plans to distribute more fairly the resources that have long been hoarded by the elites of a small number of countries. Absent such redistribution, the world will remain in its traditional state of perpetual anarchy.

***

The most compelling parts of *Exercise of Power* concern Gates's descriptions of the foreign policy bureaucracy's inner workings. Anti-imperialists would be wise to take Gates's analysis seriously, as the successful implementation of a left-wing foreign policy will rest on effectively manipulating, and ultimately transforming, the machinery of the state. We learn, for example, that it's not only a chronic lack of funding that has attenuated the State Department's influence on foreign policy. Instead, most presidents for whom Gates worked have ignored the State Department because they considered it "some kind of alien entity within [their] administration" and were further able to use modern communications technologies to talk directly with their foreign counterparts.[29] As such, Gates affirms that over the past several decades "ambassadors and embassies [have] play[ed] little role in policy decisions."[30] As calls to refund the State Department gain more and more traction within Washington, D.C., those of us who want to reinvigorate American diplomacy must consider the diverse factors that limit the State's impact and appreciate that money won't solve all the department's problems.

Gates is also very critical of Congress, which he maintains has forced "a bunch of expensive programs" on an unwilling Defense Department.[31] "Both Republicans and Democrats," the former secretary laments, "cannot abide the thought of a single Defense program in their state or district being cut by a dollar, [which means that] the department is ... stuck with paying for a significant number of bases and facilities—probably 25 percent of the total—it neither wants nor needs."[32]

To decrease military spending, then, anti-imperialists will need to provide workable and compelling alternatives to the military Keynesianism that has supported so many communities throughout the United States. In this, they might look to make common cause with soldiers, sailors, airwomen and airmen, and marines. As Gates underlines, "the biggest doves in Washington wear uniforms, partly because they have seen up close the cost of war in lives broken and lost, and partly because they fear, with good reason, that if things don't go well the politicians will abandon them and whatever fight the president has started."[33] Put simply, the Left must cultivate the military; it's one of our most powerful potential constituencies. This is especially true given that the Department of Defense, as Gates highlights, "has two seats at the president's table—the secretary [of defense] and the chairman of the Joint Chiefs of Staff—an arrangement replicated at every level of the interagency process."[34]

Throughout *Exercise of Power*, Gates underlines the primacy of domestic politics in determining U.S. foreign policy. Take, for instance, his discussion of U.S.–Colombia relations. Here, the former secretary declares that "fatalistic" American officials enacted pointless anti-drug policies, such as "whack-a-mole seizures of illegal drugs by the Drug Enforcement Agency," because these were "necessitated" by "domestic politics and policy."[35] He even connects Clinton's October 1998 decision to initiate Plan Colombia to the president's desire to distract from ongoing impeachment proceedings and gin up support for the Democrats in the midterm elections. These and other examples are crucial reminders that parochial concerns oftentimes play a key role in foreign policymaking and that transforming the U.S. approach to the world will rely on transforming American domestic politics itself.

***

Ironically given that Obama's two major foreign policy achievements—the signing of the Joint Comprehensive Plan of Action with Iran and the opening to Cuba—were diplomatic in nature, Gates remains tied to the idea that defending America's "vital interests" necessitates constantly intervening in the affairs of foreign countries. This comes through vividly in his discussion of Iran. According to Gates, despite its relative weakness vis-à-vis the

United States, Iran remains a serious threat. For this reason, "the U.S. goal must be a change in regime that arises from the Iranian people themselves."[36] To help force this change, he recommends that decision-makers use "nonmilitary instruments of power to inform [Iranians] of specific abuses by their government and to convey our support for their efforts to increase pressure on the regime."[37]

It is clear that Gates has not thought through the implications of this suggestion. Here, history provides a guide. In early 1953, the U.S. government encouraged unhappy workers in East Germany to rebel against the ruling Socialist Unity Party and, by extension, the Soviet Union. Partially as the result of this encouragement, in June protests erupted throughout the German Democratic Republic. The United States was shocked at this outcome, and President Dwight D. Eisenhower, unwilling to risk World War III, refused to support the rebels. As a result, the Soviet military quickly quashed the uprising and further clamped down on East Germany. Absent massive U.S. weapons transfers—which are very unlikely—it's difficult to imagine a similar scenario playing out any differently in modern-day Iran.

Like most members of the foreign policy establishment, Gates is obsessed with Iran because he fears that it might one day achieve a nuclear breakout that will threaten Israel, the centerpiece of U.S. strategy in the Middle East. This is a genuine anxiety, but it's worth questioning whether or not that breakout would encourage or discourage peace. A major reason the United States felt comfortable toppling Saddam Hussein and Muammar Gaddafi was that neither Iraq nor Libya had nuclear weapons. In contrast, the United States will never invade North Korea because the country recently acquired nuclear capabilities. It's thus possible that a nuclear Iran would encourage peace by making it unlikely that the United States would attack it. It is obvious that promoting nuclear proliferation is a very dangerous proposition that increases the risks of both accidental and planned nuclear wars. Still, for the foreseeable future, an anti-imperial policy might ironically be synonymous with a pro-nuclear proliferation one. To put it even more starkly, in order to save lives, it might be necessary for other countries to develop the capabilities to defend against us.

***

The more time one spends in Gates's head, the more one is struck by the increasingly nihilistic quality of the American exceptionalist creed. Gates and his ilk remain committed to the idea that when there are problems in the world, the United States must "do something." What is that something? It usually doesn't matter much. In his discussion of Syria, for instance, Gates notes that "there is little assurance" that anything the United States could have done "would have made a significant difference" in the civil war.[38] Nevertheless, he declares that something "should have been tried."[39] Why? Because the United States is the global leader.

This is argument without argument, made by a person who doesn't feel the need to rationalize American action in the world. Gates's claims reflect power shorn of any substantial justificatory logic, which, ironically, is a defining feature of the post–Cold War American Empire that the former secretary spends *Exercise of Power* lambasting. The original Wilsonian case for American domination, which held that U.S. hegemony would benefit everyone, is barely even made. Now, the United States acts because it's the United States. Liberal internationalism, in short, has become a zombie ideology thoughtlessly consuming the world.

Like Gates—and like the previous four Presidents—the United States' new President has been raised completely in the era of U.S. Empire, and it's highly unlikely that he will be willing to criticize its foundational assumptions. The same is true of many of his younger advisers, who ascended to their positions by flattering the sensibilities of those in power. Would a President Harris upend the order that Robert M. Gates has worked so hard to defend and cultivate? A President Buttigieg? One closes *Exercise of Power* desperately hoping that it is the last book of its kind and that Gates is the last of an aging breed. But as recent events have indicated, this is, tragically, a naive hope. For the moment, at least, the Empire is here to stay.

Endnotes

1 Robert M. Gates, *Duty: Memoirs of a Secretary at War* (New York: Alfred A. Knopf, 2014); Robert M. Gates, *A Passion for Leadership: Lessons on Change and Reform from Fifty Years of Public Service* (New York: Alfred A. Knopf, 2016).

2 Robert M. Gates, *Exercise of Power: American Failures, Successes, and a New Path Forward in the Post–Cold War World* (New York: Alfred A. Knopf, 2020).

3 Ibid., 4.

4 Ibid., 5.

5 Ibid.

6 Ibid., 390, 392.

7 Madeleine K. Albright, interview by Matt Lauer, *The Today Show*, NBC-TV, Columbus, OH, February 19, 1998, https://1997-2001.state.gov/statements/1998/980219a.html.

8 Gates, *Exercise of Power*, 47, 11.

9 Ibid., 389.

10 Ibid.

11 Ibid., 415.

12 Ibid., chapter 12.

13 "The Chargé in the Soviet Union (Kennan) to the Secretary of State [The Long Telegram]," February 22, 1946, *Foreign Relations of the United States*, 1946, Eastern Europe, the Soviet Union, Volume VI, ed. Rogers P. Churchill and William Slany (Washington, D.C.: Government Printing Office, 1969), Document 475, https://history.state.gov/historicaldocuments/frus1946v06/d475.

14 Gates, *Exercise of Power*, 365.

15 Ibid., 365–366.

16 Ibid., 27.

17 Ibid., 374, 33.

18 Ibid., 18.

19 Ibid.

20 See Harold M. Barger, *The Impossible Presidency: Illusions and Realities of Executive Power* (Glenview, IL: Scott, Foresman and Company, 1984); Jeremi Suri, *The Impossible Presidency: The Rise and Fall of America's Highest Office* (New York: Basic Books, 2017).

21 Gates, *Exercise of Power*, 58–59.

22 Ibid., 59.

23 Ibid., 398.

24 Ibid., 399.

25 Ibid., 74.

26 Ibid., 187.

27 Sidita Kushi and Monica Duffy Toft, "Introducing the Military Intervention Project: A New Dataset on U.S. Military Interventions, 1776–2019," *Journal of Conflict Resolution* 67, no. 4 (April 2023), 753.

28 Gates, *Exercise of Power*, 124. Elsewhere, in an Orientalist vein, Gates refers to Afghanistan as a "primitive" and "staggeringly backward nation," in which "corruption oozed from every pore." Ibid., 174, 188, 189.

29 Ibid., 65.

30 Ibid., 67.

31 Ibid., 68.

32 Ibid.

33 Ibid., 69.

34 Ibid.

35 Ibid., 146.

36 Ibid., 117.

37 Ibid.

38 Ibid., 312.

39 Ibid., 313.

SAMANTHA POWER AND THE FOG OF INTERVENTION

Let's say it's January 2021, and President Bernie Sanders has just assumed office. On his second day as commander-in-chief of the most powerful military in world history, Bernie and his foreign policy team are ushered into the White House Situation Room. After being seated at a long wooden table, a group of diplomats and military officers informs Bernie that armed militants in the Central African Republic have placed artillery around a town and are threatening to bombard its 10,000 inhabitants. The townspeople have requested that the United States destroy the weapons and save their lives. What should Bernie do?

For Samantha Power, who served as U.S. ambassador to the United Nations during Barack Obama's second term, this really is no question at all: you eliminate the weapons. Power has dedicated her life to promoting humanitarian intervention—the idea that the United States, as the world's "indispensable nation," has the moral duty to use its awesome military capabilities to prevent or halt atrocities.[1] First as a war reporter covering the Balkans in the 1990s, then as the Pulitzer Prize–winning author of *"A Problem from*

Hell": America and the Age of Genocide, and finally as a government official herself, Power has insisted that the "responsibility to protect" innocents from slaughter is sacrosanct, even if it means U.S. military adventurism or violating foreign nations' sovereignty.[2] When civilians are threatened, Power believes that we must save them.

For this position, she has been both praised and lambasted. Power's supporters see her as a moral beacon in a world focused on power politics at the expense of human rights. In the last two decades, she has shaped how a generation of liberal analysts and policymakers understand international relations and their role within it: Barack Obama has called her "one of our foremost thinkers on foreign policy," while Ben Rhodes has said she was "who I wanted to become when I moved down to Washington."[3] Meanwhile, critics such as the law professor Aziz Rana understand her as a "pro-war face" who employs the discourse of human rights to mask American imperialism.[4] For them, Power embodies the contradictions of liberal geopolitics, in which lofty rhetoric is used to justify military action in regions where the United States has, at best, tangential interests.

Power's memoir arrives at a time when she and her approach have fallen from favor—both with the current administration, which has adopted a nakedly transactional approach to foreign affairs, and with left-wing foreign policy thinkers, who want to dismantle U.S. military dominance. Against these tides, Power's new book seems intended to rehabilitate both her agenda and her own reputation, as she narrates in vivid and engaging prose her rapid rise to some of the most influential positions in U.S. foreign policymaking. It's the story of a sympathetic protagonist just trying to save innocent lives—yet one that inadvertently demonstrates the lethality of good intentions. The most startling thing about a book titled *The Education of an Idealist* is that Power appears not to have learned very much.[5]

***

Power's early years exemplified the peripatetic privilege of the global bourgeoisie. She was born in Ireland in 1970, the daughter of a doctor mother and a dentist father. In 1979, after her father's alcoholism destroyed her parents' marriage, Power's mother moved with Samantha and her brother to the United States. Power quickly acclimated to American life; she lost her Irish accent, began a lifelong love affair with baseball, and started on her high school's basketball team. She also studied hard for the SAT and, in 1988, was accepted to Yale University.

During Power's sophomore year, the Berlin Wall came down, the Cold War ended, and she became a political junkie who quizzed herself on the news of the day. In the summer of 1990, she took a trip to Europe that would transform her life. Power began her journey with a visit to the Anne Frank House in Amsterdam. Walking through the bleak Secret Annex drove home to Power "the horror of Hitler's crimes," and after her visit she started to keep a list of books she wanted to read on "what U.S. officials knew about the Holocaust and what they could have done to save more Jews."[6] Soon after, she traveled to Dachau, where she "wondered aloud how the modern world would look if President Roosevelt had not finally entered the war."[7] (Ignoring, naturally, the Soviet Union's role in ending World War II and that it was the Red Army that liberated Auschwitz.)

Power's trip persuaded her that U.S. military force could legitimately be used to save innocent lives. The Holocaust became for her the moral justification for American Empire in an era in which the United States no longer faced any perceived existential threats. Power concluded that if the United States didn't rule the world, genocide was inevitable, and for the remainder of her career she would view atrocities in the Balkans, Africa, and the Middle East through the prism of the Holocaust: after all, if the U.S. military had liberated victims of genocide in the 1940s, why couldn't it do the same in the 1990s, 2000s, and 2010s?

The timing of Power's trip was also crucial for her intellectual development. Before the disintegration of the Soviet Union in the early 1990s, it was difficult to argue that the U.S. military could serve as a neutral arbiter of human rights. Not only was the nation engaged in an avowedly political struggle with an existential communist enemy, but the Vietnam War and several other failed interventions underlined the dangers of using military force for ideological ends. Communism's collapse made it possible for Power to imagine the U.S. military as a nonideological guarantor of broadly accepted human rights. The empire could act for humanity, not politics. For Power—and for many in her generation—the U.S. military was the base upon which the liberal international order of free markets, democracy, and human rights would be constructed.

***

By her senior year at Yale, Power had determined that she "wanted to end up in a position to 'do something'" about humanitarian crises.[8] After graduating, she interned at the Carnegie Endowment for International Peace, where Mort Abramowitz, the endowment's president and a former ambassador to Turkey, was turning his attention to the incipient Bosnian War. The more Power learned about the conflict and its atrocities, "the more unnerved" she became.[9] The war, she writes, provided her with "a focus—a specific group of people in a specific place who were being pulverized."[10] To publicize their suffering, she decided to become a war reporter, and in late 1993 she moved to the Balkans, armed with little more than a laptop.

Power was in Zagreb, Croatia, when on February 5, 1994, Bosnian Serbs mortared the Markale market in Sarajevo, killing 68 civilians. As she watched "CNN footage of market vendors carrying away the bloodied remains of their mutilated friends," she found herself "rooting for the first time in [her] life for the United States to use military force."[11] She spent the next year and a half writing pieces on civilian suffering that she hoped would engender a domestic outcry and convince President Bill Clinton to forcibly end the siege of Sarajevo.

As time went on and Clinton refused to intervene (the U.S.–led NATO Operation Deliberate Force would not commence until August 1995), Power began to consider a new track that was "less about describing events and more about directly trying to shape them."[12] The decisive moment came in July 1995, when she learned that the Bosnian Serb army murdered more than 8,000 Bosnian Muslims in Srebrenica. The sheer brutality of the genocide compelled Power to take up a place at Harvard Law School (she had applied and been accepted earlier that year), with the intention of "becom[ing] a prosecutor who could bring murderers to justice."[13]

At Harvard, Power returned to the question that had haunted her at the Anne Frank House and Dachau: Don't Americans, as citizens of the world's greatest power, have a personal responsibility to save lives if we have the capacity to do so? She enrolled in a class on the ethics of using force, and, most important for her future career, she wrote a paper that examined "what U.S. policymakers *themselves* were thinking when they responded to" twentieth-century genocides.[14] This paper was her first step toward her 2002 book *"A Problem from Hell,"* which codified a decade of liberal thinking about humanitarian intervention and which transformed Power into an internationally renowned expert on human rights and genocide prevention.

"A Problem from Hell" had two main arguments. First, it claimed that throughout the twentieth century "the United States has consistently refused to take risks in order to suppress genocide" and, by not acting, had failed the people of Armenia, Cambodia, and Rwanda, among other places.[15] Second, the book maintained that in the future, U.S. decision-makers should take steps to prevent or halt atrocities "along a continuum of intervention—from condemning the perpetrators or cutting off U.S. aid to bombing or rallying a multinational invasion force."[16] Power did not, as many critics later avowed, unthinkingly advocate military intervention; rather, she considered intervention as the final in a series of graduated steps intended to avert or stop genocide. But as Power herself would soon learn, when Americans were presented with the hammer of military force, many atrocities began to look like nails.

Power's book was perfectly primed for the post-9/11 moment, during which the question on many Americans' minds was not whether the United States should remake the world, but how. *"A Problem from Hell"* quickly became a cudgel in the debate over invading; as Power notes, several pundits clamoring for war invoked her book, arguing that the 1980s "Iraqi campaign of genocide against the Kurds" gave the United States a *casus belli*.[17] Even though Power herself opposed the invasion, the writers who referenced *"A Problem from Hell"* were not exactly misreading the book: Power had placed U.S. military intervention on the menu of options available to policymakers who said they wanted to protect human rights.

In a moment defined by paranoia, revenge fantasies, and a sense of moral crusade, it is not particularly surprising that *"A Problem from Hell"* was employed to rationalize war. The book's relevance at the time, in fact, helps explain why it won the Pulitzer Prize for general nonfiction in April 2003, one month after the George W. Bush Administration invaded Iraq.

***

With Barack Obama's election in 2008, Power got the chance to use her ideas to shape U.S. policy more directly. Obama and Power first met in the spring of 2005, when Obama was an ambitious junior senator from Illinois. They worked together for a year (Power volunteered to serve in his office), and when Obama won the Democratic primary in 2008, he hired her as a foreign policy adviser, later appointing her to the National Security Council (NSC) as senior director for multilateral affairs and senior director for human rights.

In government, Power swiftly learned that few officials cared about human rights; many, in fact, deemed them a distraction from more important issues of power politics. Nevertheless, while at the NSC, Power helped expand by $50 million U.S. aid to Iraqi refugees, increased the number of Iraqis allowed to resettle in the

United States, and doubled the government's refugee stipend. She also advocated for the United States to run for a seat on the U.N. Human Rights Council, which it won in 2009. From this perch, U.S. officials spurred a number of resolutions focused on revealing human rights abuses in various nations, including Iran, Syria, Sudan, and North Korea. Moreover, Power proudly emphasizes, the United States "succeeded in getting the Human Rights Council to reduce by half the share of country-specific resolutions on Israel."[18]

As this last comment indicates, for Power, protecting human rights means disciplining nations of the Global South that are not U.S. allies. Throughout *The Education of an Idealist*, she barely mentions Israel or Saudi Arabia—she says nothing about Israel's occupation of the West Bank or the Saudi war on women and LGBTQI+ people. These silences are deafening, because the type of world that Power wants to build will never be realized if only certain countries—namely, those that stand outside America's imperial sphere—are held to account. Her approach does not make much sense from a pragmatic perspective either: U.S. officials have the highest likelihood of ending human rights abuses in countries that depend on us; there is little point in spending political capital in a mostly quixotic attempt to transform antagonists such as North Korea.

Meanwhile, Power completely ignores the human rights violations that took place in her own country under Obama's watch; like many liberal interventionists, she is far more vexed by suffering abroad. Nowhere does she address police violence against African Americans, mass surveillance, refugee detention, or mass incarceration. Nor does she give much thought to the colonial violence that defines American history: In *The Education of an Idealist*, she recalls inviting a Serbian official to meet with her in the so-called Indian Treaty Room, where she lectured him on the importance of apprehending the war criminal Ratko Mladi. Somehow, Power overlooks the irony of championing justice in a room named for repeatedly broken treaties that the U.S. government made with the native population against which it committed genocide.

Power's most consequential decision during Obama's first term displayed a shortsightedness that has often accompanied her faith in U.S. military power. With the outbreak of civil war in Libya, Power began to advocate vociferously in favor of intervention to stop a potential massacre at Benghazi. In particular, during a March 15, 2011 meeting, Power endorsed U.N. Ambassador Susan Rice's proposal to establish a no-fly zone over Libya and attack Muammar Qaddafi's forces. Obama approved Rice's plan, and on March 19, a U.S.–led NATO coalition began bombing Libya, initiating a process that concluded with Qaddafi's death. Despite the war's expansion and the chaos that ensued, Power remains proud of her contribution. For her, "once the revolution spread, the real question became how to use the tools at our disposal to bring about the best possible—or the least bad—outcome."[19]

But was that the real question? Here are some other questions that are equally important that she should have taken more seriously before Obama commenced Operation Odyssey Dawn: Is the war likely to expand? If the war expands and Qaddafi is deposed, who will govern Libya? Is the United States—especially the American public—willing to commit itself to reconstruction efforts? What precedent does the intervention potentially set? Power never really asked these questions, because ultimately, as the historian Stephen Wertheim has argued, she considers humanitarian intervention a categorical imperative (as long as it doesn't involve U.S. allies, of course).[20] For this reason, throughout her time in office Power regularly encouraged war.

***

In Obama's second term, Power left the NSC to become U.S. ambassador to the United Nations. In this position, she won many admirable victories: she aided in establishing a U.N. post dedicated to monitoring global LGBTQ+ rights; brought countries together to end the deadly Ebola outbreak of 2014; and promoted a resolution that demanded the United Nations deport any peacekeeping units from countries in which U.N. soldiers were reported to have committed sexual assault.

Yet it was also during Obama's second term that Power found herself less able to convince the president of the moral necessity of intervention. In her memoir, she relates that when she first learned that Bashar al-Assad's government had employed chemical weapons in the Syrian civil war, she "hope[d] that Obama would respond forcefully" and was disappointed when he didn't.[21] Nevertheless, in August 2013, Power was heartened to discover that Obama intended to answer the Syrian government's murder of 1,400 people in a chemical weapons attack with airstrikes of military targets.

Power's expectations, however, were dashed when she was informed that Obama had decided to seek congressional authorization for the airstrikes. "'What happens if Congress doesn't support you?'" she asked the president. "'Does that mean Assad could just keep using chemical weapons, and they would become like a conventional weapon of war?'"[22] In the end, Obama determined that Congress would rebuff his plan and chose not to go ahead with a vote; against Power's wishes, he also refused to intervene. Instead, the president accepted Russia's offer to work together to disable Assad's chemical weapons program. For her part, Power "shuddered at the inadequacy of the effort" to decrease Assad's stockpile, despite the fact that U.S.–Russian collaboration provided an opportunity to build the trust necessary to reach a political resolution of the conflict.[23]

Power's recollection of the Syria debate highlights her meritocratic skepticism of democratic politics. She writes that she "regretted that our administration had not ascertained whether we had the votes *before* the President announced he was going to Congress. Had he known he would fail, [she] did not believe he would have chosen the path he did."[24] Power, in other words, wanted Congress to rubber-stamp Obama's decision to intervene; she wasn't interested in having a real public discussion about the potential benefits and drawbacks of using military force. In fact, Power has the temerity to express disappointment with the U.S.

public for refusing to support intervention. Most Americans, she laments, "wanted no part of Syria. The student activists, civic groups, churches, mosques, and synagogues that had come out en masse to demand help for the people of Darfur [where in the mid-2000s a genocide erupted] were largely silent."[25] Such a statement evinces the privilege of an individual who has no reason to fear the effects that another Middle Eastern intervention might have on her own family—or on the people of the Middle East.

***

The assumption running through Power's career is that the American Empire is able to act as a force for good in the world. At her memoir's end—and in the wake of Afghanistan, Iraq, Libya, and Syria—she affirms that "on issue after issue, either the United States brought a game plan to the table or else the problem worsened."[26] Though this might be true in some cases, it is certainly not the rule, especially when one considers the disastrous effects of the nation's wars in the greater Middle East; its pointless antagonism of China, Russia, and Iran; its unwillingness to take the business-unfriendly steps required to arrest climate change; and its unhesitating promotion of a capitalist system that has exploited the labor of untold millions. The last several decades have taught us that the world needs far less American "leadership" than it has enjoyed.

If you accept Power's premises, then humanitarian intervention boils down to a purely philosophical inquiry: Is it right to save lives if one has the capacity to do so? The answer, of course, is yes. The problem, though, is that intervention is not a thought experiment; it takes place in a world of brutal realities. In particular, humanitarian forces confront radical uncertainty. Is intervention likely to impel more violence in the long term? Do policymakers actually know enough about the situation on the ground to make the "right" decisions? Is the American public willing to commit itself to yearslong reconstruction efforts? Honest answers here may not sit well with idealism. In many instances, the most moral act is not to act at all.

Simply maintaining an enormous military able to intervene anywhere in the world carries its own set of malign consequences: endless wars, global arms proliferation, a militaristic political culture, the diversion of resources from welfare to weapons, and the strengthening of the military-industrial complex, to name just a few. *The Education of an Idealist* does not account for these social ills, or consider that the only way we can avoid them is by giving up the capacities that enable us (theoretically, if not in practice) to alleviate foreign suffering.

The historian Samuel Moyn has warned that we must be careful not to privilege "the narrow and rare problem of when to send the military to help strangers into the decisive one around which the future of American foreign policy revolves."[27] Power's memoir shows how much the discourse of humanitarian intervention obscures. By focusing on the question "Do we save innocent lives?" liberal interventionists such as Power shift our attention from an equally important query: "How do we change conditions so lives don't need to be saved?" A world oriented around this last question would look very different from the one we have now.

Endnotes

1 Madeleine K. Albright, interview by Matt Lauer, *The Today Show*, NBC-TV, Columbus, OH, February 19, 1998, https://1997-2001.state.gov/statements/1998/980219a.html.

2 Samantha Power, *"A Problem from Hell": America and the Age of Genocide* (New York: Perennial, 2003 [2002]). On the "responsibility to protect," see Office on Genocide Prevention and the Responsibility to Protect, United Nations, "About the Responsibility to Protect," United Nations, accessed July 30, 2025, https://www.un.org/en/genocide-prevention/responsibility-protect/about.

3 Barack Obama, "Remarks by the President in Personnel Announcement" (remarks, Washington, D.C., June 5, 2013), https://obamawhitehouse.archives.gov/the-press-office/2013/06/05/remarks-president-personnel-announcement; Ben Rhodes, *The World as It Is: A Memoir of the Obama White House* (New York: Random House, 2018), 18.

4 Aziz Rana, "The Left's Missing Foreign Policy: On the Pressing Need, Fifteen Years After the Iraq Invasion, for a Non-Imperial Vision of the U.S. and the World," March 28, 2018, *n+1*, https://www.nplusonemag.com/online-only/online-only/the-lefts-missing-foreign-policy/.
5 Samantha Power, *The Education of an Idealist: A Memoir* (New York: Dey St., 2019).
6 Ibid., 45.
7 Ibid., 46.
8 Ibid., 49.
9 Ibid., 56.
10 Ibid., 61
11 Ibid., 78.
12 Ibid., 86.
13 Ibid., 103.
14 Ibid., 121.
15 Power, *"A Problem from Hell"*, 503.
16 Ibid., 504.
17 Power, *Education*, 133.
18 Ibid., 222.
19 Ibid., 308.
20 Stephen Wertheim, "When Humanitarianism Hurts," March 26, 2010, *The Utopian*, https://www.the-utopian.org/post/2340512569/when-humanitarianism-hurts.
21 Power, *Education*, 362.
22 Ibid., 376.
23 Ibid., 386.
24 Ibid., 384.
25 Ibid., 382.
26 Ibid., 550.
27 Samuel Moyn, "Old Rivals, New Allies?", review of *A Foreign Policy for the Left*, by Michael Walzer, *Modern Age* 60, no. 3 (Summer 2018), 75.

THE WORLDS OF NOAM CHOMSKY

Noam Chomsky is the most famous critic of U.S. Empire in the world. No single living intellectual comes close. Even John Mearsheimer, the international relations theorist well-known for his critiques of U.S. foreign relations, can't hold a candle to Chomsky: a Google Ngram search quickly reveals how many more times Chomsky's name appears in English-language texts than Mearsheimer's.[1]

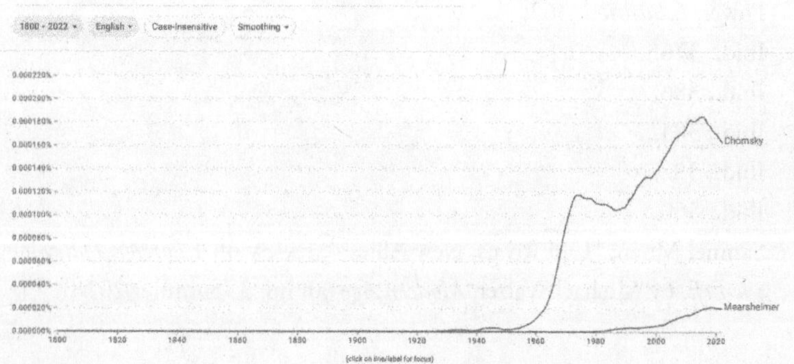

And Chomsky is not just one of the most cited writers on the subject of U.S. foreign relations; he's that rare scholar who has made the leap from academia to popular culture. His name appears in songs by the punk band NOFX ("And now I can't sleep from years of apathy / All because I read a little Noam Chomsky") and the comedian Bo Burnham ("My show is a little bit silly / And a little bit pretentious / Like Shakespeare's willy / Or Noam Chomsky wearing a strap-on").[2] Robin Williams's psychologist character in *Good Will Hunting* brings up Chomsky to demonstrate his intellectual bona fides to Will himself.[3] And in my favorite reference, on the TV show *Community*, the character Britta—an annoying lefty poseur whose claim to fame is that she "lived in New York"—has a cat named Chomsky.[4] If ordinary Americans know one critic of the American Empire, it's almost certainly Chomsky.

Though he was trained as a linguist, it's not especially surprising that Chomsky has become best known for his political opinions. Born in 1928 and raised in Philadelphia, he wrote his very first article—which appeared in the February 1939 edition of his fifth-grade newspaper—on, as he remembers, "the spread of fascism in Europe and its apparently inexorable conquest and the terror this incited."[5] Indeed, the essay that made Chomsky's name was not an esoteric piece on linguistics but rather his 1966 "The Responsibility of Intellectuals," a manifesto that lambasted those scholars who, Chomsky believed, were more interested in cozying up to power than speaking truth to it.[6]

Like many great essays, "The Responsibility of Intellectuals" was Chomsky's response to something that annoyed him: how academics around Harvard and MIT (where he taught) aligned themselves with the John F. Kennedy Administration regardless of its policies. "There was a kind of Camelot fever," Chomsky recalls. "Great excitement among, say, Cambridge intellectuals … There was a shuttle, [an] airline shuttle … that went from Boston to Washington, up and back through the day. In the morning, you could literally see the intellectual elite lining up at the shuttle so they could go to Washington and rub shoulders with the great and the powerful, [and they would] come back in the evening on the shuttle all excited."[7]

As the Vietnam War heated up, so did Chomsky's righteous rage. It galled him that scholarly war hawks such as Harvard historian Arthur M. Schlesinger Jr.—JFK's confidant—and MIT economic historian Walt Rostow—Lyndon Johnson's national security adviser—used their considerable brainpower to grease the wheels of the imperial war machine, oftentimes through propagandistic statements to the public. This, Chomsky insisted, betrayed the intellectual's duty. "It is the responsibility of intellectuals," he avowed in no uncertain terms, "to speak the truth and to expose lies."[8]

Ever since that essay, Chomsky has done exactly that, dedicating himself to the task of speaking truth, if not to power, then to the tens of millions of people in the United States and abroad who want to understand why the so-called indispensable nation has acted in the world as it does. In his dozens of books on U.S. foreign policy, Chomsky has painstakingly elucidated the many crimes committed by the United States all over the globe. Beyond his criticisms, he has also articulated a democratic alternative to the present world order, one in which ordinary people come together to resist the American Empire and the incredible damage it causes.

The Myth of American Idealism: How U.S. Foreign Policy Endangers the World is Chomsky's latest book and, given his advanced age, probably his last.[9] Coauthored with Nathan Robinson, the prolific editor of the left-wing magazine *Current Affairs*, it contains all of Chomsky's hallmarks. Written in a direct, no-nonsense style, full of shrewd analysis and layered with potent details, it is an excellent summary—and condemnation—of how the United States has shaped the world since it became a global superpower after World War II. Like almost all of Chomsky's books, it fulfills the intellectual's responsibility to speak the truth and to expose lies—including what Chomsky considers the biggest falsehood of them all: Americans' naive belief that their country "is committed to promoting democracy and human rights" around the world.[10] This is the "myth of American idealism" referenced in the book's title, and it is a myth that Chomsky and Robinson dismantle piece by piece.

***

The case that Chomsky and Robinson lay out is difficult to deny, if familiar to those aware of the ignominious history of U.S. foreign relations since 1945. The book presents a horrifying chronology: our 1947 intervention in Greece to suppress a popular communist uprising; our subversion of Italy's 1948 election; our repression of democratic and left-wing groups in postwar Japan and South Korea; our participation in the 1953 overthrow of Iran's Mohammed Mossadegh, the 1954 overthrow of Guatemala's Jacobo Árbenz, and the 1961 assassination of the Democratic Republic of the Congo's Patrice Lumumba; our many failed attempts to murder or overthrow Cuba's Fidel Castro; our participation in the annihilation of Indonesian communists and fellow travelers; our destruction of North and South Vietnam, Cambodia, and Laos; our involvement in the 1973 overthrow of Chile's Salvador Allende; our provision of aid to Guatemala as its government perpetrated a genocide; and so on, down to the present day.

After finishing *The Myth of American Idealism*, no honest reader could possibly deny that the United States has been involved in some of the worst crimes of the twentieth and twenty-first centuries and is directly and indirectly responsible for the death and dispossession of tens of millions of people. The truth is obvious for those with eyes to see: since its rise to global power in the 1940s, the United States has not been a benevolent hegemon. Rather, and like the many empires that preceded it, the American Empire is a cruel one that resorts to violence and subterfuge whenever we Americans deem it necessary. And we do deem it necessary. A lot.

Chomsky and Robinson tell this story in the sharp, serious, and to-the-point tones of a biblical prophet, a figure that Chomsky, with his long and snowy beard and hair, has come to resemble. We

Israelites have sinned, and in addressing us, the pair's prose simmers with a bracing anger that few modern writers are willing to adopt.

Problems emerge, however, when Chomsky and Robinson relate the practice of U.S. foreign policy to the myth of American idealism that they rightly deplore. In effect, the two maintain that most ordinary Americans embrace an idealistic view of their nation that "excuse[s] behavior that has caused colossal amounts of death and destruction."[11] There is no doubt that the myth of American idealism is repeated ad nauseam by politicians and their stenographers in the mainstream media. But do most people truly believe it?

***

Chomsky's most influential book is his 1988 *Manufacturing Consent: The Political Economy of the Mass Media*, which he cowrote with the economist Edward S. Herman.[12] In it, Chomsky and Herman argue that Americans are the victims of propaganda and misinformation that for decades have "manufactured consent" for an obviously rapacious, ruinous, and even evil U.S. foreign policy.

For Chomsky and Herman, the primary manufacturer of this consent is not the American state itself but the supposedly private media. The idea of a "free press," they insist, has always been misleading: While it is true that in American society there is little "formal censorship," media organizations have nonetheless sought "to inculcate and defend the economic, social, and political agenda of privileged groups that dominate the domestic society and the state."[13] Ironically, it is the very lack of official censorship that provides the news with a patina of objectivity and has made the American mass media so effective at manufacturing consent for elite interests. Americans, in short, are regularly fed (and unknowingly consume) a steady diet of propaganda; as in authoritarian societies, they are "managed and mobilized from above."[14]

To some degree, Chomsky and Herman are correct in their claims. As Chomsky and Robinson note in *The Myth of American*

Idealism, mainstream media organizations have dedicated themselves to "reinforcing and spreading the basic doctrines of U.S. foreign policy, portraying our aggression and terror as self-defense"; have "helped the state manufacture new enemies"; have insisted that whichever adversaries we are presently fighting are "diabolical and bent on our destruction"; and have ensured that American "wrongdoing is consigned to the memory hole or recast as another 'noble mistake.'"[15]

There is no doubt that all this is true. But even if propaganda abounds, is it accurate to say that most Americans believe it? Do Americans really consider U.S. power abroad to be a beneficent force? There is ample evidence to suggest they do not.

To start, one could go back to the 1960s, when a massive movement against the Vietnam War spread across much of the United States and demonstrated just how many Americans had come to doubt the notion of U.S. benevolence. Or one could look at the 1980s, which witnessed significant protests against U.S. policy in Central America. Even in the wake of the September 11, 2001 attacks—a period in which many Americans were baying for blood—a large protest movement erupted in an attempt to prevent the U.S. invasion of Iraq.

Today, the myth of American idealism is in even less repute. Simply put, the Global War on Terror and its myriad and manifest failures have revealed to Americans the damage their nation has done, and continues to do, abroad.

Take, for example, the use of the term "American Empire," a pejorative phrase that implicitly places the United States in a violent, imperial lineage. Whereas the term had previously been confined to the radical socialist and libertarian fringes, in the past two decades it has gone mainstream. Books with titles like *The Secret History of the American Empire* and *How to Hide an Empire* have become bestsellers, while outlets such as National Public Radio host interviews on subjects like "The History of U.S. Intervention and the 'Birth of the American Empire.'"[16] At the same time, mainstream cultural products such as the movie *Captain America:*

Civil War and the *Call of Duty: Black Ops* video game series portray the United States as either a rogue nation or run by a bunch of ne'er-do-well psychopaths who embrace violence for violence's sake.

If Americans' language and pop culture suggest anything, it is that many of us do not believe that our country is an idealistic one focused on doing good in and for the world. We may support it; we may trust that it does what is necessary. But we no longer accept its benevolence. We know that we're an empire, and not an especially kind one at that.

Intriguingly, polling data shows that Americans are slowly turning away from the idea that the security and prosperity of both our nation and the world depend on U.S. global "leadership." A recent poll by the Chicago Council on Global Affairs, for example, reveals that "fewer than six in 10 Americans think the United States should play an active role in world affairs."[17] Another poll, this time by Gallup, puts that number at 66 percent.[18] While these polls still do indicate that most Americans believe that the United States should remain involved in international politics, things look different when you divide Americans by age. A Pew poll, for instance, discovered that just 33 percent of adults under the age of 35, and 49 percent of those between the ages of 35 and 49, consider it "extremely or very important that the U.S. play an active role in world affairs," compared with 66 percent of those in the 50–64 age group and 74 percent of those above 65.[19]

The fact that young people have become ever more skeptical of U.S. hegemony indicates that Chomsky and Herman's propaganda model no longer accurately reflects reality. Besides the undeniable damage caused by American belligerence worldwide, a major reason for this is that the era of mass media in which Chomsky and Herman wrote has ended. Essentially, the "mass" media has been displaced by a "social" media that skirts many of the norms that had previously enabled mainstream newspapers and television news programs to manufacture consent for U.S. Empire.

Whereas in the past it was difficult for Americans to access evidence of U.S. violence abroad, today all one has to do is scroll through X or Instagram or TikTok to see horrifying images of U.S.-sponsored war crimes. It is just not true, as Chomsky and Robinson declare, that "the human costs of the pursuit of dominance … do not reach most of the public."[20] Anyone with a smartphone who is interested in international politics has seen the terrible images of Gazan children ripped apart by U.S.-supplied bombs—images that in the era of mass media would have been unlikely to appear in *The New York Times* or on Walter Cronkite's *CBS Evening News*. The widespread dissemination of these appalling photos and videos is a likely reason why a Chicago Council poll found that "slightly more Americans think Israel has gone too far and its military actions in Gaza are not justified (32%) than think Israel is justified in defending its interests (27%)."[21] In the 2020s, the brutality of U.S. Empire is no longer hidden but rather available to all.

***

For years, Chomsky has argued that the truth will set us free—that when enough Americans learn about the crimes their nation commits overseas, they will organize and reshape the empire from within. But we all know about the horrors of the American Empire, and yet these horrors persist. This raises the question: If the truth is known but has not transformed U.S. foreign policy in any discernible way, how can critics of empire actually change the United States' approach to the world?

Predictably, Chomsky and Robinson offer a traditional left-wing answer to this question: They argue that "necessary social change happens because of large numbers of dedicated people … working together at all levels, day in and day out."[22] To prove their point, they highlight a number of anti-war movements, including those against the Vietnam and Iraq wars, that, they claim, altered the course of U.S. foreign policy. But when one interrogates these examples, it becomes clear that Chomsky and Robinson's proposed solution to the problem of American Empire—mass protest movements—has never been enough on its own.

The movement against the Vietnam War provides a case in point. Despite how this movement is remembered, it had little policy influence. Historical scholarship, in fact, suggests that the most immediate effect of the anti-war movement was to shift military strategy in Southeast Asia to focus more on bombing than ground troops, which tragically increased the violence that the people of North and South Vietnam, Laos, and Cambodia suffered. The movement's most lasting impact was that it helped end the draft, but this had the ironic consequence of making it easier for U.S. presidents to deploy force abroad, because without a draft, the children of the bourgeoisie no longer fought America's wars. Even more, the anti-war movement appears not to have significantly hastened the war's end. A number of scholars, the historian Sean Fear explained to me, link the U.S. withdrawal from Southeast Asia less to the anti-war movement and more to, as Fear put it, "conservative concerns over the cost of Vietnam and its seeming irrelevance to broader Cold War strategy" that became significant after the election of Richard M. Nixon to the presidency in 1969.[23]

Similarly, though the protest movement against the war in Iraq may have gotten millions of people into the streets both in the United States and abroad, this, too, failed to prevent or end the war. Simply if starkly put: When it comes to changing U.S. foreign policy, mass action alone has never realized the dreams its advocates have set out for it. While protest movements are preferable to lethargy, inaction, and nihilism, by themselves they are just not enough.

If the Left ever hopes to change U.S. foreign policy, it needs to move beyond the shibboleths of the past. We must stop fetishizing information politics and mass protests and instead must develop an institutionalist understanding of how state power functions. And when we look to institutions, we can see that the U.S. national security state has been specifically designed to prevent the solutions that Chomsky and Robinson propose from working.

To make a long story short: In the late 1940s and early '50s, the architects of the national security state, anxious about the impact that a supposedly ignorant public could have on U.S. foreign affairs, established a series of institutions—from the National Security Council to the Central Intelligence Agency to the National Security Agency—that were intentionally insulated from public opinion and, in many instances, from Congress itself. Marches and publicity campaigns alone will not turn these institutions around; only political—that is, state—power might.

Though Chomsky and Robinson acknowledge that foreign-policy decision-making is "heavily concentrated in the hands" of the U.S. ruling elite, and though they concede that this elite operates "within institutions that reflect existing power structures," they remain convinced that these "institutions can be modified or replaced," because "citizens can easily act to create alternatives even within existing formal arrangements."[24] Unfortunately, nothing in the history of the post–World War II United States indicates that this is the case.

None of these criticisms is intended to take away from the achievement of *The Myth of American Idealism*, which should become required reading for those seeking to learn about the U.S. Empire's blood-soaked history. Without a doubt, Chomsky and Robinson have fulfilled their responsibility as intellectuals to speak the truth and to expose lies.

In fairness, too, the problem of converting criticism into policy has bedeviled the anti-imperialist left for decades; no one knows the precise way to go about it. But what is clear is that the Left needs to spend less time disabusing people of myths they no longer believe and organizing mass protests that go nowhere. Instead, we must formulate a more effective strategy for shaping state behavior. Reforming, and eventually ending, the American Empire will not be easy, and if history teaches us anything, it is that we may fail. But we must try: the fate of the world might actually depend on it.

Endnotes

1 "Google Ngram Viewer," accessed August 4, 2025.

2 "Franco Un-American," track 3 on NOFX, *The War on Errorism*, Fat Wreck Chords, 2003, Genius, https://genius.com/Nofx-franco-un-american-lyrics; "What's Funny," track 3 on Bo Burnham, *Words Words Words*, Comedy Central Records, 2010, Genius, https://genius.com/Bo-burnham-whats-funny-lyrics.

3 *Good Will Hunting*, directed by Gus Van Sant (Miramax, 1997), 126 minutes, Amazon Prime Video (streaming).

4 *Community*, season 6, episode 2, "Lawnmower Maintenance & Postnatal Care," directed by Nat Faxon and Jim Rash, written by Dan Harmon, Alex Rubens, and Carol Kolb, aired March 17, 2015, Amazon Prime Video (streaming).

5 Noam Chomsky, "We Talk to Chomsky, Pt. 1," interview by Daniel Bessner and Derek Davison, *American Prestige*, June 8, 2024 [originally released January 8, 2022], https://americanprestige.substack.com/p/unlocked-we-talk-to-chomsky-pt-1.

6 "The Responsibility of Intellectuals" began life as a speech that Chomsky delivered at the Harvard Hillel Foundation in March 1966. It was then published in *Mosaic*, the journal of Harvard's Hillel. Soon after, Chomsky's friend, the literary critic Frederick Crews, brought the piece to the attention of the *New York Review of Books*, where it was republished in expanded form. In this essay, I quote from the expanded version of the piece. See Noam Chomsky, "The Responsibility of Intellectuals," *Mosaic* 7, no. 1 (Spring 1966), 2–16; Noam Chomsky, "A Special Supplement: The Responsibility of Intellectuals," *New York Review of Books*, February 23, 1967, https://www.nybooks.com/articles/1967/02/23/a-special-supplement-the-responsibility-of-intelle/. Also see Robert F. Barsky, *Noam Chomsky: A Life of Dissent* (Cambridge, MA: MIT Press, 1998), 122; Noam Chomsky, *Noam Chomsky: A Personal Bibliography, 1951–1986*, comp. Konrad Koerner and Matsuji Tajima, with the collaboration of Carlos P. Otero (Amsterdam, NL: John Benjamins Publishing Company, 1986), 91.

7 Chomsky, "We Talk to Chomsky, Pt. 1."

8 Chomsky, "The Responsibility of Intellectuals."

9 Noam Chomsky and Nathan J. Robinson, *The Myth of American Idealism: How U.S. Foreign Policy Endangers the World* (New York: Penguin Press, 2024).

10 Ibid., 4.

11 Ibid., 20.

12 Edward S. Herman and Noam Chomsky, *Manufacturing Consent: The Political Economy of the Mass Media* (New York: Pantheon Books, 1988).

13 Ibid., 1, 298.

14 Ibid., 303.

15 Chomsky and Robinson, *The Myth of American Idealism*, 285, 286.

16 John Perkins, *The Secret History of the American Empire* (New York: Dutton, 2007); Daniel Immerwahr, *How to Hide an Empire: A History of the Greater United States* (New York: Farrar, Straus and Giroux, 2019); Stephen Kinzer, "The History of U.S. Intervention and the 'Birth of the American Empire,'" interview by Terry Gross, *Fresh Air*, NPR, January 24, 2017, https://www.npr.org/2017/01/24/511387528/the-history-of-u-s-intervention-and-the-birth-of-the-american-empire.

17 Dina Smeltz, "American Support for Active U.S. Global Role Not What It Used to Be," Chicago Council on Global Affairs, August 22, 2024, https://globalaffairs.org/research/public-opinion-survey/american-support-active-us-global-role-not-what-it-used-be.

18 Jeffrey M. Jones, "Steady 66% Want Leading or Major World Role for U.S.," Gallup, March 6, 2025, https://news.gallup.com/poll/657725/steady-leading-major-world-role.aspx.

19 Hannah Hartig, "Views on America's Global Role Diverge Widely by Age and Party," Pew Research Center, August 2, 2024, https://www.pewresearch.org/short-reads/2024/08/02/views-on-americas-global-role-diverge-widely-by-age-and-party/.

20 Chomsky and Robinson, *The Myth of American Idealism*, 12.

21 Dina Smeltz and Lama El Baz, "American Public Divided over U.S. Approach to Israel's War in Gaza," Chicago Council on Global Affairs, April 4, 2024, https://globalaffairs.org/research/public-opinion-survey/american-public-divided-over-us-approach-israels-war-gaza.

22 Chomsky and Robinson, *The Myth of American Idealism*, 297.

23 Sean Fear, email message to author, October 28, 2024.

24 Chomsky and Robinson, *The Myth of American Idealism*, 239, 20.

ON JOHN J. MEARSHEIMER AND MICHAEL WALZER

On February 2, 2003, the political scientist John J. Mearsheimer published a coauthored op-ed in *The New York Times* that lambasted the Bush Administration's case for invading Iraq.[1] In a carefully laid out argument, Mearsheimer and Stephen Walt, a fellow scholar of international relations, predicted that deposing Saddam Hussein would cause more problems than it solved. They argued that the dictator needed to be contained, and that preventative war was not just unnecessary but also harmful.

Of course, neither Bush nor his cronies listened, and on March 20, the Iraq War began. When it was officially wound down in December 2011 (note that we still retain thousands of troops in the country), the war had cost almost $1 trillion; resulted in the deaths of hundreds of thousands of Iraqis and about 4,500 U.S. soldiers; generated untold suffering among people who lost limbs, family members, and their mental health; and destabilized the region by empowering the Islamic State and engendering a massive refugee crisis.

Since then, Mearsheimer, a West Point graduate who served in the Air Force, has been a stalwart opponent of U.S. military adventurism, particularly in Eastern Europe and the Middle East. His latest book, *The Great Delusion: Liberal Dreams and International Realities*, is his attempt to explain why so few people in the U.S. foreign policy establishment—a loose network of government bodies, think tanks, NGOs, lobbying groups, and research organizations—seem to agree with him.[2] Doing so, Mearsheimer maintains, will help us understand "why post–Cold War U.S. foreign policy was so prone to failure" and will (hopefully) help the nation chart a better path forward in an era when the United States' relative power position is in decline.[3]

According to Mearsheimer, U.S. foreign policy has failed because after the Cold War, and especially after 9/11, elites in both parties embraced a grand strategy of "liberal hegemony" that seeks "to turn as many countries as possible into liberal democracies while also fostering an open international economy and building formidable international institutions."[4] This strategy is doomed, he argues, because it is insufficiently attuned to two realities of international politics. First, it does not take into account the power of nationalism, which causes foreign peoples to reject U.S. attempts to intervene in their affairs. Second, and more important, Mearsheimer believes that liberal hegemony ignores the centrality of balance of power politics to international relations.

Like many realists before him, from Hans Morgenthau to Henry Kissinger, Mearsheimer considers "international anarchy"—a term that simply refers to the fact that there is no world state able to legitimately adjudicate international disputes—the primary determinant of geopolitics. Because there is no world state, war is an ever-present possibility, which means that wise states must always focus their attentions on the "balance of power"—the power relationships that exist between states—and attempt to increase their relative positions within it. For realists, these are the fundamental, tragic, and untranscendable realities of international politics that prevent the realization of perpetual peace.

But the United States has not been a wise state. To explain why, Mearsheimer argues that sometimes a liberal state is so much more powerful than any potential challenger that its elites can disregard the balance of power and embrace the quixotic notion that they can make the world in their liberal, democratic, and capitalist image. This, obviously, was the position the United States found itself in after the collapse of the Soviet Union, and everyone reading this knows where the story ends: in the mountains of Afghanistan, the streets of Iraq, and the deserts of Libya, where U.S. intentions have gone to die.

These failures lead Mearsheimer to advise that the United States abandon liberal hegemony and embrace a grand strategy of "restraint" characterized by a much more limited use of U.S. power abroad.[5] Specifically, he affirms that the United States should stop provoking Russia by encouraging the expansion of NATO and the European Union; should stop promoting democracy in Russia's neighbors; and should end the permanent war in the Middle East.

Mearsheimer, however, by no means advocates a full retrenchment of U.S. power. Indeed, he is quite concerned about the rise of China, which he considers the only nation able to potentially challenge U.S. hegemony. As such, he maintains that the United States "must prevent China from becoming a regional hegemon in Asia."[6] This presumably means that Americans should retain their presence in East Asia, especially the South China Sea. If the United States prevents China's ascent, Mearsheimer suggests we could reap the benefits of hegemony without suffering the drawbacks of overextension.

There is much to admire in Mearsheimer's case against liberal hegemony, which has time and again failed to achieve its grand ambitions. I have no doubt that the United States has little to gain by provoking Vladimir Putin or striking weddings in Yemen with drones. On balance, a strategy of restraint would be far superior to one characterized by disastrous interventions, and those who envision more robust social welfare services at home should consider building bridges with realists such as Mearsheimer who want to contain the U.S. military and its ballooning budget.

However, there are significant problems with Mearsheimer's ontology—and, indeed, with the ontology of realism in general. To understand why, we must examine realism's midcentury origins. Realism was developed in the 1940s and 1950s by a cohort of German émigrés scarred by the international relations of the 1930s, a decade in which two great powers—Nazi Germany and Imperial Japan—launched a devastating world war that killed and maimed tens of millions. It is not surprising that in response to the horrors of World War II—and the inability of the League of Nations to prevent it—thinkers such as Morgenthau, John Herz, Hans Speier, and Arnold Wolfers developed a theory of international politics that was incredibly pessimistic about the possibilities of international cooperation and which considered great power wars endemic features of geopolitics. These beliefs formed the core of realism and remain at the center of its philosophy.

These convictions are problematic, however, because they reify a peculiar historical moment as ontological reality. As Mearsheimer succinctly puts it, "realism is a timeless theory" that is true throughout all eras of history.[7] But as the historian Nicolas Guilhot has shown, this belief "places limits upon the kind of political goals that one can pursue and indeed makes it difficult if not impossible to pursue positive or transformative goals."[8] Thus Mearsheimer maintains that human beings will never be able to create a world state capable of transcending international anarchy and are instead doomed to fight war after war until one, presumably, finally wipes out the entire species. There is a reason that Mearsheimer's most famous book is titled *The Tragedy of Great Power Politics*.

From a historical perspective, though, Mearsheimer's pessimism appears unwarranted. If anything, the broad sweep of human history evinces a trend toward ever-larger political units that encompass wider and wider geographic and cultural spaces. Human beings, in other words, have repeatedly built new solidarities that at one time appeared impossible. Why would this process stop at the nation-state, a political form that is only 225 years old? Even if one believes a world state is an unrealistic fantasy, why is it impossible to create novel political constellations based on mutual respect and cooperation? Simply put, I am not convinced that Mearsheimer is correct to claim that human beings are congenitally unable to build regional, continental, and, perhaps, global political communities that, eventually, transcend war. While this process will no doubt be difficult and painful, there is no reason to believe it is impossible—unless you think it always is, and will forever be, the 1930s.

Realism's midcentury origins also lead Mearsheimer to emphasize worst-case scenarios. This is clear in his anxiety over China's rise, which he considers a threat to U.S. hegemony and thus to the U.S. national interest. Beyond the fact that it seems to me profoundly unrealistic to believe that Americans will indefinitely support a U.S. military presence in East Asia, it is unclear why, exactly, the emergence of another great power far from our shores threatens the United States. Indeed, a negotiated security transition in East Asia (the United States maintains approximately 375,000 personnel in its Indo–Pacific Command) would free up funds that could be used to bolster the social safety net and address domestic income inequality, two of the most pressing issues of our time. It could also make China a true stakeholder in maintaining international peace. Furthermore, there are historical reasons to be wary of worst-case scenarios. During the Cold War, the mistaken belief that the Soviet Union was necessarily an existential enemy bent on the United States' destruction engendered costly arms races, prevented the sort of honest negotiations that could have ended the U.S.–Soviet struggle in the 1950s, and encouraged Americans to create a massive global basing system (currently about 750 bases in dozens of countries). More recently, the fear of another 9/11 led to the fruitless "War on Terror" and its many violations of civil liberties that Mearsheimer rightly deplores. This is all to say that we must not allow worst-case scenarios to determine U.S. foreign policy.

In the entirety of its existence, one could argue that the United States' survival has been urgently threatened by external forces only twice: during the War of 1812 and during the Cuban missile crisis of 1962. Our average condition is one of safety, and it is from this base that we must develop our grand strategy.

Mearsheimer's—and many realists'—obsession with worst-case scenarios emerges from the assumption "that most states, most of the time, follow balance-of-power logic."[9] This is simply not true. As manifold historians have demonstrated, decision-makers pursue policies for a diversity of reasons, whether they be ideological, economic, developmentalist, racial, gendered, or, perhaps most importantly, political. To take a famous example, Lyndon B. Johnson escalated the Vietnam War not only—or even mostly—because of the "domino theory" but also because he was anxious about his political future. In retrospect, even the Cold War—the balance-of-power struggle par excellence—seems to have been mostly about the ideological fight between capitalism and communism. Ironically, Mearsheimer himself has recognized the limits of the balance of power as an explanans of state behavior, cowriting a book about the pernicious effects of the "Israel lobby" on U.S. foreign policy.[10] Indeed, in *The Great Delusion* he admits that "the best way to undermine liberal hegemony is to build a counter-elite that can make the case for a realist-based foreign policy."[11] By Mearsheimer's own admission, then, the balance of power often does not explain U.S. international relations. A central category of realist thinking about geopolitics is thus undercut, which implies that realism's pessimism might be unwarranted.

***

Despite its flaws, Mearsheimer's realism provides a much better guide for making foreign policy than the one presented in Michael Walzer's strange *A Foreign Policy for the Left*.[12] Walzer, one of the most prominent political theorists of the twentieth century, unfortunately seems stuck in that era: his recommendations atavistically reflect the hopes of the "long 1990s" (1989–2001), when Americans believed that they could use their awesome power to do whatever they wanted in the world.

Walzer's primary concern is humanitarian intervention, which is a somewhat odd focus in 2018. As Samuel Moyn aptly put it in his review of *A Foreign Policy for the Left*, "Walzer elevates the narrow and rare problem of when to send the military to help strangers into the decisive one around which the future of American foreign policy revolves."[13] Walzer's understanding of foreign policy, in short, is parochial; one might even say it exists outside history. Since the end of the Cold War, policymakers have been forced to answer the question of humanitarian intervention fewer than a dozen times. Compare this to the fact that in 2017 alone U.S. Special Forces were deployed to 149 countries. Given this record, should the resurgent left be focusing its energies on humanitarian intervention or U.S. militarism?

From a biographical perspective, it is easy to see why Walzer is preoccupied with humanitarian intervention. Born to Jewish parents in New York City in 1935, Walzer's early political development was defined by an ethical confrontation with World War II and the Holocaust. The source of his interventionism becomes obvious in *A Foreign Policy for the Left* when he warns that "anti-militarism … produced one of the worst moments in left history—the opposition of many, though not all, British, French, and American leftists to rearmament against Nazi Germany in the 1930s."[14] Similar to realists such as Mearsheimer, the bogeyman of Hitler continues to shape Walzer's understanding of geopolitics. While leftists would be foolish to argue that a Hitler-esque figure will never again emerge, they should also not pretend that tin-pot dictators such as Putin, Kim Jong Un, and Bashar al-Assad are existential threats akin to the Nazi tyrant. The same is true for the "Islamist zealotry" against which Walzer wants to prosecute an "ideological war."[15] It is perhaps time for younger leftists, less traumatized by events that happened over seven decades ago, to begin asserting their voice in foreign policy discussions.

In several instances, Walzer appears not to have a full grasp of contemporary geopolitics. This becomes disappointingly clear when he claims that "a very limited (and ineffective) American intervention" in the Syrian civil war "was overwhelmed by the massive interventions of other states."[16] Walzer seems to be arguing that more military investment in Syria would have ended, or at least attenuated, the violence. This is twice wrong. First, the United States continuously intervened in Syria from the start by financing regime opponents, backing the actions of regional allies, and eventually arming local proxies. These policies, alongside an "Assad must go" posture and an initial refusal to include Iran in negotiations, may not have put U.S. boots on the ground, but they exacerbated the growing militarization of the conflict in ways that escalated and prolonged the bloodshed. It is difficult to see what adding U.S. troops to the maelstrom would have accomplished.

Second, and more important, Walzer's position ignores the balance of power. As Asli Bâli and Aziz Rana have noted, the U.S belief "that with enough [military] pressure a tipping point could be reached and the Assad regime would fall ... ignored the obvious fact that Syria's centrality to Iranian and Russian regional security interests meant that these countries would not allow the regime to fall without being given a stake in the future governing arrangement."[17] While it is true that Assad and his external backers bear the overwhelming responsibility for the violence in Syria, the U.S. decision to treat the nation as a regional chess piece without reckoning with the interests of competing states proved disastrous. Unless the United States was willing to fully commit its military to Assad's overthrow—which was politically unlikely in the wake of Afghanistan and Iraq—Iran and Russia were not going to allow it to happen. As this suggests, Walzer's understanding of foreign policy would benefit from a hefty dose of Mearsheimerian realism.

Walzer, however, is right to criticize those American leftists who believe that "Americans will be more safe in the world and the world will be better off ... if we concentrate on creating a just society at home."[18] (Though he does go too far in referring to this position as the "default"; to my knowledge, few young leftists defend isolationism.) He is also correct to argue that the United States is simply too powerful, too influential, and too embedded in the globe's political, economic, and cultural systems to retreat from international relations. But it is unclear why leftist internationalism must center on military intervention, as opposed to, say, closing down overseas bases—a topic Walzer barely addresses and which to me seems like a pressing problem. Though Walzer honestly desires to "help people in faraway countries escape poverty and terror," he never considers that the best means to do so is to remove a U.S. military that has repeatedly caused the very horrors he wants to assuage.[19]

In spite of its significant problems, *A Foreign Policy for the Left* does contain several insights. Perhaps the most important is Walzer's argument that the Left should focus both on "what our own state is doing in other people's countries" and on what "our [i.e., leftist] parties, unions, and nongovernmental organizations" should do in the world.[20] In other words, Walzer usefully highlights the distinction between state foreign policy and what might be termed the foreign policy of civil society. Though these are related, they are not the same. In the former, the central actors are elites—analysts, experts, bureaucrats—which underlines the need for the Left to develop a cadre capable of effectively manipulating the levers of state power should a democratic socialist government be elected. In the latter, the central actors are ordinary people who have the capacity to build transnational solidarities based on anti-militarist, anti-imperialist, postcapitalist politics. The question for the Left is how to integrate these two types of foreign policies into a coherent program that is popular, effective, and wise—no easy task, and one to which leftists must dedicate themselves in the coming years.

***

Unfortunately, neither Mearsheimer nor Walzer offer recommendations for how to reform the foreign policymaking process. For both scholars, foreign policy centers on what the United States should or shouldn't do in the world. Yet, today, several of the most important questions of foreign policy lie at home. Since at least 1945, U.S. foreign policy has been made by a small group of nonelected elites ensconced in executive agencies and free from public and Congressional accountability. In the wake of the myriad foreign policy disasters since 9/11, from Afghanistan to Iraq to Libya to Syria to Yemen, this elite has unsurprisingly lost its legitimacy. Indeed, during his primary campaign President Donald J. Trump made hay by lambasting the establishment for its many failures. And he wasn't wrong. Given that the United States is entering a new geopolitical era defined not by unipolarity and hegemony but by multilateralism and power sharing, it might be time for Americans to rethink how U.S. foreign policy is made. How can we ensure that U.S. foreign policymaking is more democratic? How can we guarantee that foreign policymakers are held to professional and legal account? These are critical questions that foreign policy thinkers, who for too long have focused on the world and not the United States, must begin to address in earnest.

Mearsheimer and Walzer represent two important sides of the mainstream foreign policy debate. Though at first glance they have little in common, in significant ways both are responding to the geopolitics of the 1930s and 1940s. But the world of 2018 is manifestly not the world of 1945—let alone of 1933—and it is time to develop a new geostrategy unencumbered by past traumas. While international relations are sometimes nasty and brutish, we must never assume that they always are. If we give up on transformational politics, as Mearsheimer does, and if we remain mired in the stale platitudes of the 1990s and 2000s, as Walzer is, our foreign policy will continue to be defined by failure, destruction, and death. For the sake of Americans and those living abroad, we cannot allow this to happen.

Endnotes

1 John J. Mearsheimer and Stephen M. Walt, "Keeping Saddam Hussein in a Box," *New York Times*, February 2, 2003, https://www.nytimes.com/2003/02/02/opinion/keeping-saddam-hussein-in-a-box.html.
2 John J. Mearsheimer, *The Great Delusion: Liberal Dreams and International Realities* (New Haven, CT: Yale University Press, 2018).
3 Ibid., vii.
4 Ibid., viii.
5 Ibid., chapter 8.
6 Ibid., 228.
7 Ibid., 135.
8 Nicolas Guilhot, *After the Enlightenment: Political Realism and International Relations in the Mid-Twentieth Century* (New York: Cambridge University Press, 2017), 4.
9 Mearsheimer, *The Great Delusion*, 171.
10 John J. Mearsheimer and Stephen M. Walt, *The Israel Lobby and U.S. Foreign Policy* (New York: Farrar, Straus and Giroux, 2007).
11 Mearsheimer, *The Great Delusion*, 231.
12 Michael Walzer, *A Foreign Policy for the Left* (New Haven, CT: Yale University Press, 2018).
13 Samuel Moyn, "Old Rivals, New Allies?", review of *A Foreign Policy for the Left*, by Michael Walzer, *Modern Age* 60, no. 3 (Summer 2018), 75.
14 Walzer, *A Foreign Policy for the Left*, 25.
15 Ibid., 152.
16 Ibid., 6.
17 Asli Ü. Bâli and Aziz Rana, "Remember Syria?", *Boston Review*, July 18, 2018, https://www.bostonreview.net/articles/asli-bali-aziz-rana-trump-putin-syria/.
18 Walzer, *A Foreign Policy for the Left*, 3.
19 Ibid., 8.
20 Ibid.

PART III
POLITICS

ENDING PRIMACY TO END U.S. WARS

The United States has been a territorially, culturally, and economically expansionist power for its entire history. In the early 1940s, decision-makers in Washington embraced a grand strategy of "armed primacy"—that is, the pursuit of global dominance based on military superiority and expressed in policies that presume that domestic and global peace and prosperity depend on the United States' being the world's strongest power. Throughout the Cold War and post–Cold War periods, U.S. officials pursued primacy, which engendered numerous wars and interventions.[1] The Gulf War of 1990–1991 was of particular importance in this context: It was the opening salvo in an attempt to create a post–Cold War order with the United States as its sole center of power. The quick victory over Iraq, its popularity among elites and the public, and broad international participation in the operation demonstrated to U.S. officials that wars could be fought relatively cheaply, humanely, and easily. The Gulf War also provided a bête noire for policymakers in the person of Saddam Hussein—whose bravado and anti-American attitude led many U.S. elites to compare him with Adolf Hitler as an existential threat to U.S. security interests. Put another way, the Gulf War indicated to many observers that the United States could serve as the world's policeman and, in President George H.W. Bush's evocative phrase, establish a "new world order" with the nation as the prime military power.

As U.S. elites embraced the new world order, it was crucial to them that America brook no challenges to it, even by smaller states. Though defeated in the Gulf War, Iraq was such a state throughout the 1990s and early 2000s: Saddam remained in power and in control of a strong military that served as a constant (perceived) threat to U.S. dominance in the region. This was a major reason that only a pretextual incident was needed to produce a confrontation, which the September 11, 2001 attacks provided.

Despite the failures that the pursuit of primacy generated—most obviously the 2003 invasion of Iraq, but also the invasion of Afghanistan two years earlier and the NATO intervention in Libya in 2011—the United States remains committed to the primacy grand strategy. This is especially apparent in its increasingly hostile relationship with China, a country that many U.S. elites argue seeks hegemony in East Asia—an outcome that the Trump and Biden Administrations have both attempted to prevent. It is inevitable, given the present geopolitical context, that the United States and China will compete for regional and even global influence. But this competition must not be allowed to explode into war.

Indeed, the United States must reconceive its fundamental commitment to primacy and recognize that, in the emergent multipolar world, it can no longer dictate terms in its relations with others as it has in the past. The U.S.–China competition presents the most pressing case in point. The United States must embrace a more constructive position toward the People's Republic that respects its emergent status and creates the conditions that will enable the cooperation necessary to address the primary threats of the twenty-first century: inequality, population movements, pandemics, and climate change. This holds not only in East Asia but also in other regions and relationships as well.

Competition, in other words, must not be allowed to prevent cooperation. Even as the United States competes with China, it needs to establish conditions that, first, ensure that this competition is constrained and, second, enable the creation of novel international and regional institutions that incentivize exchange. The coming multilateral world has the potential to engender innovative forms of transnational and international interaction. For this to occur, however, the United States must rethink its commitment to a strategy of armed primacy.

To take another obvious case, it is important to recognize that Washington's response to Russia's recent invasion of Ukraine must not be to sustain American military hegemony. On the contrary, the pursuit of primacy is a key reason the United States' global position has declined—which, in turn, arguably emboldened the Kremlin's ambitions in Ukraine. Additional investments in the illusion of global American hegemony will only advance this trend.

***

From its beginnings as a settler-colonial nation, the United States has been an expansionist power. Over the course of the nineteenth century, it pressed its boundaries relentlessly westward across the continent, displacing Indigenous tribes. It then dominated the Western Hemisphere through both economic and military means. After the Spanish–American War of 1898, U.S. officials seized Spain's colonies in the Philippines, Puerto Rico, and Guam. Today, the United States retains formal control over five populated territories: American Samoa, Guam, the Northern Mariana Islands, Puerto Rico, and the U.S. Virgin Islands.

By World War I, the United States was the unquestioned hegemon in the Western Hemisphere. But it was only in 1940 that U.S. elites began to believe that global primacy was possible. The main cause for this shift was the fall of France in the summer of 1940. As Stephen Wertheim has documented, France's rapid collapse in the face of the Nazis' onslaught persuaded American elites in and out of government that America's and the world's peace and prosperity depended on the achievement of U.S. "armed primacy"—not only in the Western Hemisphere but in most of the rest of the world as well.[2] The fact that France's fall rapidly followed the radical expansion of Japan's war against China in 1937—when the Imperial Army moved from low-level skirmishes around Manchukuo to a full-scale invasion of the mainland—underlined the perceived need for global dominance in the face of authoritarian militarism. The idea was that if the United States failed to achieve primacy, an anti-liberal and antidemocratic power would do so, engendering war, economic competition, and other deleterious outcomes.

This belief intensified considerably during the early Cold War, when U.S. policymakers were convinced that containing and reducing Soviet power around the globe was essential for the United States' security. They thus pursued armed primacy around the world through U.S. military buildups and expansive and novel military alliances such as NATO, SEATO (Southeast Asia's short-lived equivalent of NATO), and CENTO (otherwise known as the Baghdad Pact, which brought together countries in the Middle East and Central Asia). For much of the Cold War period, however, it was not possible for the United States to dominate regions in the communist sphere of influence. U.S. elites thus refused to intervene overtly when the Soviet Union put down resistance in East Germany (1953), Hungary (1956), and Czechoslovakia (1968), as decision-makers considered these states to be in the Soviet sphere.

But in regions or nations that American policymakers believed were under their rightful purview—Korea and Vietnam, for instance—decision-makers spent an enormous amount of time and money, and deployed increasing amounts of force, to keep countries on their side. As Lindsey O'Rourke has shown, during the Cold War the United States attempted to overthrow foreign regimes dozens of times.[3] In the cases of North Korea (1950), Lebanon (1958), the Dominican Republic (1965), Grenada (1983), Libya (1986), and Panama (1989), the United States did so overtly.[4] But in most instances, U.S. officials preferred covert means to impose regime change. In an astonishing 64 cases, the United States planned or tried to topple regimes covertly; it succeeded 25 times.[5] To take a related dataset, Sidita Kushi and Monica Duffy Toft of Tufts University's Military Intervention Project have established that between 1946 and 1989 the United States mounted foreign military interventions 104 times, including full-scale wars in Korea (1950–1953) and Vietnam (1954–1975).[6] Compared with earlier eras of U.S. history, the Cold War decades—the first period in which the United States attempted to secure armed primacy—were by far the most violent when it came to foreign affairs.[7]

***

When the Berlin Wall fell in 1989, European communist regimes disintegrated and the Cold War ended. Two years later, the Soviet Union collapsed, leaving the United States the undisputed global superpower. But even before the Soviet Union's final downfall, the Gulf War of 1990–1991 made two things clear to the world. First, it demonstrated that the United States would remain militarily predominant in global affairs whether or not it confronted an existential enemy of the kind that policy elites had historically used to justify America's post–1945 search for armed primacy. Second, it revealed that U.S. elites intended to establish a world order with America as its undisputed head. As President George H.W. Bush announced on September 11, 1990—a little more than a month after Iraqi President Saddam Hussein invaded Kuwait—"the crisis in the Persian Gulf" would result in the creation of "a new world order … freer from the threat of terror, stronger in the pursuit of justice, and more secure in the quest for peace." Crucially, Bush also made clear that "our involvement in the Gulf is not transitory" and that "long after all our troops come home … there will be a lasting role for the United States in assisting the nations of the Persian Gulf."[8] Put another way, Bush connected an intervention to stop a specific incursion to the larger project of global primacy, embodied here in the assurance that the United States would continue to dominate the Middle East into the foreseeable future.

Of special importance were the lessons U.S. elites drew from the conflict, which suggested that primacy was politically and militarily feasible. In particular, the rapid success of Operation Desert Storm, which resulted in only 143 American combat deaths, indicated to many observers that a "revolution in military affairs" (RMA) had made military intervention—and primacy itself—humane and easy.[9] As H.R. McMaster, an officer in the Gulf War and later one of President Donald Trump's national security advisers, described it, RMA advocates insisted "that new technologies in the areas of surveillance, communications, long-range precision weaponry, and stealth made possible a new way of waging war."[10] Stated simply, the revolution in military affairs was understood to have made war cheap (at least in terms of American lives and expenditure) and primacy politically and diplomatically viable.[11]

The Gulf War was also critical in providing a bête noire for U.S. foreign policy in the person of Saddam Hussein. Ever since policymakers decided to pursue a grand strategy of global armed primacy in the 1940s, U.S. foreign policy has been predicated on identifying an existential enemy.[12] Oftentimes, this enemy is personalized. Hitler, Mussolini, and Hirohito played this role during World War II; Stalin and his successors assumed it afterward. But the Soviet Union's collapse removed the threat (whether perceived or actual) that had justified the large military expenditures that Washington's pursuit of primacy required. A new enemy was needed, and Saddam Hussein quickly became that enemy. In fact, in the run-up to and after Iraq's invasion of Kuwait, Saddam was regularly compared with Hitler—a salient indication of the Iraqi leader's place in the American imagination.[13] George H.W. Bush drew this analogy most notably in October 1990, when he referred to Saddam as "Hitler revisited."[14] In Saddam, who remained in power after the Gulf War, U.S. officials and ordinary Americans found someone whose threat justified the continued search for primacy.[15]

The "easy" U.S. success in the Persian Gulf War and the absence of a peer competitor combined to encourage reckless adventurism.

In the three decades after the Gulf War, the United States pursued a staggering number of global military interventions—112 from 1990 to 2019, more than 28 percent of all interventions the U.S. had undertaken since 1776.[16] The war also strengthened jingoist and nationalist tendencies among senior policymakers, who argued that, when using force, the country could do no wrong. The late Madeleine Albright, then serving as secretary of state, embodied the spirit of the age when she declared in 1998 that the United States had the right to use force "because we are America; we are the indispensable nation. We stand tall and we see further than other countries into the future."[17]

Iraq occupied a central place in U.S. foreign policy throughout the 1990s, in part because of its symbolic significance in legitimizing the strategy of armed primacy after the Cold War. And in many ways, the country served as an American punching bag. After the war, the United States imposed extensive economic sanctions on Iraq, as well as no-fly zones.[18] In 1996, President Bill Clinton ordered a missile strike on Iraq to respond to Baghdad's attack on Erbil, an Iraqi Kurdish city; in 1998, he ordered air strikes on Iraq for its failure to comply with various United Nations resolutions that required the country to allow inspectors access to its weapons facilities. That same year, Clinton also signed the Iraq Liberation Act into law. This act stated unequivocally that it was "the policy of the United States to support efforts to remove the regime headed by Saddam Hussein from power in Iraq and to promote the emergence of a democratic government to replace that regime."[19] Clinton further pursued a strategy of "dual containment" against Iraq and Iran that, as former Secretary of Defense Robert M. Gates summarized, "meant relying on military force to prevent Iraq from attacking its neighbors, combined with stricter enforcement of the no-fly zones, additional economic sanctions, and support for Iraqi opposition groups."[20]

As this record makes plain, years before the U.S. invasion of 2003, policymakers were set on a course of confrontation with Iraq because they were committed to a strategy of U.S. primacy;

were persuaded that war could be fought cheaply and with few consequences for Americans; had made it difficult to back down or compromise with Saddam, having compared him to Hitler; and had instituted sanctions and no-fly zones that were effectively war by another name.

The Iraq War from 2003 to 2011, therefore, was not an aberration or the isolated mistake of an especially reckless George W. Bush Administration: It was the consequence of the broad U.S. commitment to primacy and more proximate developments in the U.S.–Iraq relationship that occurred after the Cold War's end. One cannot easily dismiss the possibility that a Gore Administration, if elected in 2000, would have also invaded the country after the September 11, 2001 attacks. Al Gore had voted for the Gulf War, favored intervention throughout the 1990s, endorsed the Iraq Liberation Act, and said in 2002 "that the goal of removing Saddam Hussein from power is a worthy objective, and I support that."[21] Put another way, the Iraq War was overdetermined and was likely to occur after some inciting incident set it in motion.

***

It is painfully obvious today that U.S. officials remain committed to primacy, even though the strategy has led the United States into several expensive wars of questionable value to the nation's fundamental security interests—Iraq, Afghanistan, Libya, Syria—all of which have diverted resources that could have been better spent on improvements at home. Moreover, polling suggests that younger generations are becoming increasingly skeptical of primacy and more interested in participating in international organizations, which indicates that now is an apt time to reconsider a grand strategy that decision-makers embraced more than 75 years ago.[22] Biden's August 31, 2021 speech announcing the U.S. withdrawal from Afghanistan makes Washington's continued devotion to primacy very clear. The president declared that the United States remains committed to combating threats from "across the world," from Somalia to Syria, from Iraq to Africa and Asia, and will use its "over-the-horizon capabilities" to launch attacks when and where it thinks it should.[23] The entire globe, it appears, remains within the U.S.' ambit. Thus the United States retains 750 military bases and other facilities abroad, and thus the nation devotes almost $800 billion per annum to its military budget.[24]

In his Afghanistan speech, Biden cast China as a central threat to U.S. interests.[25] Indeed, in his first speech to Congress as president, on April 28, 2021, Biden affirmed that the United States is "in competition with China and other countries to win the twenty-first Century."[26] While competition does not necessarily imply military conflict, Biden's speech was followed by an increased military budget as opposed to other sorts of investments—in science, technology, and education, for instance. In April 2022, Biden approved an additional $29 billion increase in defense spending.[27] This suggests that the Biden Administration remains fundamentally committed to primacy—that is, armed global domination. The idea seems to be that either the United States militarily dominates China or China militarily dominates the United States. Among the policy planners, no third scenario can be imagined.

According to primacy's advocates, the globe cannot peacefully encompass a plurality of powers and interests: it can accommodate only one power that rules through domination, or what is euphemistically termed "leadership." This is why primacists are so worried about China: they view international relations as a zero-sum game. As Ivo Daalder and James Lindsay argue in *The Empty Throne*, "a world with no leader would leave the United States poorer and less secure than if it continued to lead globally."[28] Indeed, Daalder and Lindsay are quite worried about China, affirming in no uncertain terms that "a Chinese-dominated world would not be friendly to the United States."[29] When making arguments such as this, primacists fail to consider that a more multilateral world might be defined by cooperation instead of security competition.

Rush Doshi, who is currently a member of Biden's National Security Council, likewise frames international relations in zero-sum terms. In *The Long Game*, Doshi worries that China has developed "a grand strategy to displace American order" and become "the world's leading state."[30] The only thing the United States can do, Doshi concludes, is "adopt an asymmetric approach that blunts Chinese advances at lower cost than China expends in generating them."[31] Cooperation is barely thinkable.

Over the past several years, U.S.–China relations have soured markedly. The Trump Administration, which was replete with China "hawks," instituted several tariffs on Chinese imports that provoked retaliatory measures and resulted in a minor trade war between the two countries. Trump also undertook several other actions that indicated his administration's hostility toward China. He launched a vigorous campaign to limit the reach of Huawei, the highly competitive telecommunications giant, eventually pressuring Canadian authorities to arrest Meng Wanzhou, the company's chief financial officer, on bank fraud charges (charges since dropped). In 2019, Trump's Treasury Department officially labeled China a currency manipulator; that same year, the president signed the Hong Kong Human Rights and Democracy Act, which authorized sanctions against those who commit human rights abuses in Hong Kong. Trump's insistence that COVID-19 was a "Chinese virus" was merely the crudest reflection of his administration's view that China was the main threat to U.S. supremacy.[32]

The Biden Administration has similarly pursued a number of policies intended to counter China's rise. The Federal Communications Commission, the Commerce Department, and the Treasury have blacklisted numerous Chinese companies as the administration has sanctioned several individuals in connection with Beijing's Hong Kong policy and its treatment of the Uighur population in Xinjiang Province. The administration has also prevailed upon NATO to declare China a security risk. Moreover, Biden has continued Trump's ban on U.S. investment in Chinese defense-technology companies and, earlier this year, forbade U.S. officials from attending the Winter Olympics in Beijing.[33] Finally, last June the Senate passed the U.S. Innovation and Strategic

Competition Act, which is specifically intended to combat China (particularly in the technological sphere); the House approved a related America COMPETES Act in February 2022.[34]

It is clear that the United States remains committed to retaining its hegemony in East Asia and, indeed, primacy on a global scale. But this grand strategy might result in pernicious consequences. If the United States fails to recognize China's legitimate interests in East Asia and Beijing's understandable desire to participate in shaping the global order, the U.S. might wind up fighting it. As with the Gulf War of 1990–1991 and the Iraq War of 2003–2011, an ill-considered commitment to primacy might engender violent conflict by pushing the United States toward confrontation instead of cooperation and engagement. This is especially worrisome given Biden's portrayal of China as an existential threat to U.S. interests. As the president remarked to reporters in March 2021, he believes that "China has an overall goal … to become the leading country in the world, the wealthiest country in the world, and the most powerful country in the world," and he is personally dedicated to ensuring that this doesn't "happen on my watch."[35] What, exactly, is Biden willing to risk in his attempt to ensure that the U.S. remains the prime power wherever and forever? Might he, or a future president, risk war?

There are, of course, obvious differences between the Iraq and China cases. Unlike Iraq, China is a peer competitor, has nuclear weapons, and is a genuine threat to U.S. regional hegemony in East Asia. Furthermore, China is the world's largest economy in terms of purchasing-power parity. The United States and China are also far more economically interdependent than the United States and Iraq ever were.

If the two wars with Iraq were destructive, a war with China would be catastrophic. The value of continued U.S. primacy in East Asia is insufficient to justify the enormous cost of such a conflict. For this reason, the United States must adjust to new geostrategic realities, abandon the illusion of indefinitely sustained primacy, and work with allies, partners, and China itself to avoid a deleterious competition that will divert attention from the truly existential threats of our era: inequality, population movements, pandemics, and above all, climate change.

***

The United States learned the wrong lessons from the Gulf War and the Iraq War that followed. A "cheap" primacy was never achievable, and while many analysts and decision-makers today accept the latter intervention as an unprecedented strategic mistake, it has nevertheless been treated as an isolated event disconnected from the United States' broader grand strategy. In reality, the Iraq War grew out of the U.S.' search for primacy. Fundamentally, U.S.–Iraq tensions were rooted in Iraq's challenge to U.S. dominance in the Middle East. Consequently, a U.S. effort to change the regime in Baghdad was likely to occur after some inciting incident, regardless of which political party was in power.

This insight provides guidance for how to navigate current U.S.–China tensions. The United States and China will be on a collision course if U.S. policy is driven by a desire to sustain primacy in East Asia. U.S. and Chinese leaders must accept that neither country can dominate the other and that mutual recognition is essential if we are to avoid a disastrous, potentially nuclear war.

Endnotes

1 While primacy had been adopted as a strategy in the 1940s, the existence of the Soviet Union meant that, in practice, the United States did not have the ability to be a genuinely global hegemon until after the U.S.S.R.'s collapse.

2 Stephen Wertheim, *Tomorrow, the World: The Birth of U.S. Global Supremacy* (Cambridge, MA: Harvard University Press, 2020), 4, chapter 2.

3 Lindsey A. O'Rourke, *Covert Regime Change: America's Secret Cold War* (Ithaca, NY: Cornell University Press, 2018), 3.

4 Ibid.

5 Ibid.

6 Sidita Kushi and Monica Duffy Toft, "Introducing the Military Intervention Project: A New Dataset on U.S. Military Interventions, 1776–2019," *Journal of Conflict Resolution* 67, no. 4 (April 2023), 767.

7 Between 1776 and 1864, the United States militarily intervened abroad 64 times; between 1865 and 1917, 82 times; between 1918 and 1945, 30 times; between 1990 and 2000, 46 times; and between 2001 and 2019, 66 times. Ibid.

8 George H.W. Bush, "Address Before a Joint Session of the Congress on the Persian Gulf Crisis and the Federal Budget Deficit" (speech, Washington, D.C., September 11, 1990), in John T. Woolley and Gerhard Peters, ed., *The American Presidency Project* (Santa Barbara, CA, 1999–2025), https://www.presidency.ucsb.edu/documents/address-before-joint-session-the-congress-the-persian-gulf-crisis-and-the-federal-budget.

9 "U.S. Military Casualties-Persian Gulf War-Casualty Summary Desert Storm (as of July 7, 2025)," Defense Casualty Analysis System, U.S. Department of Defense, accessed July 28, 2025, https://dcas.dmdc.osd.mil/dcas/app/conflictCasualties/gulf/stormsum.

10 H.R. McMaster, *Crack in the Foundation: Defense Transformation and the Underlying Assumption of Dominant Knowledge in Future War* (Carlisle Barracks, PA: Center for Strategic Leadership, U.S. Army War College, Student Issue Paper, Volume S03-03, November 2003), 13, https://media.defense.gov/2023/May/02/2003213354/-1/-1/0/3177.PDF.

11 The Gulf War, in reality, was hardly "clean." It inflicted tremendous suffering on the Iraqi people; for instance, there are an estimated 142,500–206,000 "Iraqi deaths directly attributable to the Gulf War." See Jane Salvage, *Collateral Damage: The Health and Environmental Costs of War on Iraq* (London, UK: Medact, November 12, 2002), 2, https://web.archive.org/web/20200719070432/https://www.ippnw.org/pdf/medact-iraq-2002.pdf.

12 Daniel Bessner, "The American Empire and Existential Enemies," *Foreign Exchanges*, September 7, 2020, https://www.foreignexchanges.news/p/the-american-empire-and-existential.

13 See, e.g., Charles Krauthammer, "Nightmare from the '30s," *Washington Post*, July 27, 1990, https://www.proquest.com/docview/140181358?sourcetype=Newspapers; Robin Wright, "Hussein Invasion Mimicks [*sic*] Hitler in Central Europe," *The Windsor Star*, August 3, 1990, https://www.proquest.com/newspapers/hussein-invasion-mimicks-hitler-central-europe/docview/253883680/se-2; Floyd Norris, "How Much Will Hussein Try to Grab?" *New York Times*, August 5, 1990, https://www.proquest.com/newspapers/how-much-will-hussein-try-grab/docview/108502215/se-2; Andrew B. Schmookler, "Hussein as Hitler," *The Sun* (Baltimore, MD), January 12, 1991, https://www.baltimoresun.com/1991/01/12/hussein-as-hitler-2/; A.M. Rosenthal, "On My Mind; Always Believe Dictators," *New York Times*, March 29, 1994, https://www.nytimes.com/1994/03/29/opinion/on-my-mind-always-believe-dictators.html.

14 George H.W. Bush, "Remarks at a Republican Campaign Rally in Manchester, New Hampshire" (speech, New Hampshire, 1990), in John T. Woolley and Gerhard Peters, ed., *The American Presidency Project* (Santa Barbara, CA, 1999–2025), https://www.presidency.ucsb.edu/documents/remarks-republican-campaign-rally-manchester-new-hampshire.

15 The United States was historically committed to dominating the Persian Gulf region for several strategic reasons, which waxed and waned over time. First, it wanted to ensure the free flow of oil to the United States and the global economy. Second, the Middle East is strategically positioned, and U.S. dominance of the region allows the nation to project power into Russia and Central Asia. Third, in the 1990s, U.S. strategy was at least partially oriented toward defending human rights, which Saddam Hussein regularly violated, and it was therefore believed to be the "mission" of the United States to overthrow him. Fourth, U.S. decision-makers were dedicated to preventing the emergence of a regional hegemon able to displace the United States as the Gulf's preeminent power.

16 Kushi and Toft, "Introduction to the Military Intervention Project," 767.

17 Madeleine K. Albright, interview by Matt Lauer, *The Today Show*, NBC-TV, Columbus, OH, February 19, 1998, https://1997-2001.state.gov/statements/1998/980219a.html.

18 Joy Gordon, "The Enduring Lessons of the Iraq Sanctions," *Middle East Report* no. 294 (Spring 2020), https://merip.org/2020/06/the-enduring-lessons-of-the-iraq-sanctions/.

19 Iraq Liberation Act of 1998, Pub. L. No. 105–338 (1998), 3, https://www.govinfo.gov/content/pkg/PLAW-105publ338/pdf/PLAW-105publ338.pdf.

20 Robert M. Gates, *Exercise of Power: American Failures, Successes, and a New Path Forward in the Post–Cold War World* (New York: Alfred A. Knopf, 2020), 205.

21 "Gore Talks of Iraq, al Qaeda—and What He'd Do Differently," *CNN*, November 20, 2002, https://www.cnn.com/2002/ALLPOLITICS/11/19/lkl.gore/. See also Frank P. Harvey, "President Al Gore and the 2003 Iraq War: A Counterfactual Test of Conventional 'Wisdom," *Canadian Journal of Political Science/Revue canadienne de science politique* 45, no. 1 (March 2012), 1–32.

22 *In a Politically Polarized Era, Sharp Divides in Both Partisan Coalitions* (Washington, D.C.: Pew Research Center, December 2019), 14, https://www.pewresearch.org/politics/wp-content/uploads/sites/4/2019/12/PP_2019.12.17_Political-Values_FINAL.pdf; Christine Huang and Laura Silver, "U.S. Millennials Tend to Have Favorable Views of Foreign Countries and Institutions—Even as They Age," Pew Research Center, July 8, 2020, https://www.pewresearch.org/short-reads/2020/07/08/u-s-millennials-tend-to-have-favorable-views-of-foreign-countries-and-institutions-even-as-they-age/.

23 Joseph R. Biden, Jr., "Remarks by President Biden on the End of the War in Afghanistan" (speech, Washington, D.C., August 31, 2021), Biden White House, https://bidenwhitehouse.archives.gov/briefing-room/speeches-remarks/2021/08/31/remarks-by-president-biden-on-the-end-of-the-war-in-afghanistan/.

24 David Vine, Patterson Deppen, and Leah Bolger, *Drawdown: Improving U.S. and Global Security Through Military Base Closures Abroad,* Quincy Brief No. 16 (Washington, D.C.: Quincy Institute for Responsible Statecraft, September 20, 2021), https://quincyinst.org/research/drawdown-improving-u-s-and-global-security-through-military-base-closures-abroad/#; Kanishka Singh, "U.S. President Biden Signs $770

Billion Defense Bill," *Reuters*, December 27, 2021, https://www.reuters.com/world/us/us-president-biden-signs-770-billion-defense-bill-2021-12-27/.

25 Similar claims have been made in the 2018 National Defense Strategy and in the 2021 Interim National Security Strategic Guidance. See U.S. Department of Defense, *Summary of the 2018 National Defense Strategy of the United States of America: Sharpening the American Military's Competitive Edge* (Washington, D.C.: U.S. Department of Defense, 2018), https://media.defense.gov/2020/May/18/2002302061/-1/-1/1/2018-NATIONAL-DEFENSE-STRATEGY-SUMMARY.PDF; Joseph R. Biden, Jr., *Interim National Security Strategic Guidance* (Washington, D.C.: White House, March 2021), https://irp.fas.org/offdocs/inssg.pdf.

26 Joseph R. Biden, Jr., "Address Before a Joint Session of the Congress" (speech, Washington, D.C., April 28, 2021), in John T. Woolley and Gerhard Peters, ed., *The American Presidency Project* (Santa Barbara, CA, 1999–2025), https://www.presidency.ucsb.edu/documents/address-before-joint-session-the-congress-3.

27 Shannon Bugos, "Biden Approves $29 Billion Increase in Defense Budget," Arms Control Association, April 2022, https://www.armscontrol.org/act/2022-04/news/biden-approves-29-billion-increase-defense-budget.

28 Ivo H. Daalder and James M. Lindsay, *The Empty Throne: America's Abdication of Global Leadership* (New York: PublicAffairs, 2018), 171.

29 Ibid., 173.

30 Rush Doshi, *The Long Game: China's Grand Strategy to Displace American Order* (New York: Oxford University Press, 2021), 332.

31 Ibid., 333.

32 "U.S.–China Relations, 1949–2025," Council on Foreign Relations, accessed July 28, 2025, https://www.cfr.org/timeline/us-china-relations.

33 Michael Martina and Karen Freifeld, "Biden Order Bans Investment in Dozens of Chinese Defense, Tech Firms," *Reuters*, June 4, 2021, https://www.reuters.com/legal/government/biden-order-ban-investment-59-chinese-defense-tech-firms-2021-06-03/; Jennifer Conrad, "A Year In, Biden's China Policy Looks a Lot Like Trump's,"

Wired, December 30, 2021, https://www.wired.com/story/biden-china-policy-looks-like-trumps/.

34 David Shepardson, "U.S. Senate Passes Sweeping Bill to Address China Tech Threat," *Reuters*, June 9, 2021, https://www.reuters.com/world/us/us-senate-set-pass-sweeping-bill-address-china-tech-threat-2021-06-08/; Patricia Zengerle and Michael Martina, "U.S. House Backs Sweeping China Competition Bill as Olympics Start," *Reuters*, February 4, 2022, https://www.reuters.com/world/us/us-house-set-pass-sweeping-vote-china-competition-bill-2022-02-04/.

35 Jarrett Renshaw, Andrea Shalal, and Michael Martina, "Biden Says China Will Not Surpass U.S. as Global Leader on His Watch," March 25, 2021, https://www.reuters.com/article/world/biden-says-china-will-not-surpass-us-as-global-leader-on-his-watch-idUSKBN2BH32Z/.

UKRAINE AND THE RETURN OF THE UNITED STATES

The United States' dedication to arming Ukraine in its attempt to repel the Russian Federation's invasion presents a puzzle: Why, exactly, has the nation been so committed to this effort?

To answer that question, I explore how the Biden Administration—above all, Secretary of State Antony J. Blinken—has talked about the U.S. project in Ukraine. By analyzing Blinken's rhetoric, we are able to examine how U.S. elites understand the conflict, at least discursively and in public settings, thus providing a first-run attempt at explaining the U.S. decision to back the Ukrainian military and rally international support to its cause. This analysis, in turn, provides important insights into the Biden Administration's overall foreign policy strategy and goals.

A detailed examination of Blinken's speeches reveals that the United States remains dedicated to the war in Ukraine primarily because the Biden Administration views it as a means to shore up a weakening American hegemony. In effect, U.S. rhetoric and actions serve to remind U.S. allies, partners, and even those not formally associated with the United States that U.S. primacy remains the defining feature of international relations. In particular, the Biden Administration appears to believe that support for Ukraine is a primary means to restore the so-called "rules-based international order," which its members came into office insisting was in crisis.

Donald Trump's ascension to the presidency in 2017 contributed to a significant uptick in chatter in Washington, D.C., about the decline of the "rules-based international order." The just-so story told by those who valorize such an order goes as follows: after World War II, the United States, in concert with Western European allies, constructed an international system in which liberal norms of engagement and exchange, and institutions such as international law and the United Nations, helped end major wars and ensure (relative) geopolitical stability. Though those who promote this tale often admit that mistakes were made in the Cold War and post–Cold War periods—the Korean, Vietnam, and Iraq Wars are usually highlighted as especially egregious errors—they nevertheless claim that, on balance, the rules-based international order proved a force for good in the world.

Trump's victory took the wind out of the sails of this triumphalist narrative. The reality star's willingness to openly criticize his forebears' launching of endless wars as well as his vulgarity, xenophobia, and discursive insouciance toward traditional American ideas about global power and responsibility generated an almost hysterical panic among defenders of the liberal order. Trump, it seemed to many, was a harbinger of U.S. hegemony's end, or at least its attenuation. And it wasn't only Americans who worried; U.S. allies likewise fretted about the end of the era of U.S. "leadership."[1]

When President Joseph R. Biden assumed office in 2021, his primary foreign policy goal was to reinvigorate the rules-based order by persuading allies that the United States was committed to reinvigorating its "leadership." The war in Ukraine provided Biden, Blinken, and other key members of the administration with a seemingly ideal opportunity to show the world that the United States wasn't going anywhere. Unsurprisingly, the administration seized this opportunity with aplomb.

***

Even before the war in Ukraine began, Secretary of State Antony Blinken repeatedly claimed that supporting the defense of Ukraine was first and foremost about defending the rules-based international order. On February 22, Blinken made an argument that he would repeat ad infinitum over the next year: Russia's war, the secretary declared, presented "the greatest threat to security in Europe since World War II" because Putin was "blatantly and violently breaking the laws and principles that have kept the peace across Europe and around the world for decades."[2] Blinken affirmed that the invasion threatened not only Europe but also "nations everywhere that have been made safer and more secure by the international rules- based order."[3]

This rhetoric indicates that for Blinken, and indeed the Biden Administration, the defense of Ukraine was about far more than just protecting one country; it was about, as the secretary declared in early March,

> principles like the notion that one country can't simply commit acts of aggression on another, changing its borders by force; that one country can't dictate to another its choices, its decisions, its policies, with whom it will associate; principles like one country can't exert a sphere of influence to subjugate its neighbors to its will.[4]

Blinken warned nations around the globe that if they failed to confront Putin in Ukraine, they risked "opening a Pandora's box in every corner of the world for this to happen again and again and again."[5] This rhetoric transformed support for Ukraine into support for the global order—and, implicitly, U.S. hegemony—itself.

Intriguingly, Blinken rarely discussed why, exactly, the world required U.S. "leadership." As far as I can tell, he only did so in the immediate period after the conflict began. According to the secretary, "one of the principles" that the Biden Administration has been "animated by, is that … when the United States is not leading … then one of two things" occurs:

> Either someone else is [leading] and doing things in a way that may not actually advance the interests of the American people or the values that we hold, or maybe no one is and then you tend to have vacuums and chaos and that usually has a way of coming back and biting us.[6]

As presented by Blinken, the nations of the world were faced with a stark choice: either they submit to U.S. hegemony and live in peace, or they accept that, absent the United States, international relations will become far more dangerous and unstable. Vladimir Putin's invasion of Ukraine, the secretary insisted, was a harbinger of what would happen in a world in which the United States retreated from its role as international leader. Simply put, the choice was between Hobbesian chaos and American imperialism.

***

Despite that it was Russia which had trampled on the liberal order's rules, for Blinken, the main threat facing the United States, and the world, was China, which he claimed would perhaps "fil[l] the void" should the nation surrender its hegemony.[7] From the war's onset, Blinken frequently criticized China. In early March 2022, the secretary informed CNN's Jake Tapper that he had told Wang Yi, China's then minister of foreign affairs, that the United States "would expect China … to stand up and make its voice heard" by condemning Russia's aggression.[8] Just over a week later, after China did not condemn Putin's invasion, Blinken told CNN's Wolf Blitzer that "the fact that China has not denounced what Russia is doing in and of itself speaks volumes"; China was not genuinely committed to the rules-based order and was, as a result, not genuinely committed to peace.[9]

Beyond criticizing China's foreign policy, on more than one occasion Blinken attacked the People's Republic on moral grounds. In mid-March, he told NPR's Steve Inskeep that China was "already on the wrong side of history when it comes to Ukraine," and in an April talk at the University of Michigan, he remarked that condemning Russia was "not about siding with the United States. It's about siding with right versus wrong."[10] As these comments indicate, the secretary framed China's decision not to reproach Russia as an immoral one. (The hypocrisy of an American official who works for a government that supports wildly oppressive regimes from Saudi Arabia to Djibouti castigating a nation for immoral behavior hardly needs to be pointed out.)

To demonstrate to the world what would happen if a nation dared to challenge perceived U.S. interests, from the war's start the Biden Administration intended to make Russia pay an enormous price for its aggression. On the day the invasion began, Blinken informed CBS's Norah O'Donnell that the administration desired to "inflict maximum pain on Russia."[11] A little over two months later, Secretary of Defense Lloyd Austin declared that the United States hoped "to see Russia weakened to the degree that it can't do the kinds of things that it has done in invading Ukraine."[12]

But what did any of this actually mean in practice? First, the United States made a concerted effort to wean its European allies off Russian energy. Since the war's beginning, Blinken declared that the nation retained "a strong interest … in degrading Russia's status as a leading energy supplier" and hoped to enable Europe to "accelerate its diversification away from Russian gas."[13]

The United States thus encouraged Germany to close the Nord Stream 2 pipeline; sent significant quantities of liquified natural gas to Europe; "den[ied] critical technologies to Russia for further energy exploration"; and stabilized oil markets by releasing part of its Strategic Petroleum Reserve and increasing its own oil production.[14] This effort proved remarkably successful. By late June 2022, the European Union had decided "to cut Russian oil imports by 90 percent by the end of the year and to ban EU firms from carrying Russian crude [oil]," and by September, the United States was "the leading supplier" of liquified natural gas to Europe.[15] Beyond punishing Russia, the United States hoped to use the war to consolidate Ukraine's status as an American client. In September, Blinken affirmed that the nation was committed to helping Ukrainians develop "a strong defensive and deterrence system that makes it less likely in the future that Russia will act aggressively toward Ukraine."[16] This would, of course, take years, which was just fine with Blinken, who had declared in early March that the United States was in the war for "the short-run, the medium-run, the long-run."[17] U.S. support for Ukraine was obviously not only about repelling Russia but also about making the country even more economically and militarily dependent on the United States than it already was.

To justify the United States' increasingly hands-on role in Ukraine, Blinken repeatedly attempted to place Russia beyond the geopolitical and moral pale. Before the war began, the secretary affirmed in no uncertain terms that Russian actions vis-à-vis Ukraine had "never been about Ukraine and NATO [expansion] per se."[18] This idea, Blinken told Wolf Blitzer, was simply "a lie."[19] According to Blinken, NATO was a mere defensive alliance that "never sought and will not seek conflict with Russia."[20] Putin was thus not reacting to U.S. encroachment on Russia's southwestern border. Rather, Blinken avowed, the invasion was primarily "about conquest," Putin's "conviction that Ukraine is not a sovereign, independent country," and "reconstituting the Russian empire or, short of that, a sphere of influence, or, short of that, the total neutrality of countries surrounding Russia."[21] While there is some truth to Blinken's claims about Putin's goals and his intentions on Russia's western borders, the secretary refused to acknowledge that the Russian president might have had any legitimate concerns about his nation's security, especially given the repeated Russian experience of being invaded by Western and Central European powers. Strategic empathy, it seems, is not Blinken's strong suit.

In a further effort to depict Russia as a so-called "rogue nation," Blinken consistently referenced Russia's untrustworthiness and barbarism. In February, he argued that Putin's "complete abdication of Russia's commitments under the Minsk Agreements is just the latest demonstration of Russia's hypocrisy when it comes to the agreements that it claims to seek and to uphold."[22] He also repeatedly brought up past Russian war crimes. During the invasion's first week, for instance, Blinken declared that Russia had used "grisly tactics before in Syria, in Chechnya," and it would likely do so again in Ukraine.[23]

After the war broke out, Blinken made it a point to underline Russia's many war crimes, avowing that the United States was documenting these "to ensure … that there's accountability" so "that Russia cannot escape the verdict of history."[24] Of course, this is not to deny the terrible human rights abuses committed by Russia in Ukraine and elsewhere; these are numerous and brutal, and those who perpetrated them should be investigated and put on trial. But it is hardly unique for crimes to be committed in war—the United States and its allies have committed their fair share—and Blinken's emphasis on human rights primarily served as a means to exorcise Russia from the international community by transforming it into an outcast. This exorcism, predictably, also had the benefit of reinforcing the necessity of U.S. hegemony.

***

For the United States, the most important effect of the war was that it allowed the nation to reassert and consolidate its "leadership" over Europe. Since the invasion began, NATO, under U.S. direction, "activated and deployed parts of its response force"; Denmark, France, Germany, the Netherlands, Spain, and the United Kingdom "sent troops and aircraft and ships" to NATO's "eastern flank"; every member of NATO "provid[ed] either military or humanitarian aid to Ukraine"; and the European Union, for the first time in its history, began "financing the purchase and delivery of military assistance to a country under attack."[25] The war in Ukraine reinvigorated the U.S.–Europe relationship by allowing countries to commit to a common project. Without a doubt, the response to the invasion was the most important post-Trump reaffirmation of North Atlantic solidarity.

Outside Europe, Blinken used the war to encourage other nations to remain in or join the U.S. orbit. When the secretary traveled to Algeria in late March, for example, he reminded Algerians that nations in the so-called MENA region "have experienced themselves the consequences of Russian military campaigns before—for example, in Syria and Libya, where Russian military and paramilitary forces exploited conflicts for Moscow's gain, with deadly consequences for citizens and communities."[26] This, Blinken maintained, was happening again, "with rising food prices, especially [the price of] wheat," being the latest instance of Russia negatively impacting the Muslim world.[27] The only way to avoid such pain in the future, of course, was to line up behind the United States.

In a similar vein, during a visit to India in April, Blinken praised the nation (and Russia's fellow BRICS partner) for its "very strong statements … condemning the killing of civilians in Ukraine."[28] While Blinken declared that he appreciated that "India's relationship with Russia has developed over decades at a time when the United States was not able to be a partner to India," he also averred that "times have changed"—the United States was now "able and willing to be a partner of choice with India across virtually every realm—commerce, technology, education, and security."[29]

Put in cruder terms, U.S. leadership was back, baby. Better get behind Uncle Sam.

***

The most significant example of the United States' successful effort to get Europe to affirm all of its strategic priorities was the June 2022 NATO *Strategic Concept*. This paper endorsed all of

Blinken's arguments and preferences: it insisted that "a strong, independent Ukraine is vital for the stability of the Euro-Atlantic area"; claimed that "Moscow's behavior reflects a pattern of Russian aggressive actions against its neighbors and the wider transatlantic community" that could not be ignored; warned that Russia might "attack ... Allies' sovereignty and territorial integrity"; and, in an obvious nod to American rhetoric, avowed that Russia had revealed its desire to "undermine the rules-based international order."[30] Strikingly, the *Strategic Concept* further asserted NATO's continued commitment to an "Open Door policy," avowing that NATO members remained dedicated to "the decision we took at the 2008 Bucharest Summit and all subsequent decisions with respect to Georgia and Ukraine."[31] NATO expansion, a significant cause of the war, was thus rearticulated with relish.

Even more tellingly, the *Strategic Concept* also expressed a deep hostility toward China. For the first time in its history, NATO declared that China's "stated ambitions and coercive policies challenge our interests, security and values."[32] China, the report maintained, "employs a broad range of political, economic and military tools to increase its global footprint and project power"; uses "confrontational rhetoric and disinformation [to] target Allies and harm Alliance security"; and "seeks to control key technological and industrial sectors, critical infrastructure, and strategic materials and supply chains."[33] As such, it was clear to NATO members that China "strives to subvert the rules-based international order."[34] What this document represented was nothing less than NATO's endorsement of the United States' effort to prevent China from challenging its hegemony. Europe, it seemed, was just fine being the United States' lackey.

The *Strategic Concept* seems to have significantly emboldened Blinken. After its release, the secretary adopted a more aggressive attitude toward China's behavior with regard to Ukraine, declaring "that it's pretty hard to be neutral when it comes to this aggression":

> There is a clear aggressor. There is a clear victim. There is a clear challenge not only to the lives and livelihoods of people in Ukraine, but there is a challenge to the international order that China and the United States as permanent members of the Security Council are supposed to uphold.[35]

According to Blinken, China's support of Russia in the United Nations, combined with the fact that it had "amplified Russian propaganda" and "announce[d] the 'no limits partnership' with President Putin," demonstrated that the People's Republic was "shirking its responsibility as a P5 member [i.e., one of the five permanent members of the United Nations Security Council]" to defend global peace.[36]

Put another way, the nations of the world could only rely on one country: the United States.

In October 2022, the Biden Administration released its *National Security Strategy* (NSS). In effect, the NSS codified the arguments that Blinken had been making since the war's outbreak. It maintained that the United States was "in the midst of a strategic competition to shape the future of the international order"; proclaimed that "the need for American leadership is as great as it has ever been"; insisted that "Russia poses an immediate threat to the free and open international system"; and affirmed that the "most consequential geopolitical challenge" came from China.[37]

The NSS also emphasized the importance of the U.S.–Europe relationship. Europe, the report declared, was "our foundational partner," and as such, the United States was devoted to "broadening and deepening the transatlantic bond—strengthening NATO, raising the level of ambition in the U.S.–EU relationship, and standing with our European allies and partners in defense of the rules-based system that underpins our security, prosperity, and values."[38]

When it came to Ukraine, the NSS unsurprisingly adopted an aggressive tone, insisting that the United States would not only support Ukraine in the war but also "encourage its regional integration with the European Union."[39] Beyond Ukraine, the report announced that the United States would also "support the European aspirations of Georgia and Moldova."[40]

All told, the NSS revealed that the United States' primary goal was "to prevent competitors from altering the status quo."[41]

But, ironically, the report itself demonstrated that if any nation wanted to transform the status quo, it was the United States. Specifically, the NSS avowed that the Biden Administration intended to "place a premium on growing the connective tissue ... between our democratic allies and partners in the Indo–Pacific and Europe."[42] In this way, the Biden Administration announced its desire to construct a genuinely integrated global structure that would enable it to combat Russia and, more importantly, China, thus ensuring U.S. hegemony in the coming decades.

One of the more unexpected consequences of the war is that it appears to have engendered a shift in the Biden Administration's rhetoric concerning the supposed Manichaean struggle between democracy and authoritarianism. Biden, Blinken, and the rest of the administration's foreign policy team entered office claiming they were committed to shoring up democracy in its international fight against autocracy. In fact, in a March 2022 speech Biden gave addressing Russia's invasion of Ukraine, he explicitly framed U.S. support for Ukraine in the context of this struggle. "Today's fighting in Kyiv and Mariupol and Kharkiv," the president averred, "are the latest battle [*sic*] in a long struggle" between Western democracy and Russian authoritarianism that previously encompassed "Hungary, 1956; Poland, 1956 then again 1981; [and] Czechoslovakia, 1968."[43] In other words, the United States' support for Ukraine was a continuation of its Cold War struggle against Soviet tyranny.

Nonetheless, in September 2022, the president gave a speech before the UN in which he softened his "democracy versus autocracy" framing. In this speech, Biden noted that "the United Nations Charter was not only signed by democracies of the world, it was negotiated among citizens of dozens of nations with vastly different histories and ideologies, united in their commitment to work for peace."[44] He continued:

> To stand against global politics of fear and coercion; to defend the sovereign rights of smaller nations as equal to those of larger ones; to embrace basic principles like freedom of navigation, respect for international law, and arms control — no matter what else we may disagree on, that is the common ground upon which we must stand. If you're still committed to a strong foundation for the good of every nation around the world, then the United States wants to work with you.[45]

Beyond this speech, the administration's *National Security Strategy* declared that the United States "will partner with any nation that shares our basic belief that the rules-based order must remain the foundation for global peace and prosperity."[46] In short, the war in Ukraine helped the Biden Administration identify its primary goal: to retain, and perhaps even expand, U.S. hegemony, regardless of who it needed to ally with to do so.

The Biden Administration's efforts have been rather successful in shoring up U.S. "leadership," especially in Europe. In January 2023, Biden elucidated the many ways in which European countries had aided the war effort:

> The UK—the United Kingdom—recently announced that it is donating Challenger 2 tanks to Ukraine. France is contributing AMX-10s, armored fighting vehicles. In addition to the Leopard tanks … Germany is also sending a … Patriot missile battery. The Netherlands is donating a Patriot missile and launchers. France, Canada, the UK, Slovakia, Norway, and others have all donated critical air defense systems to help secure Ukrainian skies and save the lives of innocent civilians who are literally … the target of Russia's aggression. Poland is sending armored vehicles.

> Sweden is donating infantry fighting vehicles. Italy is giving artillery. Denmark and Estonia are sending howitzers. Latvia is providing more Stinger missiles. Lithuania is providing anti-aircraft guns. And Finland recently announced its largest package of security assistance to date.[47]

The United States and Europe are now united in a way they have not been in years.

Simply put, the war in Ukraine has so far proved a remarkably effective means for the United States to rearticulate the reasons for its primacy and to encourage allies and partners to line up behind its goals. Ironically, given Putin's desire to challenge U.S. hegemony, the major consequence of Russia's invasion of Ukraine has been the reaffirmation of both American power and the transatlantic alliance. From this perspective, the war has been a strategic disaster for Russia and has done little but weaken Putin's position.

Endnotes

1 Kori Schake, "The End of the American Order: At An International Conference, Allies Grieved the Loss of the United States They Had Believed In," *The Atlantic*, November 19, 2018, https://www.theatlantic.com/ideas/archive/2018/11/halifax-forum-allies-mourn-pre-trump-america/576154/.

2 Antony J. Blinken and Dmytro Kuleba, "Secretary Antony J. Blinken and Ukrainian Foreign Minister Dmytro Kuleba at a Joint Press Availability" (remarks, Washington, D.C., February 22, 2022), U.S. Department of State [2021–2025], https://2021-2025.state.gov/secretary-antony-j-blinken-and-ukrainian-foreign-minister-dmytro-kuleba-at-a-joint-press-availability-2/.

3 Ibid.

4 Antony J. Blinken and Ursula von der Leyen, "Secretary Blinken and European Commission President Ursula von der Leyen Before Their Meeting" (remarks, Belgium, March 4, 2022), U.S. Department of State [2021–2025], https://2021-2025.state.gov/secretary-antony-j-

blinken-and-european-commission-president-ursula-von-der-leyen-before-their-meeting-2/.

5 Ibid.

6 Antony J. Blinken, "Secretary Antony J. Blinken Roundtable with Journalists" (interview, Washington, D.C., March 18, 2022), U.S. Department of State [2021–2025], https://2021-2025.state.gov/secretary-antony-j-blinken-roundtable-with-journalists/.

7 Antony J. Blinken, "Secretary Antony J. Blinken Virtual Remarks on 21st Century Diplomacy and Global Challenges, The Gerald R. Ford School of Public Policy at the University of Michigan" (remarks, Washington, D.C., April 14, 2022), U.S. Department of State [2021–2025], https://2021-2025.state.gov/secretary-antony-j-blinken-virtual-remarks-on-21st-century-diplomacy-and-global-challenges-the-gerald-r-ford-school-of-public-policy-at-the-unive-rsity-of-michigan/.

8 Antony J. Blinken, "Secretary Blinken With Jake Tapper of CNN" (interview, Moldova, March 6, 2022), U.S. Department of State [2021–2025], https://2021-2025.state.gov/secretary-antony-j-blinken-on-cnn-state-of-the-union-with-jake-tapper/.

9 Antony J. Blinken, "Secretary Antony J. Blinken With Wolf Blitzer of The Situation Room on CNN" (interview, Washington, D.C., March 15, 2022), U.S. Department of State [2021–2025], https://2021-2025.state.gov/secretary-antony-j-blinken-with-wolf-blitzer-of-the-situation-room-on-cnn/.

10 Antony J. Blinken, "Secretary Antony J. Blinken With Steve Inskeep of NPR's Morning Edition" (interview, Washington, D.C., March 16, 2022), U.S. Department of State [2021–2025], https://2021-2025.state.gov/secretary-antony-j-blinken-with-steve-inskeep-of-nprs-morning-edition/; Blinken, "Virtual Remarks on 21st Century Diplomacy and Global Challenges."

11 Antony J. Blinken, "Secretary Antony J. Blinken On CBS Evening News with Norah O'Donnell" (interview, Washington, D.C., February 24, 2022), U.S. Department of State [2021–2025], https://2021-2025.state.gov/secretary-antony-j-blinken-on-cbs-evening-news-with-norah-odonnell/.

12 Antony J. Blinken and Lloyd Austin, "Secretary Antony J. Blinken and Secretary Lloyd Austin Remarks to Traveling Press" (remarks, Poland, April 25, 2022), U.S. Department of State [2021–2025], https://2021-2025.state.gov/secretary-antony-j-blinken-and-secretary-lloyd-austin-remarks-to-traveling-press/.

13 Antony J. Blinken, "Secretary Blinken's Press Availability" (remarks, Belgium, March 4, 2022), U.S. Department of State [2021–2025], https://2021-2025.state.gov/secretary-antony-j-blinken-at-a-press-availability-15/.

14 Ibid.

15 Antony J. Blinken, "Secretary Antony J. Blinken at a Press Availability" (remarks, Germany, June 24, 2022), U.S. Department of State [2021–2025], https://2021-2025.state.gov/secretary-antony-j-blinken-at-a-press-availability-19/; Antony J. Blinken and Mélanie Joly, "Secretary Antony J. Blinken and Canadian Foreign Minister Mélanie Joly at a Joint Press Availability" (remarks, Washington, D.C., September 30, 2022), U.S. Department of State [2021–2025], https://2021-2025.state.gov/secretary-antony-j-blinken-and-canadian-foreign-minister-melanie-joly-at-a-joint-press-availability/.

16 Blinken and Joly, "Joint Press Availability."

17 Antony J. Blinken and Dmytro Kuleba, "Secretary Blinken and Ukrainian Foreign Minister Dmytro Kuleba at a Joint Press Availability" (remarks, Poland-Ukraine border, March 5, 2022), U.S. Department of State [2021–2025], https://2021-2025.state.gov/secretary-antony-j-blinken-and-ukrainian-foreign-minister-dmytro-kuleba-at-a-joint-press-availability-3/.

18 Blinken and Kuleba, "Joint Press Availability," February 22, 2022.

19 Blinken, "The Situation Room."

20 Blinken, "Press Availability," March 4, 2022.

21 Blinken, "Press Availability," June 24, 2022; Antony J. Blinken, "Secretary Antony J. Blinken at a Press Availability" (remarks, Indonesia, July 9, 2022), U.S. Department https://2021-2025.state.gov/secretary-antony-j-blinken-at-a-press-availability-21/ [2021–2025]; Blinken and Kuleba, "Joint Press Availability," February 22, 2022.

22 Blinken and Kuleba, "Joint Press Availability," February 22, 2022.

23 Blinken, "Press Availability," March 4, 2022.

24 Antony J. Blinken, "Secretary Antony J. Blinken at a Press Availability" (remarks, Washington, D.C., March 2, 2022), U.S. Department of State [2021–2025], https://2021-2025.state.gov/secretary-antony-j-blinken-at-a-press-availability-14/; Antony J. Blinken, "Secretary Antony J. Blinken Press Availability at the Meeting of NATO Foreign Ministers" (remarks, Belgium, April 7, 2022), U.S. Department of State [2021–2025], https://2021-2025.state.gov/secretary-antony-j-blinken-press-availability-at-the-meeting-of-nato-foreign-ministers/.

25 Blinken, "Press Availability," March 4, 2022.

26 Antony J. Blinken, "Secretary Antony J. Blinken at a Press Availability" (remarks, Algeria, March 30, 2022), U.S. Department of State [2021–2025], https://2021-2025.state.gov/secretary-antony-j-blinken-at-a-press-availability-17/.

27 Ibid.

28 Antony J. Blinken, Lloyd J. Austin III, S. Jaishankar, and Rajnath Singh, "Secretary Antony J. Blinken, Secretary of Defense Lloyd J. Austin III, Indian Minister of External Affairs Dr. S. Jaishankar, and Indian Minister of Defense Rajnath Singh at a Joint Press Availability" (remarks, Washington, D.C., April 11, 2022), U.S. Department of State [2021–2025], https://2021-2025.state.gov/secretary-antony-j-blinken-secretary-of-defense-lloyd-austin-indian-minister-of-external-affairs-dr-s-jaishankar-and-indian-minister-of-defense-rajnath-singh-at-a-joint-press-availability/.

29 Ibid.

30 North Atlantic Treaty Organization, *NATO 2022 Strategic Concept: Adopted by Heads of State and Government at the NATO Summit in Madrid, 29 June 2022* (Brussels, BE: NATO, 2022), 1, 3, 4, https://www.nato.int/en/about-us/official-texts-and-resources/strategic-concepts/nato-2022-strategic-concept.

31 Ibid., 9, 10.

32 Ibid., 5.

33 Ibid.

34 Ibid.

35 Blinken, "Press Availability," July 9, 2022.

36 Ibid.

37 Joseph R. Biden, Jr., *National Security Strategy* (Washington, D.C.: White House, October 2022), 2, 8, 11, https://bidenwhitehouse.archives.gov/wp-content/uploads/2022/10/Biden-Harris-Administrations-National-Security-Strategy-10.2022.pdf.

38 Ibid., 38.

39 Ibid., 26.

40 Ibid., 39.

41 Ibid., 22.

42 Ibid., 11.

43 Joseph R. Biden, Jr., "Remarks by President Biden on the United Efforts of the Free World to Support the People of Ukraine" (speech, Poland, March 26, 2022), Biden White House, https://bidenwhitehouse.archives.gov/briefing-room/speeches-remarks/2022/03/26/remarks-by-president-biden-on-the-united-efforts-of-the-free-world-to-support-the-people-of-ukraine/.

44 Joseph R. Biden, Jr., "Remarks by President Biden Before the 77th Session of the United Nations General Assembly" (speech, New York, September 21, 2022), Biden White House, https://bidenwhitehouse.archives.gov/briefing-room/speeches-remarks/2022/09/21/remarks-by-president-biden-before-the-77th-session-of-the-united-nations-general-assembly/.

45 Ibid.

46 Biden, *National Security Strategy*, 3.

47 Joseph R. Biden, Jr., "Remarks by President Biden on Continued Support for Ukraine" (speech, Washington, D.C., January 25, 2023), Biden White House, https://bidenwhitehouse.archives.gov/briefing-room/speeches-remarks/2023/01/25/remarks-by-president-biden-on-continued-support-for-ukraine/.

AMERICA HAS NO DUTY TO RULE THE WORLD

The United States is the world's overwhelming military power, and it's not even close. The country controls about 750 overseas bases (China, by comparison, has only one foreign base, in Djibouti). It spends around $730 billion on its military, which is more than China, India, Russia, Saudi Arabia, France, Germany, the United Kingdom, Japan, South Korea, and Brazil combined. It has over 190,000 soldiers deployed in 140 foreign countries—around 70 percent of the world's total. To many Americans and foreigners alike, this power appears as a natural fact of international relations. Very few people alive today can remember a time when the United States did not have the ability to destroy much of the globe.

There are various ways to narrate why the United States, a nation-state founded in an anti-colonial revolution, became the most powerful empire in history. You may call it destiny, the fulfillment of the country's millenarian promise to become, as the Puritan leader John Winthrop declared in a 1630 sermon, "a city upon a hill" for the world's benighted.[1] Or you may claim it was the United States' vast material resources and its geographical luck, surrounded by two vast oceans and weak neighbors, that enabled it to develop its capacities to govern the world. Perhaps if you're a

Marxist, you'll insist that it was capitalism's unquenchable appetite that drove U.S. elites to expand from sea to shining sea before turning their gaze abroad in search of more territory to exploit. And if you're an apologist for U.S. power, you can affirm that dominance was forced upon the United States by Europe's two world wars, which impelled the mantle of "Western civilization" to pass from the Old World to the New, or by the attack at Pearl Harbor, to which any reasonable nation would have replied with force.

In *Tomorrow, the World: The Birth of U.S. Global Supremacy*, historian Stephen Wertheim highlights an overlooked cause of the United States' ascendance: the fall of France in June 1940.[2] When the French military collapsed in the face of Adolf Hitler's blitzkrieg, a generation of American foreign policy elites worried that if the British Empire also fell, there would be no great power left to challenge Nazi dominance and ensure liberalism's future. The United States, they concluded, needed to fill that role, and the only way to do so was for it to become a major military power dedicated to protecting the free exchange of ideas, people, and, especially, goods. At first, Americans mostly confined their vision of a U.S.-led order to the Western Hemisphere. But after the nation entered World War II in December 1941, and Nazi success seemed less assured, those visions expanded to encompass most of the globe. Peace, prosperity, and liberalism itself depended on world-spanning U.S. armed primacy.

This conviction became an essential component of the imperialist ideology that U.S. elites developed and institutionalized during the Cold War, and it remains widely held today. Because Americans identify stability with dominance, the United States spends an unconscionable amount on its military and pursues a series of endless wars that have little strategic benefit, do nothing to improve the lives of Americans or those suffering abroad, and, ironically, engender instability. Wertheim, one of the founders of the Quincy Institute for Responsible Statecraft, an anti-militarist think tank backed by George Soros and Charles Koch, has devoted his career to challenging the shibboleths that surround U.S. primacy. Just as

Americans once chose to rule, he argues, they can likewise choose not to.

***

The first centuries of U.S. history underline how strange the country's bid for hegemony was. As Wertheim notes, before the mid-twentieth century Americans tended to claim that "their nation was exceptional because it did *not* covet armed supremacy over the rest of the world."[3] They recoiled from so-called foreign entanglements—imbrication in the power politics of other countries, especially in Europe. This became such an important element of U.S. nationalism that even when Americans used their military for expressly political purposes—Indigenous genocide, colonialism, resource extraction—they did so, Wertheim maintains, "in the name of ending power politics."[4]

Americans were some of the world's most vocal advocates of "internationalism"—the idea that reason, rules, and discussion could enable nations to avoid or attenuate the scourge of war. At the turn of the century, Progressives including Vice President (later President) Theodore Roosevelt and Secretary of War (later State) Elihu Root promoted international conferences such as the Hague Conventions of 1899 and 1907, which established the Permanent Court of Arbitration and created several laws of war. Soon thereafter, in the maelstrom of World War I, Progressive President Woodrow Wilson furthered the internationalist cause by developing the idea for the League of Nations, which, he averred, would be the mechanism for transcending power politics itself.

Unfortunately for Wilson and other internationalists, the United States never joined the League, rejecting the Treaty of Versailles because it threatened to impinge on U.S. sovereignty. But American internationalists continued to promote mechanisms and plans for geopolitical cooperation. In 1921, Secretary of State Charles Evans Hughes called the Washington Naval Conference, which established a framework for great powers to discuss disagreements about the

Pacific Ocean. In 1924 and 1929, U.S. bankers and industrialists spearheaded the Dawes and Young Plans to stabilize European economies, and in 1928, the nation signed the Kellogg–Briand Pact (named after Secretary of State Frank B. Kellogg and French Foreign Minister Aristide Briand) to outlaw war. On the eve of the 1930s, Americans were at the forefront of internationalist efforts to replace geopolitical conflict with reason, arbitration, and law.

The 1930s was the decade that dashed the internationalist dream. Both Nazism and Soviet communism, valorizing strength and developing cults of personality around charismatic dictators, were plainly and avowedly irreconcilable with American ideas of liberalism. Because, as the title of a famous book from the era put it, "you can't do business with Hitler" (or Stalin), internationalists began to doubt the potential of discussion to guarantee global peace.[5] Furthermore, the internationalist institutions that had emerged were foundering. Most dramatically, the League of Nations failed to prevent or halt Japan's 1931 invasion of Manchuria and Italy's 1935 invasion of Ethiopia. To many contemporary internationalists, the successes of fascism, Stalinism, and Japanese imperialism suggested that force, not reason, ordered international politics. If this was true, they concluded, then military power was stability's indispensable handmaiden, and sometimes the United States would need to use or abet force outside the traditional hemispheric bastion it had defined in the Monroe Doctrine of 1823.

This *volte-face* was a difficult one to make: How could someone who had argued that reason, law, and discussion could end war suddenly defend the use of force beyond the Western Hemisphere? To do so, pro-force internationalists created the category of "isolationism," accusing anyone who opposed military power of rejecting *all* forms of international engagement outside the hemisphere.[6] In this way, pro-force Americans claimed the mantle of internationalism even as they rejected its foundational assumption that the United States remain militarily apart from Europe and Asia. The historic struggle between internationalists and so-called isolationists was, in fact, a debate between two types of internationalists—those who defended coercive force across the globe and those who did not. Simply put, no group of Americans ever insisted that the United States remain aloof from the rest of the world; the question was how, exactly, the United States should engage.

Confronted with the rise of Hitler, pro-force internationalists defeated their "isolationist" opponents relatively easily. By the late 1930s, isolationism had become a powerful term of opprobrium. Robert Sherwood, the playwright who served as Franklin Delano Roosevelt's speechwriter (and who later became director of the Office of War Information's Overseas Branch), lambasted "isolationists" for desiring to "keep us out of everything."[7] Secretary of State Cordell Hull worried that if "isolationist" dreams were realized, they would "carry the whole world back to the conditions of medieval chaos."[8] In internationalists' opinion, force was needed to ensure progress both in the United States and abroad. Still, few American internationalists imagined that the United States itself would become the world's dominant power anytime soon—Great Britain already occupied that position.

***

When World War II erupted in Europe in September 1939, members of the emergent foreign policy establishment—a loose agglomeration of East Coast lawyers, businessmen, and bureaucrats—recognized that the United States would come out of the war more powerful than ever before. And, if the nation wanted to wield this power effectively, it needed to develop plans for the postwar world. One week after Germany invaded Poland, Hamilton Fish Armstrong, a founder of the Council on Foreign Relations (CFR), made the State Department an offer: the CFR would plan for the postwar era while the government addressed itself to the exigencies of war. With official blessing, and $300,000 in funding from the Rockefeller Foundation, the CFR got to work.

The project's membership list was like a roll call of the internationalists who would lay the intellectual foundations for American Empire: it included the economist Jacob Viner, the geographer Isaiah Bowman, and the lawyer (and later director of central intelligence) Allen Dulles. These men formed a "para"- or "pseudo"-state connected to the government but not officially a part of it, an early version of the "military-intellectual complex" that would shape U.S. foreign affairs in the Cold War and after.[9] A crucial benefit of this arrangement was that it left the group free from public scrutiny: State Department officials worried that if postwar planning was carried out in the actual government, it might, Wertheim writes, "become public knowledge and raise suspicion that the Roosevelt Administration was preparing for war."[10] From its beginnings, U.S. primacy was intimately linked with skepticism of democracy.

When they began their efforts, the CFR planners assumed that the United States would not actually send troops to Europe and Asia. But everything changed in the summer of 1940. The Nazis' swift defeat of the French military, which had halted the German advance in World War I, and which was considered among the world's strongest, shocked American internationalists. With France's collapse, Hitler dominated continental Europe. Now, if the Nazis invaded and conquered the United Kingdom (already forced to retreat at Dunkirk), then Germany would have defeated the world's most powerful empires and would be on its way to global dominance.

The CFR planners considered this unacceptable. Though they didn't believe that Hitler endangered America's physical security, Wertheim argues, "the specter of a Nazi-led world order" that "threatened to stop liberal intercourse from traversing the globe and the United States from driving world history" led them to define economic exchange and American destiny as "vital" interests worthy of armed defense.[11] For the first time in their nation's history, the CFR internationalists started to affirm that the United States needed to engage in power politics outside the Western

Hemisphere. France's collapse put a definitive end to the notion that the world was progressing toward a more peaceful and open state.

This story of the United States' bid for global power undermines the importance of the "Pearl Harbor" myth to American history. After 1945, apologists for American Empire have often argued that the surprise Japanese destruction of the Pacific Fleet at Pearl Harbor (and the simultaneous, if usually ignored, assaults on the U.S. territories of the Philippines, Guam, and Wake Island) justified the U.S. presence abroad: Didn't the attack, after all, demonstrate what happened when the United States restrained its military power? Yet Wertheim shows that more than a year earlier, prominent members of the U.S. foreign policy establishment were already arguing that their nation needed to take a leading role in world affairs. Put another way, the United States was not forced to build its global empire in reaction to a physical attack, but did so as the result of an intellectual revolution that jettisoned the liberal premises of traditional internationalism.

***

In late 1940, the CFR's Economic and Financial Group, headed by Viner and the economist Alvin Hansen, concluded that the Nazis would retain their hold on Europe (and parts of North Africa and the Middle East) for the foreseeable future. This, they determined, meant that the United States could compete with Hitler only if it controlled a "Grand Area" that connected the Americas to the British Empire and Pacific Basin. Linking these regions would provide the material basis for the United States and its junior partner, the United Kingdom, to compete with the emergent German economic juggernaut and continue to direct world history. In effect, the CFR planners were arguing that to challenge the Nazi empire, the United States needed to become the prime power everywhere else on the globe. Conceptually, they were also claiming that liberal exchange needed to be underwritten by military force.

Gone was any Enlightenment-based notion that humans could overcome their differences through discussion. Instead, the planners embraced a Hobbesian theory of human nature in which people were selfish, greedy, and prone to war, governable only through violence and its threat.

The CFR planners and fellow travelers such as Under Secretary of State Sumner Welles, however, did not want to assert simply that the power of the American–Anglo alliance justified its rule. For this reason, they laid a liberal ideology over great power dominance, avowing that the Americans and British would create and defend an international order devoted to liberal norms. This argument not only assuaged internationalists' consciences; it also allowed them to sell U.S. global supremacy to the American public. The primary mechanism of this "liberal international order," as it would later be called, was the United Nations. "By working through a universal body, with every nation a member," Wertheim maintains, "the United States would seem to lead an enlightened world order, bound by rules of law and respecting the equality of others."[12] By promoting the U.N., U.S. elites made armed primacy palatable to a public that had long rejected it.

The eventual structure of the United Nations reflected internationalists' interest in ensuring U.S. primacy. Most important, the Security Council, which consisted of the five great powers (the United States, the United Kingdom, the Soviet Union, China, and France), was far more powerful than the General Assembly, to which all nations belonged. This structure, Wertheim observes, enabled the great powers to "enjoy full discretion to identify aggressors and decide whether and how to act."[13] In other words, the U.N. was not intended to end power politics but to legitimate it. Several intellectuals and officials at the time, including Raymond Leslie Buell and the economic expert Milo Perkins (the executive director of the Board of Economic Warfare), even endorsed the idea that whenever the United States couldn't receive U.N. sanction for a given action, it should act unilaterally. Or as Wertheim puts it: "multilateralism where possible, unilateralism if necessary."[14]

It's not a surprise, then, that the United States has frequently ignored the Security Council, as it did when it led the bombing of Kosovo in 1999 and invaded and occupied Iraq in 2003. The General Assembly, for its part, has been described by critics as "a pointless gabfest and an excuse for the wives of dictators to enjoy some 5th Avenue shopping."[15] In typically colorful language, President Richard Nixon once dismissed the U.N. as "a damn debating society."[16] Like the League of Nations before it, the U.N. has proved powerless to stop rampant violations of international law, from Israel's occupation of the West Bank to Vladimir Putin's annexation of Crimea and invasion of eastern Ukraine. This doesn't mean, however, that international organization is doomed; what it suggests is that no international organization can effectively function if great powers refuse to abandon their ability to make war unilaterally.

Acting with an unparalleled degree of influence since 1945, the United States has achieved one great accomplishment: it has ended major wars in Western and Central Europe. This is a world-historical success on a continent whose history was plagued by repeated and brutal conflicts. But this triumph at the heart of the "liberal international order" should not obscure the terrible effects U.S. primacy has had on those outside the North Atlantic core. For most of humanity, the liberal international order was not particularly liberal, and as Wertheim shows, it was never intended to be.

***

Wertheim's is the only recent book to explore U.S. elites' decision to become the world's primary power in the early 1940s—a profoundly important choice that has affected the lives of billions of people throughout the globe. This is partly because internationalists who oppose the use of force have since 1945 been largely excluded from the foreign policy debate. Indeed, pro-force internationalists were so successful in expelling noninterventionists from the public sphere that, as Wertheim writes, "the *restraint* of American power" is now considered "the height of introversion and selfishness."[17] For over 75 years, to criticize armed primacy in public has been to go beyond the pale.

Tomorrow, the World is also unique in its near-exclusive focus on domestic U.S. history. In the last three decades, diplomatic history has been transformed by two intellectual "turns" that have deemphasized how domestic politics and events shaped U.S. foreign policy. On one hand, "international" historians have examined the United States' impact abroad and the influence that other countries and peoples have had on U.S. foreign affairs. On the other hand, "transnational" historians have analyzed how non-state actors, groups, and movements pushed U.S. foreign policy in particular directions. While these approaches have deepened historians' understanding of several aspects of U.S. foreign relations—most important, its effects on foreign peoples, which were too often ignored by previous generations of intellectuals—they have forced the scholars' gaze from U.S. policy elites themselves.

Wertheim represents a new generation of foreign policy thinkers—millennials for whom the invasion of Iraq was a seminal event that dispelled the notion, popular in the 1990s, that the United States was the world's "indispensable nation."[18] Like many of his contemporaries—Megan Black, Daniel Immerwahr, and Jennifer M. Miller, to name a few—he has devoted his scholarship to exploring the origins and character of a U.S. hegemony that has done more harm than good.[19] While Wertheim traces the rise of armed primacy, Black has explored the Interior Department's drive for U.S. expansion, Immerwahr has examined the United States' territorial empire, and Miller has analyzed how U.S. elites sought to create a democratic mind in the foreign populations that they governed. Together, these scholars desire to explain how, exactly, the United States came to rule the world.

With his work for the Quincy Institute (where I am a nonresident fellow), Wertheim has also attempted to transform U.S. foreign policy from inside the Beltway. In this way, he has something in common with Hamilton Fish Armstrong and the CFR planners that he writes about, who likewise wanted to have a direct effect on policy. To date, Quincy has released a number of road maps for a more "restraint"-oriented foreign policy. Its report, *A New U.S. Paradigm for the Middle East: Ending America's Misguided Policy of Domination*, for example, argues that the nation should adopt a demilitarized approach to the region, defined by drawing down troops, avoiding disputes tangential to its interests, normalizing relations with Iran, using diplomacy to end the civil wars in Syria and Yemen, and working with local partners to transfer security responsibilities.[20] These are concrete proposals that give restraint a clear meaning and make the end of primacy easier to envision.

One of very few think tanks in Washington, D.C., that is avowedly anti-militarist, the Quincy Institute has its work cut out for it. Although Donald Trump repeatedly criticized the Iraq War during his campaign for president, his foreign policy team—a grab bag of militarists and malcontents ranging from Mike Pompeo to John Bolton—has shown little affinity for dismantling hegemony. A Joe Biden Administration, meanwhile, will likely be staffed with interventionist stalwarts like Susan Rice and Samantha Power, who has passionately argued that the United States has the moral duty to use force abroad if doing so saves innocent lives. There are also important disagreements within the "restrainer" community that are not easily papered over. While Soros and Koch (and the Left and libertarian right) might agree on the desirability of avoiding war, they have wildly different visions of what an ideal world would look like. Whereas liberals such as Soros favor a regulated global economy, libertarians such as Koch embrace unrestrained free markets. Which should U.S. foreign policy pursue? Relatedly, does abandoning military primacy also mean abandoning economic primacy? It's currently unclear how the Quincy Institute will answer these questions.

The institute has already drawn criticism from the Right and Left. The militarist Senator Tom Cotton, borrowing the language of the internationalists discussed in *Tomorrow, the World,* has labeled Quincy "an isolationist blame-America-first money pit for so-called 'scholars.'"[21] For their part, some on the left have worried that the organization's "reformist perspective," to quote a *Jacobin* article, is not sufficiently radical to offer a genuine alternative to American Empire.[22] There are also many groups—such as defense contractors—that don't want to see the United States restrain its military power. In 2019, the defense industry spent about $119,000,000 on lobbying, which likely recently encouraged Congress to vote against reducing the defense budget by a modest 10 percent.[23] U.S. primacy in 2020 is much more than an ideal or assumption. It is the organizing principle for very influential and wealthy interests that will not be easily defeated.

***

Although a vast architecture provides material and ideological support for American primacy, there are signs that public support for it is attenuating. A Pew poll last year discovered that almost half of adults under 30 believe that it would be acceptable for another country to develop military capabilities equal to those of the United States.[24] That same poll also determined that 73 percent of Americans believe "that good diplomacy is the best way to ensure peace," while a poll funded by the Charles Koch Institute similarly found that around three-quarters of those surveyed want to bring the troops home from Afghanistan and Iraq.[25] During his campaign for the presidency, Bernie Sanders promoted a restraint-oriented foreign policy that was enthusiastically embraced by his supporters. And with the Quincy Institute, heterodox analysts of foreign affairs finally have a home.

Wertheim's book contributes to the effort to transform U.S. foreign policy by giving pro-restraint Americans a usable past. Though *Tomorrow, the World* is not a polemic, its implications are invigorating. Americans, Wertheim argues, are not forced to exert power, helpless to do anything but dominate. The popular notion that global "leadership" was foisted unwittingly upon a nation that wanted to remain aloof from foreign military affairs but, for the good of the world, decided otherwise is a fairy tale. By demolishing this convenient and flattering myth, Wertheim opens space for Americans to reexamine their own history and ask themselves whether primacy has ever really met their interests.

For decades, the political establishment refused to present Americans with the choice of whether they should rule the world. There was simply no alternative to armed primacy. If the failures of post–Cold War U.S. foreign policy—the disasters of Afghanistan, Iraq, and Libya; the illegal assassinations; the siphoning of resources from butter to guns—have revealed the devastating limits of power, they have finally made restraint thinkable.

Endnotes

1 John Winthrop, "Christian Charity, A Model Hereof," in *As a City on a Hill: The Story of America's Most Famous Lay Sermon*, by Daniel T. Rodgers (Princeton, NJ: Princeton University Press, 2018), 291–308.

2 Stephen Wertheim, *Tomorrow, the World: The Birth of U.S. Global Supremacy* (Cambridge, MA: Harvard University Press, 2020), chapter 2.

3 Ibid., 1.

4 Ibid., 18.

5 Douglas Miller, *You Can't Do Business with Hitler* (Boston: Little, Brown and Company, 1941).

6 Stephen Wertheim, "Internationalism/Isolationism: Concepts of American Global Power," in *Rethinking U.S. World Power: Domestic Histories of U.S. Foreign Relations* (Cham, Switzerland: Palgrave Macmillan, 2024), 49–88.

7 Wertheim, *Tomorrow, the World*, 33.

8 Ibid., 34.

9 On the military-intellectual complex, see Ron Robin, *The Making of the Cold War Enemy: Culture and Politics in the Military-Intellectual Complex* (Princeton, NJ: Princeton University Press, 2001); Daniel Bessner, *Democracy in Exile: Hans Speier and the Rise of the Defense Intellectual* (Ithaca, NY: Cornell University Press, 2018).

10 Wertheim, *Tomorrow, the World*, 37.
11 Ibid., 51, 49, 54.
12 Ibid., 119.
13 Ibid., 139.
14 Ibid., 144.
15 Ryan Heath, "Everything You Need to Know About the U.N. General Assembly," *Politico*, September 20, 2019, https://www.politico.com/newsletters/un-playbook/2019/09/20/everything-you-need-to-know-about-the-un-general-assembly-478867.
16 "Conversation Between President Nixon and the Ambassador to the Republic of China (McConaughy)," June 30, 1971, *Foreign Relations of the United States*, 1969–1976, Volume XVII, China, 1969–1972, ed. Steven E. Phillips (Washington, D.C.: Government Printing Office, 2006), Document 136, https://history.state.gov/historicaldocuments/frus1969-76v17/d136.
17 Wertheim, *Tomorrow, the World*, 148.
18 Madeleine K. Albright, interview by Matt Lauer, *The Today Show*, NBC-TV, Columbus, OH, February 19, 1998, https://1997-2001.state.gov/statements/1998/980219a.html.
19 Megan Black, *The Global Interior: Mineral Frontiers and American Power* (Cambridge, MA: Harvard University Press, 2018); Daniel Immerwahr, *How to Hide an Empire: A History of the Greater United States* (New York: Farrar, Straus and Giroux, 2019); Jennifer M. Miller, *Cold War Democracy: The United States and Japan* (Cambridge, MA: Harvard University Press, 2019).
20 Paul Pillar, Andrew Bacevich, Annelle Sheline, and Trita Parsi, *A New U.S. Paradigm for the Middle East: Ending America's Misguided Policy of Domination*, Quincy Paper No. 2 (Washington, D.C.: Quincy Institute for Responsible Statecraft, July 2020), https://quincyinst.org/research/ending-americas-misguided-policy-of-middle-east-domination/#.
21 John Podhoretz, "Tom Cotton on Anti-Semitism," *Commentary*, January 9, 2020, https://www.commentary.org/john-podhoretz/tom-cotton-on-anti-semitism/.
22 Derek Davison and Alex Thurston, "Expect More Military 'Liberal Interventionism' Under a Joe Biden Presidency," *Jacobin*, June 7, 2020,

https://jacobin.com/2020/06/joe-biden-foreign-policy-military-liberal-interventionism-obama.

23 "Sector Profile: Defense [2019]," Open Secrets, accessed July 26, 2025, https://www.opensecrets.org/federal-lobbying/sectors/summary?cycle=2019&id=d; Joe Gould, "Progressive Effort to Cut Defense Fails Twice in Congress," *Defense News*, July 22, 2020, https://www.defensenews.com/congress/2020/07/22/progressive-effort-to-cut-defense-fails-twice-in-congress/.

24 *In a Politically Polarized Era, Sharp Divides in Both Partisan Coalitions* (Washington, D.C.: Pew Research Center, December 2019), 14, https://www.pewresearch.org/politics/wp-content/uploads/sites/4/2019/12/PP_2019.12.17_Political-Values_FINAL.pdf.

25 Ibid., 80; Rebecca Kheel, "Poll: About Three Quarters Support Bringing Troops Home from Iraq, Afghanistan," *The Hill*, August 6, 2020, https://thehill.com/policy/defense/510851-poll-about-three-quarters-support-bringing-troops-home-from-iraq-afghanistan/.

THE CASE AGAINST HUMANE WAR

In May 2013, Barack Obama delivered a speech at the National Defense University in which he defended the war on terror, then in its twelfth year. Though remembered as an anti-war candidate, Obama actually had never declared opposition to the war on terror itself. Rather, the problem, as Obama saw it, was that the United States had waged its war without regard for the law. He had taken pains to change this. As he proudly trumpeted in his speech, his administration "unequivocally banned torture, affirmed our commitment to civilian courts, worked to align our policies with the rule of law, and expanded our consultations with Congress."[1] The war on terror, previously tainted with the stink of illegality, had been cleansed.

The president also proudly affirmed that he was fighting the war on terror humanely. The large numbers of boots on the ground that had defined the Iraq War, and which had resulted in the deaths of untold numbers of Iraqi civilians, had been replaced with unmanned aerial vehicles, better known as drones. "By narrowly targeting our action against those who want to kill us and not the people they hide among," Obama avowed, "we are choosing the course of action least likely to result in the loss of innocent life."[2]

Americans could rest assured that their president was defending them ethically.

In his new book, *Humane: How the United States Abandoned Peace and Reinvented War*, the Yale historian and law professor Samuel Moyn explores how American decision-makers, military officials, jurists, and activists developed what he considers a troubling obsession with "humane" war—wars in which the United States attempts to limit the suffering of troops and civilians.[3] This focus may appear counterintuitive: If wars are fought, why not make them less destructive? But *Humane* makes the case that humane warfare brings its own set of hazards. The book reconstructs a centuries-old debate between those who insisted that war be fought humanely and those who were concerned that, by making combat more palatable, humane war would do little but promote endless conflict. In this way, *Humane* is a prehistory of our era, in which the precision drone strike has replaced massive aerial bombardment, small footprint Special Forces have replaced the ground invasion, and the United States remains entangled in wars around the world.

Moyn himself has not always identified humane war, or even war itself, as a major obstacle to peace; in the 1990s, at the beginning of his career, he was a liberal internationalist who believed force was sometimes necessary to achieve greater ends. His argument in *Humane* articulates a disillusionment that many intellectuals underwent in the Obama era, as the war on terror dragged on, bringing loss of civilian life abroad and a vast surveillance apparatus at home, all under the guise of humanity. Moyn's shift from liberal internationalist to critic of humane war reflects a broader awakening of a generation of American anti-imperialists, who have begun to question many of the premises that have guided U.S. foreign policy for decades.

***

Until relatively recently, debates about humane war were largely theoretical. For much of the twentieth century's first half, the prospect of a war without brutality appeared remote. World War I's carnage—the trenches of the Western Front, the Armenian genocide, the British blockade of the European continent—made clear to many contemporary observers that war could never be fought without enormous human cost; it could only be abolished. Peace was the goal. This was especially true in the United States, which in 1917 had broken 141 years of tradition by sending troops to fight a European war that many soon viewed as pointless and illegitimate. By 1933, "Americans could boast twelve million adherents to the peace movement and an annual combined budget of more than $1 million" for pro-peace organizations.[4]

U.S. peace advocates considered international law an important mechanism for preventing conflict. Though the Senate famously refused to join the League of Nations, American elites nevertheless helped orchestrate the Kellogg–Briand Pact of 1928, which renounced "war as an instrument of national policy."[5] The pact infamously had no enforcement mechanism. Still, in the opinion of peace advocates such as the political scientist Quincy Wright, the Kellogg–Briand Pact took the important step of formally and publicly aligning the U.S. government with the cause of global peace.

World War II annihilated the peace movement. The dream that rational exchange could avoid wars was dashed by Nazi *Blitzkriege* in Europe and Japanese surprise attacks in the Pacific. To the majority of observers, the war's outbreak demonstrated that only force could tame geopolitics. For this reason, U.S. elites chose to pursue international order through armed domination of most of the world, establishing a vast network of bases across the globe. The Pax Americana that followed was a period of peace insofar as mass war did not break out between the great powers or tear across the European continent, but the United States frequently went to war, deploying troops to stamp out communism or overthrow leaders unfriendly to U.S. economic and strategic interests. As the Military Intervention Project at Tufts University has revealed, since the close of World War II, the United States has undertaken over 200 military interventions.[6]

If World War II put the United States on a permanent war footing, its inhumanity simultaneously brought about attempts to mitigate war's worst horrors. Most prominently, the Geneva Conventions of 1949 regulated the treatment of wounded troops, prisoners of war, and civilians, while the Nuremberg Charter of 1945 made crimes against humanity illegal. These measures established some of the principles of humane war, though they were rarely put into practice. For most observers, the prospect of genuinely humane war was not yet in sight.

***

The first three decades of the Pax Americana were notoriously violent, especially in Asia, a region in which the United States had long pursued a foothold. During the Korean War, the United States showed remarkably little regard for Korean life, engaging in scorched-earth air campaigns that, Moyn recounts, laid waste to "every town and even village of note in the north."[7] The war brought about 3.5 million Korean casualties, making it "the most brutal war of the twentieth century, measured by the intensity of violence and per capita civilian death."[8]

The Korean War's savagery, however, didn't stop the United States from fighting another barbarous ground war in Asia that had little connection to its vital interests. During parts of the Vietnam War, U.S. forces killed civilians based "on the barest suspicion of Viet Cong involvement"; executed and tortured POWs; forcibly relocated villages; laced the countryside with land mines; made expansive use of napalm and phosphorus; and indiscriminately bombed North Vietnam, Cambodia, and Laos.[9] While several of these activities were legal—there were no formal restrictions against aerial bombardment or napalm—many of them were not, to say nothing of the fact that all were immoral. By the time U.S. troops fully left Vietnam in 1975, millions of Vietnamese had perished in the war.

The escalation of the Vietnam War in the mid-1960s drew strong opposition from the American public—by 1968 the war was, Moyn notes, "terminally unpopular"—but the anti-war movement was largely concerned with the moral and legal basis on which the United States had entered the war rather than with the atrocities that U.S. forces committed in the fighting.[10] A turning point came in 1969, when the journalist Seymour Hersh broke the story of the My Lai massacre, which described a U.S. Army company's murder of more than 500 South Vietnamese civilians. One of the most important responses to My Lai was written by Telford Taylor, a Columbia law professor, who earlier in his career had served as chief counsel at the Nuremberg Trials. Taylor's 1970 book, *Nuremberg and Vietnam: An American Tragedy*, Moyn writes, "made allegations of war crimes 'respectable' by moving them from the far left to the liberal center."[11] Moyn maintains that Taylor's book was so consequential because he was otherwise unwilling to criticize the U.S. military; without opposing the war itself, he urged other Americans to take a stand against its extraordinary brutality.

Soon after the war ended, a novel American coalition "concerned with the fate of the innocent in war" emerged.[12] U.S. military lawyers formed a central part of this coalition and, in the late 1970s, started to take up a novel legal framework dubbed "international humanitarian law," which was embodied in the "Additional Protocols" to the Geneva Conventions, accepted in 1977.[13] The Additional Protocols made three interventions: They "clearly formalized" civilian immunity; they prohibited "excessive" collateral damage; and "they called for precautions in targeting."[14] Taken together, the protocols "affirmed that the point of war was to weaken military capacities on the other side, absolutely prohibiting the direct targeting of civilians."[15] While the United States never ratified the Additional Protocols, by the 1980s the American military had in effect embraced them.

The Additional Protocols reflected what might be termed the "de-massification" of war that started after Vietnam. World War II, Korea, and Vietnam were "total wars," involving the mass mobilization of society and the indiscriminate targeting of civilians, who produced the matériel that enabled battle. The public opposition to the Vietnam War, however, showed U.S. decision-makers that they could no longer rely on large-scale mobilization. If the United States was going to continue to dominate the world, it needed to "de-massify" its conflicts. In 1973, Congress refused to extend the draft. The military became an all-volunteer force (AVF), concluding a 33-year period in which ordinary Americans had been conscripted en masse to fight their nation's wars.

From 1973 onward, America's wars were fought only by those who volunteered to fight them, which both undercut the anti-war movement and changed Americans' relationship to their armed forces. In short, Americans no longer needed to worry about being forced to die in foreign lands for unclear purposes. The AVF's advent also began to transform the "American Way of War." Whereas the United States had previously embraced "a strategy of annihilation based upon the principle of concentration and mass," as the historian Russell F. Weigley summarized when describing the approach of Ulysses S. Grant, after Vietnam, the U.S. military started to assert itself through air power, Special Forces, and the system of international bases it had developed in the post–World War II era.[16]

The seeds of humane war were thus planted, though they would only bear fruit during the Gulf War of 1990–1991. This war, unlike any previous U.S. war, was carried out with a phalanx of military lawyers at the ready. As Moyn highlights, lawyers rapidly "became fixtures of air operations centers, advising when dual-use targets—with both civilian and military purposes—were fair game and when limits on disproportionate collateral harm were likely to be violated."[17] For the first time in American history, the military "accepted an unprecedented intrusion of legality into fighting."[18] Indeed, lawyers remained crucial participants in all post–Gulf War U.S. conflicts. Combined, the presence of lawyers and the de-massification of war persuaded American elites that their nation could dominate the world ethically, with little cost to most of them.

***

The initiation of the war on terror after the attacks of September 11, 2001 revealed a particularly troubling feature of so-called humane war: that it could go on for much longer than a mass war.

Soon after the war on terror began, the news program *60 Minutes II* revealed photos of U.S. guards torturing detainees at Abu Ghraib prison in Iraq, engendering an outcry from Americans critical of the war.[19] But instead of pulling out of Iraq or ending the war on terror, the George W. Bush Administration used lawyers such as Jack Goldsmith of the Office of Legal Counsel to bring it "within the pale of legality."[20] And the administration was successful, at least in part. Its efforts attenuated "the harshest methods of interrogation" and ensured that certain protections were granted to combatants captured in battle.[21]

These accomplishments, Moyn writes, "cleansed" the war on terror "of stigma" and had the ironic impact of encouraging "a war that became endless, legal, and humane."[22] When Barack Obama assumed office in 2009, he continued the humanization process begun under Bush. Specifically, he made extensive use of drones and Special Forces, which his lawyers deemed humane, effective, and legal. Thus Obama approved manifold precision drone strikes throughout the global south—in Afghanistan, Iraq, Pakistan, Somalia, and Yemen—and deployed U.S. Special Forces around the world. Famously a graduate of Harvard Law School, Obama established "a lawyerly institutional process" to determine whom to target; each week, he "pore[d] over 'kill lists' that he personally vetted."[23] In this way, the president personally oversaw the execution of thousands of people, many of whom were only tenuously connected to U.S. enemies.

By the time he left office, Obama had midwifed the new, de-massified, and humane American Way of War that had been gestating for years. And many in the liberal establishment lined up behind him. As the Brookings Institution's Daniel L. Byman affirmed in a 2013 article titled "Why Drones Work," Obama's use of drones hurt "terrorist" groups and gave "Washington the ability to limit its military commitments abroad while keeping Americans safe."[24] In *The Atlantic*, the international lawyer Michael W. Lewis insisted, as his piece was subtitled, that drones were "Actually the Most Humane Form of Warfare Ever."[25] For its part, *The New York Times* published an article in which experts made "The Moral Case For Drones."[26]

But not everyone paid obeisance to Obama. David Cole, the legal director of the American Civil Liberties Union, attacked the administration in *The Nation* for its "disturbing practice" of using drones "to kill thousands of our 'enemies,' and lots of civilians, many of them far from any battlefield."[27] In his 2015 book, *Power Wars*, Charlie Savage, *The New York Times*' Washington correspondent, illuminated the expansion of executive power and surveillance networks that fueled the Obama-era national security state.[28] Critics worried that Obama was institutionalizing a way of war that accorded himself and future presidents a significant amount of unaccountable power. And they were right; as many of them feared, the powers Obama wielded passed to a particularly reckless successor. Unsurprisingly, Donald Trump made extensive and expansive use of them, keeping the structure of the humane, light-footprint, but unconstrained approach to war the United States had embraced under Bush and Obama.

***

It was the turmoil of the Bush and Obama eras that reshaped Moyn's own politics. Ideologically, Moyn started his career a liberal internationalist—in *Humane*, he writes that, as a young White House intern in the late 1990s, he believed the 1999 NATO intervention into Serbia was "the final violence necessary to put right a globe that had been disfigured by the necessities of the Cold War but was now on the brink of peace."[29] But the failures of Afghanistan, Iraq, and the war on terror writ large converted him to an avowed anti-imperialist position, and he began to write more and more for the public. Whereas Moyn's early works were decidedly academic—a book on the French Jewish philosopher

Emmanuel Levinas, another on Holocaust memory in postwar France—in 2010 he published *The Last Utopia: Human Rights in History*, which insisted human rights were a relic of the 1970s that "have done far more to transform the terrain of idealism than they have the world itself."[30] In 2018, Moyn expanded upon his criticism of human rights to argue, in a book of the same title, that they were *Not Enough*—that human rights needed to be bolstered with a commitment to material equality and economic justice.[31]

Humane is a continuation of Moyn's decade-long critique of human rights and the liberal ideology that undergirds them. But, unlike his earlier books, *Humane* is explicitly anti-imperialist, looking specifically at the misplaced idealism used to justify American Empire to the nation's elites. Moyn's anti-imperialism emerged as a younger generation of thinkers, who came of age after the U.S. invasion of Iraq, were developing their own critiques of American power; many, in fact, were students at Columbia, where Moyn then taught. By 2017, "The Disillusionment of Samuel Moyn" was notable enough to warrant a feature in *The Chronicle of Higher Education*, which traced the connections among the Moyn Circle, a group that includes the historians James Chappel, Ana Keilson, Thomas Meaney, and Daniel Steinmetz-Jenkins, as well as David Marcus, the literary editor of *The Nation*; Timothy Shenk, the co-editor of *Dissent*; and Stephen Wertheim, a founder of the Quincy Institute for Responsible Statecraft, who now works at the Carnegie Endowment for International Peace.[32] In *Humane*, Moyn thanks Meaney, Shenk, and Wertheim for their notes and cites Wertheim's work several times.[33]

Several of the circle put analysis of U.S. Empire front and center, forming a loose network of left-wing critics of U.S. foreign policy that embraced an unsparing intellectual style. Many in the group published well-honed eviscerations of prominent figures in pugnacious little magazines (as one former student commented in the *Chronicle* article, Moyn made it "OK to really shred ... the book you're reviewing, if you genuinely think it's wrong and have good reason").[34] Moyn served, the *Chronicle* noted, "as a model and magnet for a generation of younger historians and public intellectuals" in increasingly angering times.[35]

In *Humane*, Moyn's wide reading in North Atlantic philosophy, legal theory, and criticism enables him to reconstruct a centuries-old debate that most scholars have downplayed or ignored. As he traces the rise of humane war, he also unearths its early critics. Moyn begins the book with the Russian novelist Leo Tolstoy, who worried that two risks accompanied the project to humanize war. First, there was the risk that humanizing war encouraged people "to tolerate an enduring evil" instead of seeking its end.[36] Second, there was the risk that people would begin "to believe that striking a blow against the cruelty of a practice made their continuing involvement in it noble."[37] Humanizing war, Tolstoy maintained, was likely to make war honorable and peace scarce.

And Tolstoy was not a voice in the wilderness. In the wake of World War I, as Moyn notes, the British novelist H.G. Wells and other like-minded thinkers expressed the opinions of many when they affirmed that attempts to humanize war were "sops to humanity, devices for rendering war barely tolerable to civilized mankind, and so staving off the inevitable rebellion against its abominations."[38] These early warnings make it difficult to argue that our "forever war" was unforeseeable. For as long as the idea of humane war has existed, there have been prominent critics who worried about the potential connections between humanization and permanent conflict.

Nonetheless, Moyn's narrow focus on the law sometimes leads him to mischaracterize parts of his story. Take, for example, his reflections on American air power in World War II. Moyn finds it puzzling that after the war, "no international lawyers rose to prominence in ethical resistance to [the] urban holocausts" caused by aerial bombardment, suggesting that this was "because the law gave them no basis to do so."[39] But this misses what was going on at the time. In fact, there were groups both within and outside the military who believed that aerial bombing campaigns were humane. In 1943, for instance, Henry Harley Arnold, the chief of the Army Air Forces, referred to the precision strategic bomber as "the most humane of all weapons" because it had the potential to make ground war a thing of the past.[40] After the atomic bombing of Hiroshima, one high-ranking air force officer went so far as to write "that the accuracy with which this bomb was placed" demonstrated that it was not an example of "wanton, indiscriminate bombing" but rather the embodiment of precision—and, by implication, humane—warfare.[41]

The willingness of an air officer to present an atomic bombing as an instance of humane warfare indicates that U.S. elites have been deceiving themselves about the "humanity" of their wars for far longer than Moyn argues. Delusions of American innocence—reflected in the idea that even atomic bombings could be humane—were baked into U.S. dominance from its beginnings. It is wrong to claim, as Moyn does, that Americans "embraced global order … as ardent foes of humane war."[42] In many cases, the opposite is true.

Relatedly, *Humane* implies that the arguments of humane war's advocates were the primary reason the United States adopted the tactics of humane war. But such arguments found purchase only when other, more causally important transformations took place—when the advent of new technologies, domestic coalitions, and state institutions encouraged and enabled the United States to dominate the world through light-footprint and "precision" wars. Furthermore, several countries, including Azerbaijan, Iraq, Nigeria, Saudi Arabia, and Turkey, have used drones without making any pretense of practicing humane war, which suggests that other factors besides the intellectual are driving the use of this especially effective technology.

A fundamental assumption of *Humane* is that arguments for humane war made U.S. imperialism palatable to the American public. This is doubtful: the public rarely places foreign policy at the center of its concerns. Depressingly, if consistently, the American public cares about war when it affects them (as it did during Vietnam) or when criticisms of war can be used as a partisan cudgel (as they were during Iraq). While it's true that arguments for humane war helped lawyers, politicians, and military officers clear their consciences, it's unclear whether the public ever really cared one way or the other.

***

Intellectually, Moyn's criticisms of humane war are spot-on. But I can't help but conclude that his focus on humane war is somewhat behind the times. Arguments for humane war no longer occupy the center of political debate as they did in the Bush and Obama years; Trump's vulgarities have given the lie to the idea that the United States is an exceptional nation able to ethically govern the world. The recently elected Joe Biden barely mentioned law, and said nothing about humane conflict, in his February speech addressing U.S. foreign policy. Critiques of humane war simply do not speak to the new era of great power competition, which pits the United States and its allies against China, Russia, and other authoritarian powers. Nor do they directly address the major, and consistent, reasons the United States acts in the world as it does: the desire and ability to dominate others.

It's heartening that the intellectual energy among critics of American power has shifted from lambasting the tactics of American warfare to advocating for strategic restraint. Moyn himself endorses this transformation, and in *Humane* he affirms that observers must focus less on how war is fought and more on whether it is fought. The concern with humane war paved the way for the more ambitious demands anti-imperialists are making today. For the first time in almost a century, we can dare to imagine peace.

Endnotes

1 Barack Obama, "Remarks by the President at the National Defense University" (speech, Washington, D.C., May 23, 2013), Obama White House, https://obamawhitehouse.archives.gov/the-press-office/2013/05/23/remarks-president-national-defense-university.

2 Ibid.

3 Samuel Moyn, *Humane: How the United States Abandoned Peace and Reinvented War* (New York: Farrar, Straus and Giroux, 2021).
4 Ibid., 67.
5 "Kellogg–Briand Pact," August 27, 1928, accessed July 29, 2025, https://avalon.law.yale.edu/20th_century/kbpact.asp.
6 Sidita Kushi and Monica Duffy Toft, "Introducing the Military Intervention Project: A New Dataset on U.S. Military Interventions, 1776–2019," *Journal of Conflict Resolution* 67, no. 4 (April 2023), 767.
7 Moyn, *Humane*, 155.
8 Ibid.
9 Ibid., 167.
10 Ibid., 162.
11 Ibid., 184.
12 Ibid., 195.
13 Ibid.
14 Ibid., 201.
15 Ibid., 202.
16 Russell F. Weigley, *The American Way of War: A History of United States Military Strategy and Policy* (Bloomington: Indiana University Press, 1973), 142.
17 Moyn, *Humane*, 216.
18 Ibid., 215.
19 Rebecca Leung, "Abuse at Abu Ghraib," *60 Minutes II*, CBS News, May 5, 2004, https://www.cbsnews.com/news/abuse-at-abu-ghraib/.
20 Moyn, *Humane*, 236.
21 Ibid.
22 Ibid., 254, 237.
23 Ibid., 269, 293.
24 Daniel L. Byman, "Why Drones Work: The Case for Washington's Weapon of Choice," Brookings Institution, June 17, 2013, https://www.brookings.edu/articles/why-drones-work-the-case-for-washingtons-weapon-of-choice/.
25 Michael W. Lewis, "Drones: Actually the Most Humane Form of Warfare Ever," *The Atlantic*, August 21, 2013, https://www.theatlantic.com/international/archive/2013/08/drones-actually-the-most-humane-form-of-warfare-ever/278746/.

26 Scott Shane, "The Moral Case for Drones," July 14, 2012, https://www.nytimes.com/2012/07/15/sunday-review/the-moral-case-for-drones.html.

27 David Cole, "What's Wrong with Obama's Drone Policy," *The Nation*, February 13, 2013, https://www.thenation.com/article/archive/whats-wrong-obamas-drone-policy/.

28 Charlie Savage, *Power Wars: Inside Obama's Post-9/11 Presidency* (New York: Little, Brown and Company, 2015).

29 Moyn, *Humane*, 7.

30 Samuel Moyn, *The Last Utopia: Human Rights in History* (Cambridge, MA: Harvard University Press, 2010), 9. Moyn's first books are Samuel Moyn, *Origins of the Other: Emmanuel Levinas between Revelation and Ethics* (Ithaca, NY: Cornell University Press, 2005); Samuel Moyn, *A Holocaust Controversy: The Treblinka Affair in Postwar France* (Waltham, MA: Brandeis University Press, 2005).

31 Samuel Moyn, *Not Enough: Human Rights in an Unequal World* (Cambridge, MA: Harvard University Press, 2018).

32 Jon Baskin, "The Disillusionment of Samuel Moyn: The Yale Historian Has Become a Prominent Critic of Liberalism. But What's He For?", October 27, 2017, *The Chronicle of Higher Education*, https://www.chronicle.com/article/the-disillusionment-of-samuel-moyn/.

33 Moyn, *Humane*, 383.

34 Baskin, "The Disillusionment of Samuel Moyn."

35 Ibid.

36 Moyn, *Humane*, 36.

37 Ibid.

38 H.G. Wells et al., "The Idea of a League of Nations. II," *The Atlantic Monthly* 123, no. 2 (February 1919), 266. For Moyn's citation of this quote, see Moyn, *Humane*, 118.

39 Moyn, *Humane*, 134.

40 H. H. Arnold to All Air Force Commanders in Combat Zones, "Evaluation of Bombing Methods and Purposes," June 10, 1943, 2, Thirteenth Air Force, box 121, Nathan F. Twining Papers, Manuscript Division, Library of Congress, Washington, D.C.

41 Lauris Norstad to Carl Spaatz, Telecon MSG NR 9–1, n.d. [August 8, 1945], Personal Collection of Conrad C. Crane, Carlisle, Pennsylvania.

42 Moyn, *Humane*, 120.

MASS DESTRUCTION

Americans live in a very limited democracy. I don't tell the Federal Reserve to raise interest rates; I don't decide where the government puts my money; and I sure as hell didn't vote to go to war in Iraq. Many of the most consequential decisions lie outside the purview of ordinary Americans, who have few means by which to make their voices heard in the corridors of power. This is by design. As numerous historians have shown, in the twentieth century's second half U.S. elites constructed a state that intentionally restricts ordinary people's ability to shape policy. Though they might disagree about a lot, the powerful in both political parties agree that, on most things, the public cannot be trusted.

This attitude is especially entrenched when it comes to foreign policy. Since World War II, elites have insisted that foreign affairs are simply too complex, and the public too volatile and too ignorant, for average Americans to have a say in its formation. As the political scientist Gabriel A. Almond declared in 1950, "the gravest general problem confronting policy-makers is that of the instability of mass moods," which made it very difficult to promote a stable foreign policy.[1] Moreover, as Almond clarified several years later, when it came to world affairs, "often public opinion is apathetic when it should be concerned, and panicky when it should be calm."[2] For Almond and many who came after him, a public-directed foreign policy was guaranteed to be a foolish and ineffective one.

Today, one rarely hears members of the foreign policy establishment discuss the idea that ordinary Americans should have a significant say in the U.S.' role in the world. A major reason for this is that Almond's generation institutionalized a system that ensured ordinary people were kept far away from foreign policy. It's not for nothing that the National Security Act of 1947, which created the modern U.S. security state, established government bodies like the National Security Council and Central Intelligence Agency, both of which have no connection to public opinion. And beyond the official organs of state, after World War II think tanks such as the RAND Corporation, which oftentimes operate outside public view, began to exert significant influence on U.S. foreign affairs. When foreign policy is made and they disagree with it, the best that Americans can do is participate in mass protests, like those that erupted during the Vietnam and Iraq Wars. Even Congress hasn't declared war since 1942.

According to those who run the U.S. national security state, foreign policy must be an elite, expert-driven affair. But this wasn't always the case. In the early twentieth century, some Americans sought to establish a system that would give the American public a say in foreign policy decision-making. In his revelatory *Every Citizen a Statesman: The Dream of a Democratic Foreign Policy in the American Century*, historian David Allen tells the story of the Foreign Policy Association (FPA), the most important group to attempt to develop a public ready and able to make foreign policy.[3]

The FPA's story allows readers to return to a moment quite unlike our own, when some elites sought to reconcile democracy with expertise. It brings us back to an era when certain well-heeled Americans, less alienated from their fellow citizens, believed that public discussion could shape how decision-makers made policy. And it enables us to trace past efforts to educate an inchoate public and make it a crucial actor in U.S. policymaking.

But most important, if most depressing, the FPA's total failure to accomplish any of its goals highlights the difficulty, perhaps impossibility, of creating a democratic foreign policy in a country whose rulers are fundamentally skeptical of the public they deign to rule.

***

The contemporary story of democratic foreign policy in the United States begins in World War I, when the nation, bucking centuries of tradition, resolutely entered a European conflict. With this decision, President Woodrow Wilson made clear that the United States would no longer stand apart from the Old World but would instead take its place among the nations as a so-called great power. This new global role raised a novel question Americans had mostly ignored since their nation's founding: Who decides how the United States acts in the world?

For many Progressive Americans who took an interest in foreign affairs—journalists such as Herbert Croly and Frank U. Kellogg, academics such as Charles Beard, Stephen Duggan, and Alvin Johnson, and philanthropists like Florence Lamont and Dorothy Payne Whitney—the answer was clear: the "public" should determine U.S. foreign policy. But when these Progressives employed the term "public," they had a specific definition in mind; they were never referring, Allen notes, to "the unfiltered will of the people," as they believed the actually existing demos was not yet mature or educated enough to make wise foreign policy choices.[4] Instead, democratic-minded Progressives insisted, only a "properly instructed" public could ever gain the capacity to make U.S. foreign policy.[5] For these Progressive elites, a period of tutelage was necessary before the reins of policymaking could be handed over to the hoi polloi.

The question, then, was how to educate a "mass public" that only recently emerged as a political force. The very notion of "mass politics" was an artifact of the fin de siècle, when urbanization combined with cheap print media to bring something called the "mass public" into being. In the 1920s, the impact and import of the so-called masses remained open questions. Should the masses be ignored or should they become a core element of politics and policymaking? Democratic-minded Progressives insisted that politics had to be organized around a mass public whose energies were channeled, through education, toward productive goals (which were, of course, defined by the Progressive elite).

But how best to educate the masses? Luckily for democratic-minded Progressives, there was an obvious institutional means to accomplish this task: the voluntary association. In the period after World War I, Americans spent a significant portion of their time hanging out with each other at a diversity of civic organizations, from churches to Elks Lodges, from VFWs to women's clubs. As political scientists Gerald Gamm and Robert D. Putnam have shown, during the Jazz Age there were about four such associations for every 1,000 Americans.[6] In that climate, Progressive elites concluded that the best way to educate the public about foreign policy was to form a voluntary association charged with doing so.

In March 1921, a number of Progressives founded the FPA out of the extant League of Free Nations Association. The group included the history professor-turned-bureaucrat James G. McDonald (the FPA's first head), the Christian ecumenicist Robert H. Gardiner (its first treasurer), and the suffragette Christina Merriman (its first secretary). For the next 50 years, the FPA would serve as the single most important institution dedicated to producing an informed public able to guide the United States as it rose to global hegemony.

Headquartered in New York City, the FPA started out as bog-standard Progressive: its members desired for the United States to join the League of Nations, supported general disarmament, and harshly criticized imperialism. From the beginning, the tension between the association's interest in educating a mass public and its actual practice was evident; the group initially focused on hosting luncheons during which experts would give talks and then be subject to audiences' questioning. While these events were often compelling and dynamic, only the well-to-do had the time and money to attend them. In effect, the FPA's luncheons functioned as high-society gatherings, where interested parties from the upper classes—many of them women—came to learn about global affairs and give an expert or two a piece of their mind.

The FPA was remarkably successful; in the Great War's aftermath, Americans, especially elites, had started to care about the world. By 1928, the New York headquarters oversaw 14 branches located in cities across the country, including Cincinnati, Columbus, Hartford, Philadelphia, Providence, Rochester, and Springfield. The group's success was embodied in the fact that, in 1930, about 37,000 people attended an FPA-associated meeting. While those who participated in the FPA were hardly the unwashed masses, they did embody a group that had previously been disconnected from international affairs.

Besides educating a bourgeois elite, the FPA also devoted itself to producing Foreign Policy Reports whose most important readers worked at the State Department. Indeed, the early FPA's influence in the corridors of power highlights the U.S. state's relatively small size before World War II, including its foreign policy apparatus. In 1920, the State Department employed a paltry 1,222 people both at home and overseas; in 1930 that number had risen to only 1,347.[7] There was simply not enough staff at State to manage the United States' ever-increasing international interests, let alone research all the information that officials needed to make foreign policy. The FPA, in effect, served as State's research department, which provided the group with a direct line to power and foreshadowed the types of "public-private" partnerships that would come to characterize U.S. foreign policymaking for the remainder of the twentieth century.

In fact, to solidify its relationship with Washington, D.C., Allen highlights how the FPA founded a "liaison office" in the capital and appointed the journalist William T. Stone to lead it.[8] Stone rapidly became a resource for both State Department officials and congressmen, who at the time, Allen notes, "lacked significant personal or committee staffs."[9] As early as the 1920s and 1930s, the peculiar nature of the national security state, which outsources many functions one might consider properly governmental, from research to war-fighting, was already evident. The line between public and private was blurry at best.

Despite its growing influence in Washington, the FPA retained its commitment to public education. In the 1930s, this commitment was embodied primarily in two forms: the discussion group and mass media, both of which attempted to expand beyond the high-society set that the group had focused on in its first decade.

In the period between the two world wars, "discussion theory" swept the Progressive imagination.[10] This theory, Allen highlights, was premised on the Deweyan idea that knowledge should be "democratized rather than merely popularized."[11] The best way to democratize knowledge, adult education specialists insisted, was in "discussion groups": expert-led, small-group discussions in which a leader taught a group but also imbibed its participants' ideas.[12] For example, a discussion leader might've asked participants to debate whether the United States should join the League of Nations. The leader was then responsible, Allen describes, for "ensuring that facts were kept to, challenging prejudices but not taking sides, and insisting that no participant dominate while not talking too much themselves."[13] Beyond this, leaders were also required to consider seriously the participants' "experience as a contribution to their expertise."[14]

The hope was that participating in discussions would accomplish two things: instill in ordinary Americans "the skills and confidence to do more than shop among products of expertise," and remind experts that citizens were the source of their power and potentially founts of good ideas.[15] In this way, Progressive education theorists intended to reconcile democracy with expertise. The FPA, for its part, enthusiastically supported discussion theory and created programs that attempted, as Allen puts it, "to inculcate discussion techniques among teachers, clubwomen, and students."[16]

In addition to the discussion group, the FPA also started trying to speak directly to the very mass public it had come into being to educate. To do so, the group published a series of easily readable and cheap "Headline Books" with titles such as *Billions for Defense*, *The Puzzle of Palestine*, *Shadow Over Europe*, and *Battles Without Bullets*, which sought to educate ordinary people about a diversity of foreign policy and security issues.[17] Furthermore, the association partnered with NBC to broadcast a radio show titled *America Looks Abroad*, which provided 15 minutes of current events analysis every week and whose slogan—"foreign affairs are your affairs"—embodied the FPA's mission.[18]

In these ways, the FPA became the most important group to attempt to resolve the tensions between mass democracy and elite expertise, even if, as Allen underlines, it was not clear whether the association's experiments in mass education were "genuinely reaching a different kind of American or just expanding its reach to the same sorts of people in new areas of the country."[19] Still, at the least, the FPA tried.

Beyond its educational efforts, by the late 1930s the group had successfully developed a working relationship with the federal government. The FPA, in fact, was as—if not more—influential than its better-known competitor, the Council on Foreign Relations, whose members insisted that an expert elite alone should guide U.S. foreign affairs. The FPA was ascendant, even though it had not yet established the educated mass public it imagined.

Unfortunately for the association, World War II would change all that.

***

In July 1939, Major General Frank R. McCoy, a protégé of Secretary of War Henry Stimson, became the FPA's president, and under him the organization abandoned the commitment to foreign policy debate displayed in its luncheons and discussion groups; instead, it began parroting the Franklin Delano Roosevelt Administration's view that the United States needed to become involved in World War II (which erupted in September). From this moment on, the FPA would, in effect, promote U.S. "primacy"—the notion that both American and global peace and prosperity depended on the United States' becoming the world's military and economic hegemon.

Yet even this alignment with the state would not ensure the FPA's lasting influence. Most immediately, throughout the war the U.S. state poached many members of the FPA and its branches. More important, though, was the fact that the war and its aftermath transformed the ideology and structure of the U.S. state. In terms of ideology, most policy elites emerged from the war convinced that it demonstrated that the very idea of a public-directed foreign policy was not only chimerical but also dangerous, especially because the advent of nuclear weapons made the stakes of foreign policy literally existential. Hans Speier, an influential sociologist and member of the RAND Corporation, crystallized this view in 1950:

> Since the end of the first World War … the faith in the power of public opinion to render world politics reasonable has been shaken. There are many events which contributed to this demoralization: the failure of the League of Nations; disillusionment concerning the lofty war aims of the Allies and the general distrust of propaganda which spread between the two world wars; the rise of fascism and national socialism in countries of old civilization and with no lack of liberal traditions; the absence of inspiring peace aims during the second World War; the sterility of the resistance movements in the realm of political ideas; the use of weapons of mass destruction in the attainment of victory; and the quick transformation of the wartime coalition into intense hostility between its main partners even before peace was formally established.[20]

"Do we still maintain," Speier asked rhetorically, "the belief in the perfectability [*sic*] of man, faced, as we are, with the overwhelming experiences of the twentieth century … and with the advances in both the technology of destruction and moral apathy?"[21]

A more damning indictment of the FPA's *raison d'être* could hardly be imagined.

But more significant than any individual's perspective was the fact that Speier's criticism of public opinion was institutionalized in the emergent national security state. To ensure that ordinary people had no say in the corridors of power, elites within and outside government created novel institutions that insulated foreign policymaking from the public. Among them was the National Security Council, which centralized decision-making in the White House; the Central Intelligence Agency, which mostly operated in secret; and the RAND Corporation, which, like the FPA before it, served as an unofficial but influential research arm of the government. Beyond this process of state-making, the administration of Harry Truman instituted a byzantine program for classifying information that made it ever harder for the public, or even Congress, to know what the national security state was up to.

These efforts, in turn, were bolstered by research that appeared to demonstrate that the very idea of an informed public opinion was ridiculous. Allen reports how, in the winter of 1946–1947, the American Association for the United Nations and the United Nations Association of Cincinnati initiated "a six-month blitz of 2,800 speeches, the printing of 59,588 pieces of literature, and the placement of ads" about international relations with the intent of demonstrating that average Americans could be made interested in foreign affairs.[22] But as Allen relays, the National Opinion Research Center found that at the end of this study the groups discovered that their effort "'did not stir the interest of those who were not interested in the first place.'"[23] Moreover, in the early Cold War social scientific analyses by thinkers such as Speier and Gabriel Almond seemed to confirm that it was very difficult, if not impossible, to educate the public about international relations. By the 1950s, most foreign policy elites had concluded that the project to create an interested foreign policy public was a relic of a more naive moment that needed to be abandoned.

After World War II, then, the FPA and its mission were clearly out of step with the times. In 1950, the Rockefeller Foundation—the FPA's longtime benefactor—stopped funding the group, having determined, Allen recounts, that what the United States needed was "expert knowledge to lead a world that even the most educated Americans knew little about."[24] The FPA went into decline; sales of its publications fell as its membership sank and some branches closed. Whereas FPA leaders used to be welcome in the corridors of power, they now found themselves on the outside, looking in. In 1951, the group's board even considered liquidating it.

The FPA would have likely shuttered were it not for the Ford Foundation, which in the late 1940s emerged as the nation's wealthiest philanthropy. In 1949, the foundation released a report that identified five "program areas" it would heavily invest in: "The Establishment of Peace," "The Strengthening of Democracy," "The Strengthening of the Economy," "Education in a Democratic Society," and "Individual Behavior and Human Relations."[25] The FPA's work fit into several of these program areas, and the group quickly established connections with the foundation, which became its primary funder.

The most important and long-lasting innovation to emerge as the result of the Ford Foundation's support was the "Great Decisions" program. Created in Oregon in early 1955, the program, Allen explains, "claimed to offer Portlanders a chance to lead the world from their living rooms."[26] Great Decisions was a significant effort, consisting of "eighty to ninety discussion groups of a dozen or so men and women [who met] in living rooms, school halls, and public libraries for about three to four hours a week" to discuss questions like, "Does U.S. security, prosperity, and freedom depend on the rest of the world?" and "How shall we deal with the U.S.S.R.?"[27] Though similar in some ways to the earlier discussion groups, Great Decisions differed in that it expected more from its participants. As Allen notes, those who took part in sessions were "supposed to have either tuned in to a dedicated radio or television program before attending their discussion group or, preferably, to have read one of the fact sheets the Association wrote to give the minimum necessary to contribute."[28] Instead of the average American, Great Decisions implicitly targeted itself to those already concerned with world affairs. In this way, the FPA attempted to fit in with the anti-mass public tenor of the era.

The FPA used Great Decisions to promote U.S. primacy. For instance, Allen observes that "the fact sheet for the [program's] session dealing with the U.S.S.R." announced that all the United States was doing in the Cold War was giving "day-to-day assistance to Western European countries where economic instability and Communist tactics threatened democratic governments."[29] The Soviet Union, in contrast, was described as engaging in "constantly shifting attacks on Europe and Asia" that were defined by "subversion, propaganda, trickery, obstruction, sabotage, and plotting through communist cells."[30] Such "facts" did not exactly set the stage for a balanced debate of the type the early FPA would have endorsed.

Though Great Decisions was a smashing success and rapidly spread across the country, it had little impact on the FPA's overall trajectory. Things came to a head in the 1960s, when Samuel P. Hayes, Jr., a social psychologist who agreed with the critics of public opinion, took over the organization. Hayes insisted that the FPA should focus its efforts solely on the Americans it determined could actually be educated about U.S. foreign affairs—citing social scientific research, Hayes concluded that this was only about 12 million people. But even this narrowing couldn't save the association. By the late 1960s, many nonprofits had begun to refocus their attention on domestic issues, and the Ford Foundation was no different. Under its new leader McGeorge Bundy, a prominent foreign policymaker in the John F. Kennedy and Lyndon B. Johnson Administrations, the foundation, Allen notes, dedicated itself to addressing "racial justice and the urban crisis."[31] Bundy, perhaps guilty about his involvement in the disastrous Vietnam War, had little interest in either foreign policy or the FPA and eliminated all of the foundation's support for the latter.

The FPA thus continued its long decline, cutting programs, publications, and regional offices. Today, it survives as a rump organization that concentrates primarily on Great Decisions, which remains its most popular offering.

***

The FPA failed to achieve its major goals: create an educated public able to help guide U.S. foreign affairs and develop mechanisms through which that public (when it came into existence) would be heard by policy elites. After the 1960s, as Allen rightly emphasizes, "the idea that foreign policy could be forged in popular participation … disappeared; there would be attempts to remake the 'establishment,' but little more."[32]

The de-democratization of U.S. foreign policy was rapidly followed by the de-massification of U.S. war. Specifically, the Vietnam War and the backlash it engendered impelled a broader shift in U.S. war-fighting away from a citizens' military and toward an "all-volunteer force," which emerged when the draft ended in 1973. Since then, most Americans have not directly felt the consequences of their nation's wars.

By the turn of the twenty-first century, the intertwined processes of de-democratization and de-massification led policy- and war-making to become entirely elite affairs, governed by an establishment whose members hailed from an ever-narrower subset of the meritocratic elite. This establishment pursued a variety of wars with only tangential connections to any possible construal of the "national interest," from the Gulf War to the invasions of Afghanistan and Iraq to the interventions in Libya, Syria, and Ukraine. Despite periodic outbursts of mass protests, especially in the run-up to the second war in Iraq, the U.S. public has been quiescent, allowing its elites to basically do what they want. The FPA and its dream of creating a democratic foreign policy are today nothing but a memory, and a fading one at that.

Though Allen spells out numerous proximate causes of the FPA's decline, its failure was overdetermined, the result of problems endemic to liberal democracy itself. Since liberalism's advent in the French Revolution's aftermath, liberal elites have been fundamentally skeptical of the public and its opinion. While this skepticism has waxed and waned over time, it became especially strong—and, more important, was institutionalized—during the early Cold War, when nervous liberals concluded that ordinary Americans could not be trusted with the responsibilities of foreign policymaking. Once this anti-public opinion became a structural feature of the U.S. state, it became very difficult for the public to shape international affairs. Simply put, any attempt to create a democratic foreign policy faces two significant obstacles: an ideological distrust of ordinary people and a state designed to ensure that they have little impact on foreign relations.

What, then, is to be done?

The answer is old and unsatisfying: build public power through organizing and transform (maybe even transcend) the antidemocratic liberalism that has defined U.S. governance since World War II. This is the only way Americans can begin democratizing their foreign policy.

But not every story has a happy ending, and I doubt this one will. While there have been a variety of recent proposals to re-democratize U.S. political life, it is difficult to imagine a world in which these efforts succeed. Most Americans don't fight and die in our nation's wars, and beyond this, many have rightly concluded that they can't affect policy, so why try. Moreover, the material degradations of the last two generations have made it so that Americans simply don't have the time or capacity to focus on making foreign policy more democratic. Without massive transformations in the U.S. state, economy, and society, there is little to be done.

Allen's book might therefore be best interpreted as a message in a bottle, waiting to be picked up in a generation or two by people who hopefully live in a less undemocratic, less unequal world. It will be up to them to begin the process of taking control of the state as they attempt to realize one of democracy's highest aims: a policy by the people, not merely for them.

Endnotes

1 Gabriel A. Almond, *The American People and Foreign Policy* (New York: Harcourt, Brace and Company, 1950), 239.

2 Gabriel A. Almond, "Public Opinion and National Security Policy," *Public Opinion Quarterly* 20, no. 2 (Summer 1956), 376.

3 David Allen, *Every Citizen a Statesman: The Dream of a Democratic Foreign Policy* (Cambridge, MA: Harvard University Press, 2023).

4 Allen, *Every Citizen a Statesmen*, 23.

5 Ibid.

6 Gerald Gamm and Robert D. Putnam, "The Growth of Voluntary Associations in America, 1840–1940," *Journal of Interdisciplinary History* 29, no. 4 (Spring 1999), 524.

7 Office of the Historian, U.S. Department of State, "Department Personnel, 1781–1997," U.S. Department of State, accessed July 29, 2025, https://1997-2001.state.gov/about_state/history/faq.html#personnel.

8 Allen, *Every Citizen a Statesmen*, 58.

9 Ibid.

10 Ibid., 65.

11 Ibid.

12 Ibid., 64–65.

13 Ibid., 65.

14 Ibid.

15 Ibid.

16 Ibid., 67.

17 Ibid., 66. For titles of books in this series, see "The Online Books Page Presents Serial Archive Listings for Headline Series," The Online Books Page, University of Pennsylvania, accessed July 29, 2025, https://onlinebooks.library.upenn.edu/webbin/serial?id=headlineseries.

18 Allen, *Every Citizen a Statesmen*, 69.

19 Ibid.

20 Hans Speier, "Historical Development of Public Opinion," *American Journal of Sociology* 55, no. 4 (January 1950), 387.

21 Ibid.

22 Allen, *Every Citizen a Statesmen*, 179.

23 Ibid.

24 Ibid., 104.

25 *Report of the Study for the Ford Foundation on Policy and Program* (Detroit, MI: Ford Foundation, November 1949), 8.

26 Allen, *Every Citizen a Statesmen*, 174.

27 Ibid., 185.

28 Ibid., 186.

29 Ibid.

30 Ibid., 187.

31 Ibid., 227.

32 Ibid., 237.

WHOSE FAULT WAS THE COLD WAR?

The Cold War—the epic struggle between the United States and the Soviet Union over the globe's resources, people, and future—shaped, and reshaped, everything. From geopolitics to public discourse to social welfare to the films, television, and music that people all over the world consumed, the Cold War defined life in the twentieth century's second half.

Unsurprisingly, a phenomenon of such importance has been the subject of a large and expansive historiography; since the Cold War began, historians have been trying to explain why, exactly, it broke out. Most American scholars initially blamed the Cold War on the Soviet Union. Joseph Stalin, these historians affirmed, was a rapacious ideologue dedicated to global revolution who was responsible for U.S.–Soviet tensions. In the 1960s, however, a group of scholars led by the University of Wisconsin's William Appleman Williams challenged this "traditionalist" perspective. Under the banner of "revisionism," they argued that, far more than Stalin, it was the United States' search for export markets, as well as the American state's close relationship with its capitalist class, that explains the Cold War.

From the 1970s to the 1990s, the next generation of historians embraced a new, "post-revisionist" synthesis that combined elements of both schools' accounts. On one hand, as John Lewis Gaddis, the most influential post-revisionist, admitted, he and his colleagues were very influenced by the traditionalists. Similar to the traditionalists, post-revisionists argued "that American officials worried more about the Soviet Union than about the fate of capitalism in designing the policy of containment," claimed "that Soviet expansionism was the primary cause of the Cold War," and contended "that American allies welcomed the expansion of US influence as a counterweight to the Russians."[1] On the other hand, and similar to the revisionists, the post-revisionists maintained that the United States deployed "economic instruments to achieve political ends," emphasized "the absence of any ideological blueprint for world revolution in Stalin's mind," agreed that sometimes the U.S. government "exaggerate[d] external dangers for the purpose of achieving certain internal goals," and acknowledged "that there was in fact an American 'empire.'"[2] Post-revisionist scholarship dominated the historiography on the Cold War for decades.

Things began to change in the mid-2000s. Under the influence of Odd Arne Westad's paradigm-shifting *The Global Cold War: Third World Interventions and the Making of Our Times* (2005), which sought to refocus historians' attention on the Cold War in the "Third World," scholars in effect stopped looking into the question of who was responsible for the U.S.–Soviet struggle.[3] Instead, they turned toward analyzing, first, how the struggle played out in the Global South; second, how non-American actors shaped world events; and, third, how non-state actors, such as nongovernmental organizations, multinational corporations, and radical political groups, reacted to and interacted with the Cold War. Unlike previous generations of Cold War historians, these "international" and "transnational" scholars never coalesced into a coherent school centered on concrete causal claims but were instead united by a common project: to show how non-American and non-state actors experienced and defined the Cold War.[4]

Nevertheless, the question of responsibility has recently reemerged as a major one for historians. Disenchantment with the fantasies of borderless globalization that characterized the 1990s and 2000s, the success of the über-nationalist Donald Trump, and the emergence of China as a threat to U.S. power in East Asia have all reignited scholars' interest in great-power politics broadly and cold wars in particular. Indeed, in the last two years two eminent historians, Columbia University's Anders Stephanson and Johns Hopkins University's Sergey Radchenko, have released books that consciously recenter the United States and the Soviet Union—and the question of responsibility—in Cold War history.

Taken together, Stephanson's *American Imperatives: The Cold War and Other Matters* and Radchenko's *To Run the World: The Kremlin's Cold War Bid for Global Power* demonstrate one thing above all: the Cold War was, to borrow Stephanson's phrasing, a "US project"—it was, ultimately, an American choice.[5] This fact has crucial implications for U.S. foreign policy in the twenty-first century, an era in which the United States faces China, a great power that, like the Soviet Union before it, has designs on its near abroad. To put it bluntly, the future of international relations will be shaped by Americans, who either will try to prevent the People's Republic from achieving dominance in its potential sphere of influence or will accept the realities of Chinese power. If Americans don't choose wisely, a third world war might very well break out.

***

To most people, the *Cold War* is a transparent term that refers to a discrete era—the period between 1947 and 1989—during which geopolitics was structured around a U.S.–Soviet antagonism that never erupted into an outright superpower war.

Stephanson, however, rejects this common sense understanding. According to him, a "cold war" is not simply a conflict in which both sides refuse to engage in a "hot" war with the other. Rather, it is a unique form of geopolitical antipathy defined by "absolute hostility"—at least one side of a cold war must view the other as fundamentally illegitimate, unworthy of genuine diplomatic engagement.[6] Crucially, cold wars aren't always symmetrical, and in Stephanson's telling, the Cold War of the twentieth century was a U.S.-driven affair: it was the Americans who decided that the Soviet project was illegitimate and could not be countenanced. Americans, in short, turned the cold war switch on. The question is why—why did a group of leaders who had only recently been allied with the Soviet Union suddenly decide that they could no longer deal with it?

Stephanson offers a two-pronged answer to this question. First, the Cold War had practical benefits for American "internationalists," those liberal elites making U.S. foreign policy in the late 1940s and early 1950s who wanted the United States to become the prime global power, a goal that starkly departed from previous American history.[7] Between the late eighteenth century, when George Washington warned his countrymen against entangling themselves in the political and military affairs of Europe, and the U.S. entry into World War I, when Woodrow Wilson committed troops to a European war, the United States mostly remained confined to the Western Hemisphere, with the acquisition of Pacific territories (the Philippines and Guam) after the Spanish–American War of 1898 being an important exception. Even after World War I, U.S. troops returned home as many elite and ordinary Americans concluded that intervening in a European conflict had been a mistake.

While World War II appeared to change all that by entangling the United States in a genuinely global conflict, policymakers were anxious that after the defeat of Germany and Japan the traditional American focus on the Western Hemisphere would rapidly reassert itself. In fact, in the war's aftermath, a demobilization fever swept the United States, with Americans, exhausted by years of service and sacrifice, wanting to do nothing more than return to normalcy. Declaring the Soviet Union a *gens non grata*—an existential threat to humanity analogous to Nazi Germany—was therefore part of an elite strategy to ensure that the United States remained heavily involved in world affairs. And it didn't hurt that the elites who made these claims, themselves scarred by two world wars, believed what they were saying.

Engendering anxieties about the Soviet Union was also a means to persuade ordinary Americans that the United States needed to mobilize its society for a prolonged conflict. The Cold War, in short, enabled the enormous defense budgets and armed forces of which Americans were typically suspicious. It also had the political benefit of making criticism of U.S. foreign policy anathema, framing critique as defeatist and anti-American. The Cold War transformed global interventionism and domestic militarism into common sense.

Second, the very concept of a "cold war" fit in well with traditional American ideology. Since the nation's founding, American culture had been permeated with a messianic fervor that insisted the United States was the embodiment of Progress and Freedom. This fervor led Americans to repeatedly frame politics in binary terms. There's not that much of a leap, Stephanson archly notes, from Patrick Henry's "Give me liberty or give me death" to "Better dead than red" (or, one might add, George W. Bush's "Either you are with us, or you are with the terrorists").[8] In effect, Americans were primed to understand the Soviet Union as the antithesis of their own nation.

For these reasons, by the early 1950s elite and ordinary Americans alike had identified the Soviet Union as an abnormal country with which they could not reach legitimate agreements.

Stephanson's most novel argument, however, is his claim that the Cold War was really only a "cold war" between 1947 and 1963. According to him, the Cold War began around the time President Harry S. Truman announced the Truman Doctrine, which promised "to help free peoples … against aggressive movements that seek to impose upon them totalitarian regimes."[9] It ended not in 1989 but in 1963, when in the wake of the Cuban Missile Crisis the Americans and the Soviets signed the Limited Test Ban Treaty on nuclear weapons, which signaled that U.S. policy elites had started to view the Soviet Union as a normal geopolitical competitor with which they could make deals. The encounter with the nuclear eschaton led U.S.–Soviet antagonism to become more akin to the great-power Concert of Europe (1815–1914) than to a genuine cold war. The Americans didn't like the Soviet Union, but from 1963 onward they recognized it as a fact of international life.

To my mind, Stephanson's periodization is broadly correct. The Cuban Missile Crisis clearly demonstrated to both American and Soviet leaders that there was nothing worth fighting a nuclear war over, and afterward, relations between the two countries improved because Americans began treating the Soviet Union like a normal antagonist. The period 1947–1963 was thus a distinctly hostile one in the history of the U.S.–Soviet rivalry and should be understood as such.

But demarcating the different phases of the U.S.–Soviet conflict is not Stephanson's most significant contribution. Far more important is his centering of the United States in the Cold War's origin story: U.S.–Soviet antagonism, Stephanson persuasively demonstrates, stemmed from an American universalism that rejected the "spheres-of-influence" thinking that has defined great-power politics since the nineteenth century. And this is crucial, because, as Radchenko shows in his monumental *To Run the World*, Stalin was ready to deal with the Americans—it's just that the Americans weren't ready to deal with him.

In 1945, the Soviet Union occupied a space in international politics no one would have predicted only a decade earlier. Under the tyrannical rule of Stalin, the country had transformed from a crumbling backwater into the second most powerful empire on Earth. And the Soviets paid for this power in blood. According to Radchenko, during World War II the Soviet Union lost an estimated 25.5 million citizens, as well as nearly 14 million children aged four and under—vastly more than the approximately 407,000 American military deaths.[10] It's therefore unsurprising that, as the war wound down, Stalin believed that he was owed quite a bit. At the very least, he insisted that his allies allow him to establish a sphere of influence in Eastern Europe that ensured his nation would never again be invaded from the west, as it had been during the Napoleonic Wars, World War I, and World War II.

As Radchenko demonstrates, Stalin was a realist to his core—he believed that power mattered, he knew that the Soviet Union had power, and he expected the Americans to respect that power. In effect, Stalin assumed that after the defeat of Nazi Germany, the United States would return to its hemisphere and that a great power concert would emerge in Europe with the Soviet Union as its conductor. Stalin believed that once Soviet security was established, he would be able to work fruitfully with the Americans, just as he had worked fruitfully with President Franklin Delano Roosevelt during the war.

Stalin, in other words, was no ideological fanatic. Well before World War II, he had abandoned the project of global communist revolution. In Stalin's mind, what victory in the war provided him with was not the opportunity to export Marxism–Leninism but rather the opportunity to establish a Monroe Doctrine-esque hegemony over Europe. The Americans, he thought, would understand and appreciate that.

Thus, as the war came to a close, Stalin embraced, in Radchenko's words, a "spirit of give-and-take"—"he was willing to recognize and accept" American gains so long as the Americans were willing to recognize and accept Soviet gains.[11] Stalin's mistake was that he didn't appreciate the degree to which the Americans, from Truman on down, had embraced a zero-sum perspective on their country's relationship with the Soviet Union. Where Roosevelt was a pragmatist, Truman and his coterie were exceptionalists *par excellence*.

Soon after Truman's ascension to the presidency in April 1945, relations between the United States and the Soviet Union deteriorated. Truman, influenced by the messianism described by Stephanson, refused to recognize the legitimacy of the emergent Soviet sphere of influence in Eastern Europe. Over the course of 1946, this encouraged an increasingly anxious Stalin to consolidate his control over the Eastern Bloc, which in early 1947 encouraged Truman to announce his doctrine, which in turn encouraged Stalin to increase his support for the Greek communist insurgency, and so on. By the outbreak of the Korean War in the summer of 1950, the Cold War was on.

Ultimately, and in my opinion incorrectly, Radchenko blames Stalin for the Cold War's outbreak. This claim, in fact, contradicts his own argument, which makes clear that Stalin was a realist who wanted to avoid postwar U.S.–Soviet antagonism. "Stalin," Radchenko affirms, "had legitimate security interests as long as looking after them did not require the imposition of a brutal Stalinist system of control and repression on the unwilling Eastern Europeans. Since Stalin did exactly that, surely he is chiefly responsible for the confrontation that ensued."[12]

Radchenko here insists that Stalin should have behaved like no other leader has behaved in world history—including, one might note, American leaders. With the Soviet Union, and before then, Russia, having been twice invaded by Germany in the span of a generation, it was reasonable for Stalin to want to create a security buffer in his near abroad. While the methods he used to impose Soviet control on Eastern Europe were brutal, and while Radchenko is right to deplore them, it is also the case that they were not so dissimilar from the violent and antidemocratic approach the United States embraced in Latin America, the Middle East, and Asia. Given that Stalin was willing to deal with the Americans in a way they weren't with him, it seems to me that responsibility for the Cold War lies, in the final analysis, with the United States.

***

Together, *American Imperatives* and *To Run the World* underline the degree to which U.S. foreign policy in the early Cold War revolved around questions related to spheres of influence, above all: Should Americans respect them?

The historical record makes clear that Americans act as if spheres of influence are legitimate. Since the early nineteenth century, Americans have formally defined the entirety of the Western Hemisphere as their sphere of influence, and one can narrate the history of the United States as a story in which the nation slowly expanded its sphere from the eastern seaboard to the entire globe. Furthermore, during the early Cold War, U.S. policymaking elites appreciated that Eastern Europe was within the Soviet sphere of influence—this is why President Dwight D. Eisenhower refused to aid rebels in East Germany in 1953 and Hungary in 1956—even as they publicly derided this sphere as illegitimate. Imagine the suffering that would have been avoided if American rhetoric reflected American strategy.

The issue is whether Americans should respect spheres of influence. Truth be told, the matter of spheres of influence raises difficult questions for those, like myself, who are committed to universalistic humanism and anti-imperialism.

On one hand, any leftist or liberal must insist that the *demoi* of the world's nation-states should be allowed to determine their futures absent coercion. It would have been better, from a humanist and anti-imperialist perspective, if the East Germans, the Hungarians, and the Czechoslovakians—and, one might add, the Iranians, the Guatemalans, and the Chileans—had been able to decide what type of government they wanted without outside interference. The same could be said for Hong Kong and Taiwan—in a just world, Hongkongers and Taiwanese would have the right and ability to choose the form their polities assumed.

On the other hand, we don't live in a just world—we live in this one, where interests and power matter more than ideals. It is simply a fact of international relations that some things matter more to some nations than others. In the second half of the twentieth century, Eastern Europe mattered more to the Soviet Union than it did to the United States. Today, the same could be said about Taiwan. Despite the bleating of various "China hawks" in both the Democratic and the Republican parties, Taiwan is of significantly more concern to China than it is to the United States. In fact, this is true for East Asia as a whole. The United States could leave East Asia without any serious fear of its physical security being threatened as a result.

This leads to an uncomfortable and tension-filled position. Leftists and liberals should reject spheres of influence as morally illegitimate as they simultaneously respect the reality of spheres of influence when making U.S. foreign policy. In a world of competing and nuclear-armed nation-states, there is no other option. Indeed, Americans should take inspiration from Roosevelt, who understood that the United States did not have the capacity to determine international relations. What was Roosevelt's Four Policemen model of geopolitics, which declared that the United States, Soviet Union, United Kingdom, and China would each be responsible for distinct world regions, but a recognition of this fact?

Moreover, appreciating the reality of spheres of influence could have the benefit of concentrating policymakers' thinking. Instead of assuming that the United States will continue to be dominant in East Asia, recognizing and respecting Chinese power could encourage U.S. decision-makers to develop a plan for leaving the region in a responsible way that doesn't abandon our allies. We should help foster a security and economic environment in which countries such as Japan, South Korea, the Philippines, and Australia are able to fend for themselves. Now is not the time to pretend that the United States remains a hyperpower; it is the time to recognize Chinese strength as a fact. If we don't, it will be our partners, and not us, who will suffer the consequences.

Endnotes

1 John Lewis Gaddis, "The Emerging Post-Revisionist Synthesis on the Origins of the Cold War," *Diplomatic History* 7, no. 3 (Summer 1983), 180.

2 Ibid., 180–181.

3 Odd Arne Westad, *The Global Cold War: Third World Interventions and the Making of Our Times* (Cambridge: Cambridge University Press, 2005).

4 For the international and transnational turns, see Daniel Bessner and Fredrik Logevall, "Recentering the United States in the Historiography of American Foreign Relations," *Texas National Security Review* 3, no. 2 (Spring 2020), 38–55.

5 Anders Stephanson, *American Imperatives: The Cold War and Other Matters* (New York: Verso, 2025); Sergey Radchenko, *To Run the World: The Kremlin's Cold War Bid for Global Power* (New York: Cambridge University Press, 2024). The first part of Stephanson's book is titled "The Cold War as a US Project."

6 Stephanson, *American Imperatives*, 46.

7 According to Stephanson, "geopolitically, the [Cold War] was indeed remarkably successful from an internationalist standpoint, above all that of the decisive Atlantic community." Ibid., 7–8.

8 Ibid., 56. For the Bush quote, see George W. Bush, "Address to a Joint Session of Congress and the American People" (speech, Washington, D.C., September 20, 2001), George W. Bush White House, https://georgewbush-whitehouse.archives.gov/news/releases/2001/09/20010920-8.html.

9 Harry S. Truman, "Special Message to the Congress on Greece and Turkey: The Truman Doctrine" (speech, Washington, D.C., March 12, 1947), in John T. Woolley and Gerhard Peters, ed., *The American Presidency Project* (Santa Barbara, CA, 1999–2025), https://www.presidency.ucsb.edu/documents/special-message-the-congress-greeceand-turkey-the-truman-doctrine.

10 Radchenko, *To Run the World*, 2; "Research Starters: U.S. Military by the Numbers," The National World War II Museum, accessed October 21, 2025, https://www.nationalww2museum.org/students-teachers/student-resources/research-starters/research-starters-us-military-numbers.

11 Radchenko, *To Run the World*, 24.

12 Ibid., 107.

IT DIDN'T HAPPEN HERE

Since the election of Donald Trump, a specter has haunted the United States—the specter of fascism. From *The New York Times* to *The Atlantic*, from CNN to *The New York Review of Books*, liberals and socialists alike have asked the same question: Is it happening here?[1]

Answers have run the gamut. Some insist that the similarities between contemporary American populism and fascism—their shared racism, reliance on the petit bourgeois, hypernationalism, and xenophobia—indicate that fascism, finally, has come to America. Others disagree, maintaining that the enabling structural conditions of classical European fascism—firsthand experience of total war, a powerful left, and a relatively weak state capable of being taken over—no longer exist, and that, whatever right-wing populism is, describing it as "fascist" occludes more than it illuminates.

Into this fray enters the intellectual historian Bruce Kuklick, whose *Fascism Comes to America* provides an entirely new perspective on a debate that's become a bit exhausting.[2] Unlike other pundits and thinkers, Kuklick is not interested in whether fascism as such has arrived in the United States. Rather, he's concerned with how the term itself has been used in the last century of American discourse.

"Fascism," Kuklick's exhaustive survey of U.S. politics and culture shows, has generally functioned as a so-called floating signifier. In the words of the anthropologist Claude Lévi-Strauss, who originated the phrase, a floating signifier is a term "devoid of meaning and thus susceptible of receiving any meaning at all."[3] At one point or another, every political perspective in the United States has been identified as fascist. In the last two decades alone, Jonah Goldberg railed against "liberal fascism" as Chris Hedges dubbed the "Christian Right" "American fascists."[4] Dinesh D'Souza claimed that Hillary Clinton was fascist; Paul Krugman said the same about Trump.[5] And even fringe ideologies weren't safe: Sebastian Gorka linked socialism with fascism, while Nouriel Roubini made similar claims about libertarianism.[6]

The one consistent quality that the term *fascism* has retained since the 1930s is its negative valence. Almost no one uses it positively; instead, to borrow Kuklick's acid description, the term is the verbal equivalent of "throwing a tomato at a speaker at a public event."[7] "Fascism," Kuklick shows, "does not so much isolate a thing as it does some stigmatizing."[8] Indeed, fascism's power in American discourse comes from the fact that it has no stable meaning—it's mostly an all-purpose curse word, a highfalutin "fuck this"—which means that the fascism debate, as currently constructed, can never end.

***

The term *fascism* first entered popular discourse in 1921, when Italian dictator Benito Mussolini christened his political party the National Fascist Party. Mussolini employed the word, which derives from the Italian *fascio*, meaning "bundle," for two reasons. First, it signified his conviction that the Italian people were stronger when individuals acted as a coherent unit. Second, it referenced the Roman *fasces*, a bundle of rods that ancient magistrates used to symbolize their strength and, if necessary, to flog wrongdoers. With this one word, Mussolini displayed both the promise and the threat of his movement.

Initially, some American intellectuals were intrigued by the romance of Italian fascism. One prominent example was Herbert

Croly—a founder of *The New Republic*—who saw in fascism a potential means to rescue a Progressivism that by the 1920s was in steep decline. Croly insisted that Mussolini's vibrant movement rhymed with American-style Progressivism: both fascism and Progressivism emphasized "supraindividual obligations" to people and nation over parochial individualistic ones and fetishized pragmatic politics.[9] Mussolini, in fact, even listed the pragmatist philosopher William James, a lodestone for Progressives, as a primary influence. To thinkers such as Croly, these similarities suggested that fascists might have something to teach Americans.

Fascism only became a dirty word in American discourse in the 1930s, as Mussolini's Italy became increasingly associated with Adolf Hitler's Germany. As they had admired Mussolini, some Americans initially admired Hitler for his seeming ability to reinvigorate German society through the establishment of programs such as "Strength Through Joy," which encouraged internal tourism. But by the mid-1930s, the luster began to come off both Nazism and Italian fascism. In 1934, Hitler violently purged his own ranks in the infamous Night of the Long Knives. A year later, the German dictator passed the Nuremberg Laws while the Italian one invaded Ethiopia; a year after that, Germany seized the Rhineland, and Hitler and Mussolini united to form the Rome–Berlin Axis.

These events led Americans to identify Mussolini with Hitler—and fascism with Nazism. Because Americans concluded that Mussolini was "in the thrall of Hitler," by the end of the 1930s "the negative connotation of fascism had become irrevocably blurred: while the Italians hardly counted, Hitler was routinely and haphazardly counted as fascist."[10] Il Duce was left in der Führer's dust.

But even at this early stage in its history, fascism functioned as more than a neutral descriptor; it instead acted as a "foul noun of preference" that Americans "deployed … against anyone with whom they disagreed politically."[11] The most popular targets of opprobrium were President Franklin Delano Roosevelt and his New Deal. At various points in the 1930s, a number of notable figures derided FDR or the New Deal as "fascist," including liberal philosopher John Dewey (who worried FDR was creating "a police state"), socialist politician Norman Thomas (who worried FDR was beginning to resemble Mussolini), former Republican President Herbert Hoover (who likewise worried FDR was too similar to European dictators), and populist Senator Huey Long (who worried FDR was too close to the business class).[12] But the president was hardly the only one ridiculed in this fashion. As Kuklick highlights, until the U.S. entry into World War II, "everyone called anyone a fascist."[13]

No incident displays the term's malleability more than an informal 1937 survey undertaken by the social theorist Stuart Chase, who asked almost 100 people "what 'fascism' meant to them."[14] The respondents offered a range of diverse, even antithetical, definitions: A lawyer said "fascism" was "a coercive capitalistic state," while a housewife identified it as the "same thing as communism"; an author answered that it was "an all-powerful police force to hold up a decaying society," while a farmer characterized it as "lawlessness"; a social worker described it as "government in the interest of the majority for the purpose of accomplishing things democracy cannot do," while a journalist insisted it was "undesired government of [the] masses by a self-seeking, fanatical minority."[15] Still, while the respondents provided diverse interpretations of fascism, most agreed that, whatever fascism was, they didn't like it. Or as a schoolboy put it with youthful bravado, fascism was "something that's got to be licked."[16]

It took the U.S. entry into World War II to solidify how the term *fascism* was used. Once the United States joined the Allied effort after the 1941 Japanese attacks on Pearl Harbor and other U.S. possessions, political categories crystallized. Now "America battled Germany, Italy, and Japan—countries all specified as fascist."[17] Though FDR still had his critics, they were less likely to designate the president a fascist. In short, the identification of the Axis as fascist and the wartime desire for unity combined to make haphazard allegations of fascism a thing of the past—at least for a time.

***

One might have expected fascism to perish in 1945 along with the Nazi regime with which it was associated. But while the term was used far less after the war than during it, *fascism* nonetheless became a permanent part of the American lexicon. Why didn't fascism die an ignoble death like once-popular but eventually discarded political identifications such as Whig, Know-Nothing, and Dixiecrat?

The reason, Kuklick argues, is that by the time the United States entered the war, American governance had begun to be defined by a novel approach to politics dubbed "welfare liberalism," whose proponents positioned themselves against "fascism on the right and communism on the left."[18]

Strange as it seems to us today, before the 1940s Americans rarely employed the European political spectrum, which pitted a reactionary "right" against a socialist "left," to understand their own politics. Instead, most literate Americans believed that their country enjoyed "its own political divisions that sat apart from those of Europe."[19] Whenever Americans did make use of the European spectrum, it was usually to point to a radical "left" of which they wanted little part.[20] In a sense, before the 1940s, the United States had an immoderate left but "no immoderate right."[21] Abhorrent tendencies in U.S. politics presently identified as on the far right, such as avowed white supremacy, resided comfortably in the mainstream, especially since the Democratic Party relied on its segregationist wing to pass and promote the New Deal.

The welfare liberals changed this by strategically utilizing the European political spectrum to define themselves as the moderate center. To do so, they needed an extreme right-wing, and they found one in fascism. By developing and promoting an American political spectrum that placed fascism on the extreme right and communism on the extreme left, liberals were able to present themselves and their platform—limited government intervention at home, support for "democracy" abroad—as the embodiment of a rational, "vital center."[22] Put differently, during and after World War II, fascism became a useful foil against which centrist liberals defined themselves and justified the creation of an expanded welfare state and U.S. Empire that, for the first time in history, spanned much of the globe.

From the late 1940s to the late 1960s, the word *fascism*—which surpassed Nazism and National Socialism in common usage—had a relatively stable meaning: it referred to the extreme right-wing of the recently adopted political spectrum. Nevertheless, one must be careful not to overstate the term's import; for most of this period, it was communism, not fascism, that preoccupied the American mind. In fact, it was primarily German exiles such as Albert Einstein, Theodor Adorno, and Herbert Marcuse who kept the term in circulation.

***

Things changed, or rather returned to their pre–World War II state, during the Vietnam War. Anti-war baby boomers, who had not fought fascism firsthand but who had grown up in its dark shadow, once again started to apply the term to politicians across the political spectrum, from Lyndon Baines Johnson to Richard Nixon. Fascism thus retained its exceedingly negative valence but was, Kuklick shows, "untethered … from the right" and even "uncoupled from any perceptible characteristics."[23] If you *really* didn't like someone or something, you called them fascist.

This is not to say that those who used the term never had noble intentions, especially from the perspective of the Left. In several instances, left-wing thinkers concluded that they needed to employ the term *fascism* to help Americans appreciate that sometimes the policies of their liberal capitalist society uncomfortably mirrored those of Nazi Germany. In particular, when Angela Y. Davis used the term in her May 1971 essay "Political Prisoners, Prisons and Black Liberation" to inveigh against "the fascist content of the ruthless aggression in Indochina" and "the fascist stronghold in the prisons," she was trying to force people to confront painful and profound instances of violence, oppression, and injustice.[24]

But Davis's form of use never predominated, and in general, for much of the 1960s onward, innumerable people deployed the term in innumerable ways. Everyone, from Ronald Reagan to Bill Clinton, from Barack Obama to George W. Bush, has at one point or another been deemed a "fascist."

Fascism, in other words, has not typically functioned as a term of analysis—as Kuklick demonstrates, it doesn't have "much empirical content."[25] It is instead "a part of language that is more evaluative than factual."[26] For most of its American history, *fascism* has been an insult, a performative reflection of the user's desire to make the object of their derision disreputable.

Kuklick is therefore "skeptical" of the mounds of scholarly research that have utilized *fascist* to describe governments, movements, and people not linked to Mussolini's Italy or Hitler's Germany.[27] Like much research into political topics, this work, he claims, "continue[s] politics by other methods" and "displays standard sentiments as much as ... disinterested information."[28]

Kuklick is especially critical of attempts to read fascism into the American past, which many scholars have done since the late 1960s. Finding fascism in U.S. history, he warns, "distances U.S. citizens from their own past" by insisting that "dangerous challenges did not come from America but must have migrated from overseas."[29] There are manifold homegrown American phenomena that shaped the past for the worse—genocidal racism, rapacious militarism, and a violent obsession with incarcerating minorities were not fascist inventions—and we hardly need to import a term with a foreign valence to explain (and thus implicitly detach ourselves from) that history.

***

Why has *fascism* been able to serve such a protean function? According to Kuklick, it's because fascism hasn't been, and never was, a real threat in the United States. As he usefully reminds us, "living, breathing Nazis—the German–American Bundists and William Dudley Pelley's Silver Legion of the 1930s; George Lincoln Rockwell's American Nazi Party of the 1960s; or the neo-Nazis of the twenty-first century"—were all minuscule groups that never came close to wielding political power.[30] The conditions that enabled fascism's rise—a broad experience of total war and a powerful left on the verge of seizing power—were just never present here. It was precisely this lack of threat that allowed fascism to become a generalized term of vilification. If there were actual fascists running around, you wouldn't go around calling everyone fascist.

Another reason fascism has been so protean is that, unlike liberalism and conservatism, it's not a living ideology—and it never really was in the United States. No self-identified fascist is taken seriously in American society. There are no genuinely fascist op-ed columnists, no fascist TV commentators, no fascist celebrities, no fascist elected officials. You're unlikely to find people reading actual fascists outside of European history courses. When a right-wing provocateur like Matt Walsh refers to himself as a "theocratic fascist," he does so with a wink and nod, knowing that he's using a term sure to rile up liberals and leftists.[31] Fascism is a dead ideology, which ironically has allowed it to rise from the grave in easily manipulable zombified form.

Beyond its versatility, there are several additional reasons why fascism has become such a powerful term in American discourse. First, as Angela Davis's use of the word suggests, sometimes left-wing thinkers have determined that to impel Americans to confront difficult truths, only the word *fascist* will do. Using the term further enables individuals to indicate that they're "one of the good guys." When anti-war activists identified George W. Bush with Hitler in the 2000s, they were not so much making a careful historical analogy as signaling their hatred of Republican warmongers and, in most cases, their allegiance to the Democratic Party.[32]

Moreover, in eras like our own, in which rampant polarization coexists with a political structure in which most citizens have no influence, it's only natural for people to construct struggles that give their lives political meaning. Identifying "fascists" allows Americans living today to imagine themselves as part of a consequential world-historical fight between good and evil. It's an ahistorical framing that gives meaning through romantic nostalgia and provides psychic succor to all of us who have no influence in the corridors of power.

The contemporary fascism debate is thus about much more than fascism—it's about people's sense of self in a moment of anti-popular politics. And it is for this reason that the debate, which on its surface is as academic as a discussion could possibly be, has engendered so much rancor: When you attack someone's identification of fascism, you're attacking more than a political diagnosis; you're attacking their very identity.

***

Nonetheless, something did change with the rise of Donald Trump, whose success reopened the floodgates of fascism talk. Not since the 1930s and 1940s have the literati obsessed so much over fascism, and not since the 1950s and 1960s has the term been so associated with the political right.

At first glance, it's not obvious why so many more critics identified Trump as fascist instead of, say, George W. Bush. Bush, after all, established government bodies such as Immigration and Customs Enforcement, the most Gestapo-like organization in the country, and the Department of Homeland Security, whose name uncomfortably echoes the German *Heimatschutz*, a term associated with the far right. Moreover, Bush's policies—undermining FEMA, invading Afghanistan and Iraq—inarguably resulted in the death and displacement of far more people than Trump's.

Some might say that the actions taken by Republicans in the years since 2016 are more dangerous than those they took in the 2000s, that the Trump GOP's claims of voter fraud and its attempts to limit voter participation threaten democracy in a way that Bush's

GOP never did. I find this hard to credit, given that Bush's many accomplishments—stealing an election, starting pointless wars, violating sundry civil liberties—are objectively more damaging (and more Nazi-like) than anything that Trump and his GOP tried to implement.

Others might argue that the rise of far-right groups like the Proud Boys and Oath Keepers, and especially their participation in the "insurrection" of January 6, 2021, suggests that there's an unprecedented threat to U.S. democracy that only the word *fascism* can describe. But organizations like these have existed for decades and undertaken numerous spectacular acts—the Oklahoma City bombing of 1995 comes immediately to mind, as do the murders of doctors providing abortions—and the term *fascist* was not usually applied to them.

A similar argument is sometimes made about the rise of far-right governments around the world in places such as Hungary, Poland, Russia, and Turkey. But, again, these types of autocratic governments have long been a feature of international politics and were not usually identified as "fascist."

It therefore seems that one must look elsewhere to explain the explosion of fascism talk since 2016.

To my mind, the major reason fascism talk has lately reached a crescendo is that, for the first time in almost a century, liberalism finds itself in crisis. The utopian promises made in the 1990s and 2000s, when liberals averred that we were at "the end of history," have not come true. The economy has collapsed multiple times. Inequality has increased. U.S. attempts to promote "democracy" abroad have failed as Eastern Europe, once the site of liberalism's greatest triumph, has lurched to the right. Bernie Sanders has reinvigorated Americans' interest in social democracy. And the loutish Trump's victory indicated that many Americans are tired of adhering to liberal norms of engagement and exchange. Liberalism is weaker than it has been since the Great Depression.

For most of the twentieth century's second half, liberalism was kept vigorous and popular because it was able to define itself against a communist enemy, which, liberals affirmed, was the primary obstacle standing in the way of a better world. But communism has been defeated, and 30 years later everything looks and feels pretty much the same, only worse. Liberals therefore need a credible enemy whose viciousness might attract Americans to the centrist cause and, in the process, help them overlook liberalism's manifold and manifest failures. Simply put, fighting fascism provides liberals with an opportunity to reinvigorate their project in a moment of crisis. This is why fascism talk exploded under Trump and not under Bush; under the latter, liberal dreams had not yet curdled.

***

But this still doesn't answer the normative question: Should we on the left use the term *fascism*?

To many, it might not matter that the word *fascism* has no coherent analytical meaning—what matters is that it's a politically useful way, first, to force people to appreciate that U.S.-style liberal democratic capitalism doesn't prevent oppression of the kind that occurred in Nazi Germany, and second, to mobilize people against right-wing extremism.

I'm not persuaded by the first argument. I have yet to see compelling evidence that indicates invoking fascism leads Americans to confront racialized state violence. Leftists have been using *fascism* as a term of abuse for decades, and it doesn't appear to have had much effect on how the population understands society.

I'm also skeptical of the claim that using the term *fascism* is an important means to mobilize people against the far right. It seems to me that there are likely more meaningful ways to rally one's side against reaction that are centered less on abstract concepts and more on promising—and giving—people money and benefits. Unfortunately, there's no extant data that can definitively settle the question: according to polls conducted for the nonprofit organization Protect Democracy by the research firm Citizen Data, in the 2022 midterm elections, "in five battleground states

… voters—especially voters who split the ticket—were strongly motivated to respond to threats to democracy."[33] Was the fascism framework an important part of the effort to make voters anxious about democracy's survival? We just don't know, though the message "we need to defend democracy" by no means depends on identifying fascism, and we could discard the latter without losing much.

As we move further into the twenty-first century, it's worth asking whether using a twentieth-century term that inevitably invokes images of brown-shirted thugs beating down doors and black-shirted psychopaths running death camps will help us solve the problems we face. Neither climate change nor inequality nor structural racism nor the general hopelessness that has permeated American society will be defeated in ways that resemble the Allies' defeat of fascism.

It may therefore be time to retire the term. Not only is its political utility doubtful, but Kuklick has demonstrated that there is no fascist object "out there" to discover. There is thus no way to end the fascist debate. Agreement or consensus is unlikely to be reached. It's time to let it go.

Endnotes

1 Michelle Goldberg, "Just How Dangerous Was Donald Trump?", *New York Times,* December 14, 2020, https://www.nytimes.com/2020/12/14/opinion/trump-fascism.html; Shadi Hamid, "Americans Are Losing Sight of What *Fascism* Means," *The Atlantic,* October 25, 2020, https://www.theatlantic.com/ideas/archive/2020/10/americans-have-lost-sight-what-fascism-means/616846/; Thomas Weber, "Trump Is Not a Fascist. But That Didn't Make Him Any Less Dangerous to Our Democracy," *CNN,* January 24, 2021, https://www.cnn.com/2021/01/24/opinions/trump-fascism-misguided-comparison-weber; Samuel Moyn, "The Trouble with Comparisons," *New York Review of Books,* May 19, 2020, https://www.nybooks.com/online/2020/05/19/the-trouble-with-comparisons/.

2 Bruce Kuklick, *Fascism Comes to America: A Century of Obsession in Politics and Culture* (Chicago: University of Chicago Press, 2022).
3 Claude Lévi-Strauss, *Introduction to the Work of Marcel Mauss*, trans. Felicity Baker (London: Routledge & Kegan Paul, 1987 [1950]), 55.
4 Jonah Goldberg, *Liberal Fascism: The Secret History of the American Left from Mussolini to the Politics of Meaning* (New York: Doubleday, 2007); Chris Hedges, *American Fascists: The Christian Right and the War on America* (New York: Free Press, 2006).
5 Dinesh D'Souza, *Hillary's America: The Secret History of the Democratic Party* (Washington, D.C.: Regnery Publishing, 2016), chapter 6; Paul Krugman, "Appeasement Got Us Where We Are," *New York Times*, January 7, 2021, https://www.nytimes.com/2021/01/07/opinion/donald-trump-fascism.html.
6 Fox News, "Gorka Says Left-Wing 'Lunatics' Have Caused Rise of Dem Socialism," Facebook, August 5, 2018, https://www.facebook.com/FoxNews/videos/gorka-says-left-wing-lunatics-have-caused-rise-of-dem-socialism/10157239230601336/; Andrew Moran, "LOL: Nouriel Roubini Claims Libertarians, Mises Are Fascists," *Economic Collapse News*, October 16, 2018, https://economiccollapsenews.com/2018/10/16/lol-nouriel-roubini-claims-libertarians-mises-are-fascists/.
7 Kuklick, *Fascism Comes to America*, 3.
8 Ibid.
9 Ibid., 19.
10 Ibid., 66.
11 Ibid., 30, 56.
12 Ibid., 26.
13 Ibid., 94.
14 Stuart Chase, *The Tyranny of Words* (New York: Harcourt, Brace and Company, 1938), 188.
15 Ibid., 189–190.
16 Ibid., 189.
17 Kuklick, *Fascism Comes to America*, 94.
18 Ibid.
19 Ibid.

20 Ibid., 95.
21 Ibid.
22 Ibid.
23 Ibid., 161, 144.
24 Angela Y. Davis, "Political Prisoners, Prisons and Black Liberation," in *If They Come in the Morning: Voices of Resistance*, ed. Angela Y. Davis, Bettina Aptheker, and other members of the National United Committee to Free Angela Davis and All Political Prisoners (New York: Third Press Publishers, 1992 [1971]), 35, 31.
25 Kuklick, *Fascism Comes to America*, 3.
26 Ibid.
27 Ibid., 4.
28 Ibid.
29 Ibid., 186.
30 Ibid., 156.
31 "Matt Walsh," Southern Poverty Law Center, accessed July 28, 2025, https://www.splcenter.org/resources/extremist-files/matt-walsh/.
32 Michael Janofsky, "The 2004 Campaign: Advertising; Bush-Hitler Ads Draw Criticism," *New York Times*, January 6, 2004, https://www.nytimes.com/2004/01/06/us/the-2004-campaign-advertising-bush-hitler-ads-draw-criticism.html; Alex Beam, "Is Bush Hitler? I Don't Think So," *New York Times*, November 23, 2007, https://www.nytimes.com/2007/11/23/opinion/23iht-edbeam.1.8452549.html.
33 Genevieve Nadeau, "How Democracy Concerns & January 6th Influenced Midterm Voting," Protect Democracy, December 16, 2022, https://protectdemocracy.org/work/democracy-concerns-january-6-midterm-voting/.

THIS IS AMERICA

Though in its early days, the second Donald Trump Administration has proved to be significantly more radical than the first. A president who, in his initial term, lacked the wherewithal and the administrative expertise to use the power of his office to transform U.S. politics now seems able and eager to fulfill his critics' darkest fantasies.

With the aid of a coterie of loyalists, most notably the South African billionaire Elon Musk, Trump is using his presidential power to begin the process of destroying certain institutions of the administrative state, especially those that have become targets in the culture war, like the Department of Education.[1] Beyond this, he has proven more than willing to break norms and even laws. At the time of writing, he has issued 178 executive orders—26 on his first day in office alone.[2] And in mid-March, his administration defied a judicial order, deporting hundreds of Venezuelan nationals to a Salvadoran prison.[3]

Especially chilling for academics like myself, the Trump Administration arrested Badar Khan Suri, an Indian postdoctoral fellow teaching at Georgetown University on a student visa, for, as Assistant Secretary for Public Affairs of the Department of Homeland Security Tricia McLaughlin put it, "actively spreading Hamas propaganda and promoting antisemitism on social media," as well as Mahmoud Khalil, a green card holder and a leader of last year's pro-Palestine protest movement at Columbia University.[4]

Trump's frightening actions have understandably engendered concern among liberals and leftists—and even some conservatives.[5] If the president's first term, during which his greatest achievement was a massive tax cut for the wealthy, hardly departed from the practices of bog-standard Republicans, his second appears motivated by a desire to transform the American state and society.[6]

What remains unclear is the extent to which Trump's anti-democratic behavior represents a break with the United States' constitutional order. Debates over this issue within the public sphere have largely revolved around the question of whether Trump 2.0 embodies a turn toward fascism.

While those who talk of fascism are honorably motivated by a desire to apprehend what's going on, use of the term obscures both the nature and the stakes of the present moment. There is a fundamental truth at the heart of Trumpism that makes comparisons to European fascism difficult to sustain. Put simply, Trump and his hangers-on are building on long-standing *American* traditions and are using the normal tools of the *American* government to dismantle democracy. Trumpism is not a foreign import. It is distinctly homegrown. And if the Left hopes to combat it now and in the future, we must focus on transforming the profoundly American sources of the president's authoritarianism.

***

At this point, readers might be asking the obvious question: Who cares what we call Trump and Trumpism? Isn't this all just pointless intra-intellectual fighting?

Indeed, at various points, observers have criticized the fascism debate for being little more than a navel-gazing academic exercise, a decadent example of scholarly disconnection in an era when the Trump Administration is causing very real human suffering. But this criticism, while understandable, misses the mark. To name something is to diagnose it, and to diagnose a malady is to identify a cure. An incorrect political diagnosis will inevitably lead to ineffective resistance. If a patient suffered from heart disease, but a doctor diagnosed them with a hemorrhoid, then eventually the patient might die from their heart disease. A similar thing could be said for democracy.

Defenders of the claim that Trump is a fascist have tended to rely on five arguments. While these have almost always been advanced out of a deep concern for the moral demands of the present, they nevertheless misread our moment and thereby militate against the type of politics capable of resisting the Republican assault on democracy.

First, some defenders of the fascism thesis insist that the analogy meaningfully illuminates processes occurring today. But the context of interwar Europe is so different from that of the United States in the 2010s and 2020s that such analogizing obscures what's going on. We are not living in the aftermath of a world war in which mass death led to social dislocation and the emergence of novel political orders. Gangs of young veterans with combat experience do not roam our streets. A powerful communist movement does not threaten entrenched capitalist interests. Our various economic downturns do not equate to the hyperinflation experienced throughout postwar Europe.

Second, others maintain that there is no need to look to Europe to make the fascism comparison because the United States has its own fascist traditions upon which Trump and his cohorts rely. To make this argument, people point to the many racist, xenophobic, and even eliminationist aspects of U.S. history, from the "three-fifths compromise" found in the U.S. Constitution to the practice and legacy of chattel slavery, from the forced removal and genocide of Indigenous peoples to the Ku Klux Klan, from Jim Crow to redlining, from Japanese incarceration during World War II to militarist policing, and beyond. For advocates of the American fascism thesis, these developments all prove that there's an unbroken line of fascism stretching back to the nation's founding.

While there is no doubt that there are deep continuities between the present moment and U.S. history, referring to American fascism ironically undermines the fascism thesis. "Fascism," in this account, emerges as a uniquely American phenomenon, both preceding and postdating its European variants, to which it has no real connection. In this instance, the term *fascism* stands as a shorthand for "extreme far-right ideology"—a very capacious definition that isn't especially useful analytically.

A third group affirms that deploying the term *fascism* is politically useful. Calling Trump a fascist, they claim, helps to mobilize mass resistance. Here, empirical analysis suggests otherwise. In the last weeks of Kamala Harris's campaign for the presidency, she called Trump a fascist.[7] The message that Trump was a fascist threat to democracy was, according to *Vox*, her campaign's "closing argument," despite the fact that the most important super PAC supporting Harris warned that "'attacking Trump's fascism is not that persuasive.'"[8] We all know how this story ended: Trump defeated Harris, winning 49.81 percent of the popular vote to Harris's 48.34 percent, and 312 electoral votes to Harris's 226.[9]

Fourth, some of those who embrace the analogy avow that the framework of fascism can help predict Trump's behavior. This would be good if it were true, but neither history nor the social sciences are predictive endeavors. Studying history and using the tools of social science allow analysts to accomplish several things: we can identify structures, processes, discourses, and patterns; we can understand the causes of past events; and we can illuminate the origins of the present. But they cannot be used to predict the future. That is simply not what they do.

Finally, a fifth group argues that calling Trump a fascist underlines the degree to which Trumpism reflects a genuinely novel innovation in American politics. This is the most politically significant claim offered by those who endorse the analogy, because it has been deployed to mobilize not just liberals and leftists but also stalwarts of the pre-Trump Republican mainstream.

In the process, those who insist that Trump is a fascist departure from U.S. history have tacitly endorsed the antidemocratic politics of people like Liz Cheney, who have had no problem defending the United States' unjust and illegal wars, the government's expansive surveillance of citizens, and neoliberalism and neoconservatism in general. Under the banner of anti-fascism, "Never Trumpers" such as Cheney have rebranded themselves as champions of democracy, a grotesquerie for all those who remember the "Global War on Terror."[10]

***

The reality is that everything Trump is doing has antecedents in U.S. history, and the best way to apprehend Trump's radicalism and organize to stop it is to place his behavior in the context of this longer history. Trumpism, in other words, is an intensification of long-standing, antidemocratic, and profoundly American trends. There is hardly a need to use the term *fascism* to understand it. This is America, and Trump is nothing if not deeply American.

Let's begin with Trump's attempted dismantling of the administrative state. To appreciate what's going on, one doesn't have to point to any foreign *Führerprinzip*; one only has to investigate the actual history of the U.S. presidency.

Since the founding of the American republic in 1776, the presidency has grown in power while Congress, the supposed representative of the people's will, has abdicated its responsibilities. This is most evident in the realm of foreign policy. Congress is constitutionally responsible for declaring war, but it has only done so 11 times, the last time in 1942.[11]

From that moment on, though, the United States has been in a state of near-constant war. In addition to the well-known Korean, Vietnam, Afghanistan, and Iraq wars, in the decades after World War II, the United States has intervened against foreign societies, according to the political scientists Sidita Kushi and Monica Duffy Toft, with "the threat, display, or direct usage of force" more than two hundred times.[12] And what is true in foreign policy is true in other issue areas: the president has increasingly become the equivalent of an elected monarch, with the political scientist Richard W. Waterman warning that the sheer power of the office means that "America has never been so close to the precipice of autocracy as we are today."[13] Put another way, there has been an ongoing, if usually ignored, constitutional crisis since at least the 1940s.

Most dramatically, in the last several decades, a radical and antidemocratic theory of presidential power, dubbed "the theory of the unitary executive," has gained increasing sway in right-wing legal circles. As Waterman notes, this theory "posits that the president has sole responsibility for the control and maintenance of the executive branch," and concomitantly claims "that Congress does not have the right to enact laws that limit the president's powers as chief executive or commander in chief" and "that the president has the same authority as the courts to interpret laws that relate to the executive branch."[14]

The theory of the unitary executive, which according to Waterman "represents a quantum expansion of the president's administrative authority," proved especially useful during the George W. Bush Administration, and it is the one upon which many of Trump's attempts to undo the administrative state rest.[15] In deploying this theory, right-wing jurists have moved beyond the "imperial presidency" to embrace an "autocratic presidency," in which the president has become a kind of dictator.[16]

To construct the argument for the autocratic presidency, jurists such as John Yoo did not refer to fascist or Nazi law; they relied on U.S. jurisprudence.[17] The autocratic presidency is a very American invention.

Even the power of the unelected and not-confirmed-by-the-Senate Elon Musk has its precedents. Unfortunately, one of the hallmarks of the U.S. system is that presidents are allowed to name people to several influential positions without the Senate's approval—these are called "non-Senate confirmed, presidentially appointed positions."[18] Here, for instance, are some individuals who served as national security advisor (NSA), a position not confirmed by the Senate: McGeorge Bundy, Walt Whitman Rostow, Henry Kissinger, Zbigniew Brzezinski, W. Anthony Lake, Condoleezza Rice, Susan Rice, John Bolton, and Jake Sullivan.[19]

In various ways, each of these individuals shaped U.S. policy and politics—none had a democratic mandate. Besides the NSA, the president appoints, without Senate confirmation, the deputy director of the Central Intelligence Agency, the deputy national security advisor, and manifold other positions.[20]

Now let's turn to the arrests of Badar Khan Suri and Mahmoud Khalil, both of which are disturbing violations of civil liberties and the principles that are theoretically the bedrock of American political life. Tragically, arrests such as these have many precedents in U.S. history; the arrest and deportation of legal residents and even citizens—oftentimes for political radicalism—has been a recurring feature of American politics for a long time.

For much of the last century, the United States has made effective use of what the historian Adam Goodman has termed "the deportation machine."[21] During and after World War I, President Woodrow Wilson, under the authority of the Espionage Act of 1917, the Sedition Act of 1918, and the Immigration Act of 1918, arrested and deported radicals and anti-war activists; as the historian Kim Phillips-Fein recently highlighted, more than 550 people accused of political radicalism were deported as the result of the infamous Palmer Raids of 1919–1920.[22] Then, between 1929 and 1939, as Goodman reports, "as many as half a million Mexicans and Mexican Americans" were "repatriated" to Mexico—and, according to the historian Francisco Balderrama, at least 60 percent of those compelled to leave the country were U.S. citizens.[23] In the early Cold War, meanwhile, the government arrested and sometimes deported "political subversives" under the authority of the Alien Registration Act of 1940, the Internal Security Act of 1950, and the Immigration and Nationality Act of 1952.[24]

For the remainder of the twentieth century, to quote Goodman, "neighborhood sweeps and expedited deportations had periodically resulted in the removal of U.S. citizens and permanent residents."[25] In fact, after Bill Clinton signed the Illegal Immigration Reform and Immigrant Responsibility Act of 1996, "*all* noncitizens, including many long-term, legal permanent residents, found themselves subject to formal deportation."[26] To take just one example Goodman highlights, "between 2005 and 2010, some 1.4 million people—half of them children born in the United States—returned to Mexico either by choice, coercion, or force."[27]

And this doesn't even address the many violations of civil liberties witnessed during the Global War on Terror, when a citizen named José Padilla, who according to Attorney General John Ashcroft "was exploring a plan to build and explode a radiological dispersion device, or 'dirty bomb,' in the United States," was held in military detention without charge for over three years, or when a green card holder named Ansar Mahmood "was detained on suspicions of terrorism ... after he took a photograph near a water-treatment plant."[28] Beyond the Global War on Terror, in the late 2010s journalists working for the *Los Angeles Times* discovered that "Immigration and Customs Enforcement [ICE] agents repeatedly target U.S. citizens for deportation by mistake."[29] In one especially dramatic instance, a citizen named Davino Watson was held by ICE for 1,273 days.[30]

***

Clearly, Trumpism 2.0 intensifies many extant precedents—each horrifying and deeply undemocratic. The second time around, Trump is being more aggressive, more flagrant, and more public in his pursuit of genuinely radical ends.

But the powers that Trump is deploying, and the laws and theories upon which he is building his attempt to reshape the U.S. state and society, are not fascist. They are American, and the danger posed by Trump is a specifically American one. Things can be scary—things *are* scary—without them being fascist. Indeed, they might even be scarier because they're homegrown.

If socialists hope to combat Trump and organize a coalition able to prevent autocrats like him from again rising to power, we must appreciate that he emerges from American history and the American system. One of the major problems of the fascism analogy is that it diverts attention from the United States to Europe. But this is not fascist Italy or Nazi Germany.

This is America, with all that implies.

Endnotes

1 Bianca Vázquez Toness, "Trump Has Ordered the Dismantling of the U.S. Education Department. Here's What That Means," *Associated Press*, March 21, 2025, https://apnews.com/article/trump-dismantling-education-department-8b5d0961700f0fe69d18ea80b437c8b8.

2 "2025 Donald J. Trump Executive Orders," Federal Register, accessed August 5, 2025, https://www.federalregister.gov/presidential-documents/executive-orders/donald-trump/2025; Sarah Fortinsky, "Trump Executive Orders and Actions: By the Numbers," *The Hill*, January 21, 2025. https://thehill.com/homenews/administration/5098445-trump-executive-orders-first-day/.

3 Marc Caputo, "Exclusive: How the White House Ignored a Judge's Order to Turn Back Deportation Flights," *Axios*, March 16, 2025, https://www.axios.com/2025/03/16/trump-white-house-defy-judge-deport-venezuelans.

4 Kyle Cheney and Josh Gerstein, "Trump Is Seeking to Deport Another Academic Who Is Legally in the Country, Lawsuit Says," *Politico*, March 19, 2025, https://www.politico.com/news/2025/03/19/trump-deportation-georgetown-graduate-student-00239754; Joseph Stepansky, "Georgetown Researcher Arrest Escalates Trump Speech Crackdown, Scholars Say," *Al Jazeera*, March 20, 2025, https://www.aljazeera.com/news/2025/3/20/georgetown-researcher-arrest-escalates-trump-speech-crackdown-scholars-say; Jake Offenhartz, "Immigration Agents Arrest Palestinian Activist Who Helped Lead

Columbia University Protests," *Associated Press*, March 9, 2025, https://apnews.com/article/columbia-university-mahmoud-khalil-ice-15014bcbb921f21a9f704d5acdcae7a8.

5 Tara Suter, "Ann Coulter Questions Arrest of Columbia Protester on Free Speech Grounds," *The Hill*, March 10, 2025, https://thehill.com/homenews/media/5187164-ann-coulter-arrest-columbia-protester-free-speech/.

6 Chuck Marr, Samantha Jacoby, and George Fenton, *The 2017 Trump Tax Law Was Skewed to the Rich, Expensive, and Failed to Deliver on Its Promises: A 2025 Course Correction Is Needed* (Washington, D.C.: Center on Budget and Policy Priorities, June 13, 2024), https://www.cbpp.org/sites/default/files/3-5-24tax.pdf.

7 Emma Bowman, "Harris Called Trump a 'Fascist.' Experts Debate What Fascism Is—and Isn't," NPR, October 29, 2024, https://www.npr.org/2024/10/29/nx-s1-5164488/harris-trump-fascist-explained

8 Christian Paz, "How 'Trump Is a Fascist' Became Kamala's Closing Argument," *Vox*, October 24, 2024, https://www.vox.com/2024-elections/379686/trump-fascist-kamala-harris-campaigns-biden-democracy-familiar-closing-argument-campaign-2024; Shane Goldmacher and Maggie Haberman, "Pro-Harris Super PAC Raises Concerns About Focusing on Trump and Fascism," *New York Times*, October 27, 2024, https://www.nytimes.com/2024/10/27/us/politics/harris-trump-campaign-fascism.html.

9 "2024 [Statistics on the 2024 Presidential Election]," in John T. Woolley and Gerhard Peters, ed., *The American Presidency Project* (Santa Barbara, CA, 1999–2025), https://www.presidency.ucsb.edu/statistics/elections/2024.

10 Alexandra Marquez, "Liz Cheney Issues Dire Warning About 'Fundamentally Cruel' Trump, Agrees He's a 'Fascist,'" NBC News, October 13, 2024, https://www.nbcnews.com/politics/2024-election/liz-cheney-issues-dire-warning-fundamentally-cruel-trump-agrees-sfasc-rcna175193.

11 "About Declarations of War by Congress," U.S. Senate, accessed August 5, 2025, https://www.senate.gov/about/powers-procedures/declarations-of-war.htm.

12 Monica Duffy Toft and Sidita Kushi, *Dying by the Sword: The Militarization of U.S. Foreign Policy* (New York: Oxford University Press, 2023), 14; Sidita Kushi and Monica Duffy Toft, "Introducing the Military Intervention Project: A New Dataset on U.S. Military Interventions, 1776–2019," *Journal of Conflict Resolution* 67, no. 4 (April 2023), 767.

13 Richard W. Waterman, *Constitutional Ambiguity and the Interpretation of Presidential Power* (Albany: State University of New York Press, 2025), 258. See also John Kruzel and Andrew Chung, "U.S. Supreme Court Rules Trump Has Broad Immunity from Prosecution," *Reuters*, July 1, 2024, https://www.reuters.com/legal/us-supreme-court-due-rule-trumps-immunity-bid-blockbuster-case-2024-07-01/; Michael Waldman, "The Supreme Court Gives the President the Power of a King," Brennan Center for Justice, July 1, 2024, https://www.brennancenter.org/our-work/analysis-opinion/supreme-court-gives-president-power-king.

14 Richard W. Waterman, "The Administrative Presidency, Unilateral Power, and the Unitary Executive Theory," *Presidential Studies Quarterly* 39, no. 1 (March 2009), 6, 8.

15 Ibid., 8; Harold J. Krent, "From a Unitary to a Unilateral Presidency," *Boston University Law Review* 88, no. 2 (April 2008), 523–560; Christopher Wright Durocher, "A Unitary Executive on Steroids Threatens to Crush the Constitution," American Constitution Society, February 4, 2025, https://www.acslaw.org/inbrief/a-unitary-executive-on-steroids-threatens-to-crush-the-constitution/; Michael Waldman, "The Extreme Legal Theory Behind Trump's First Month in Office," Brennan Center for Justice, February 19, 2025, https://www.brennancenter.org/our-work/analysis-opinion/extreme-legal-theory-behind-trumps-first-month-office; Cass R. Sunstein, "This Theory Is Behind Trump's Power Grab," *New York Times*, February 26, 2025, https://www.nytimes.com/2025/02/26/opinion/trump-roberts-unitary-executive-theory.html.

16 On the imperial presidency, see Arthur M. Schlesinger, Jr., *The Imperial Presidency* (Boston: Houghton Mifflin Company, 1973). On the autocratic presidency, see Waterman, *Constitutional Ambiguity and the Interpretation of Presidential Power*, 229, 268.

17 Waterman, *Constitutional Ambiguity and the Interpretation of Presidential Power*, chapter 8.

18 "Post-Election Transition Milestones," Center for Presidential Transition, accessed August 5, 2025, https://presidentialtransition.org/post-election-transition-milestones/.

19 National Security Act of 1947, Pub. L. No. 118–159 (1947), 8, https://www.govinfo.gov/content/pkg/COMPS-1493/pdf/COMPS-1493.pdf.

20 "Non-Senate Confirmed Presidentially Appointed Positions," Women's Foreign Policy Group, accessed August 5, 2025, https://wfpg.memberclicks.net/assets/2020/non-senate-confirmed-sample-2016.pdf.

21 Adam Goodman, *The Deportation Machine: America's Long History of Expelling Immigrants* (Princeton, NJ: Princeton University Press).

22 Alex Goodall, *Loyalty and Liberty: American Countersubversion from World War I to the McCarthy Era* (Urbana: University of Illinois Press, 2013), chapters 1–4; Kim Phillips-Fein, "Trump's Deportations Are a Throwback to Red Scare Politics," *Jacobin*, March 20, 2025, https://jacobin.com/2025/03/trump-deportations-red-scare-khalil.

23 Goodman, *The Deportation Machine*, 46; Francisco Balderrama, "America's Forgotten History of Mexican-American 'Repatriation,'" interview by Terry Gross, *Fresh Air*, NPR, September 10, 2015, https://www.npr.org/2015/09/10/439114563/americas-forgotten-history-of-mexican-american-repatriation.

24 Ellen Schrecker, "Immigration and Internal Security: Political Deportations during the McCarthy Era," *Science & Society* 60, no. 4 (Winter 1996/1997), 393–426.

25 Goodman, *The Deportation Machine*, 129.

26 Ibid., 177.

27 Ibid., 196.

28 John Ashcroft, "Transcript of the Attorney General John Ashcroft Regarding the Transfer of Abdullah Al Muhajir (Born Jose Padilla) to the Department of Defense as an Enemy Combatant" (speech, Washington, D.C. [?], June 10, 2002), U.S. Department of Justice [2001–2005], https://www.justice.gov/archive/ag/speeches/2002/061002agtranscripts.htm; Associated Press in Miami, "Terrorism Plotter Jose Padilla Has Prison Sentence Extended," *The Guardian*, September 9, 2014,

https://www.theguardian.com/world/2014/sep/09/jose-padilla-al-qaida-new-prison-sentence.Kirk Semple, "Man Arrested Over Photos After 9/11 Is Deported," *New York Times*, August 14, 2004, https://www.nytimes.com/2004/08/14/nyregion/man-arrested-over-photos-after-9-11-is-deported.html.

29 Paige St. John and Joel Rubin, "ICE Held an American Man in Custody for 1,273 Days. He's Not the Only One Who Had to Prove His Citizenship," *Los Angeles Times*, April 27, 2018, https://www.latimes.com/archives/story/2018-04-27/ice-held-an-american-man-in-custody-for-1273-days.

30 Ibid.

ABOUT THE AUTHOR

Daniel Bessner is the Anne H.H. and Kenneth B. Pyle Associate Professor in American Foreign Policy in the Henry M. Jackson School of International Studies at the University of Washington. He previously held the Joff Hanauer Honors Professorship in Western Civilization. He is also a Non-Resident Fellow at the Quincy Institute for Responsible Statecraft, an Associate of the Alameda Institute, and a Contributing Editor at *Jacobin*.

CULTURE, SOCIETY & POLITICS

Contemporary culture has eliminated the concept and public figure of the intellectual. A cretinous anti-intellectualism presides, cheer-led by hacks in the pay of multinational corporations who reassure their bored readers that there is no need to rouse themselves from their stupor. Zer0 Books knows that another kind of discourse—intellectual without being academic, popular without being populist—is not only possible but already flourishing. Zer0 is convinced that in the unthinking, blandly consensual culture in which we live, critical and engaged theoretical reflection is more important than ever before.

If you have enjoyed this book, why not tell other readers by posting a review on your preferred book site.

You may also subscribe to our Zer0 Books YouTube Channel.

Bestsellers from Zer0 Books Include:

Poor but Sexy
Culture Clashes in Europe East and West
Agata Pyzik
How the East stayed East and the West stayed West.
Paperback:978-1-78099-394-2 ebook: 978-1-78099-395-9

An Anthropology of Nothing in Particular
Martin Demant Frederiksen
A journey into the social lives of meaninglessness.
Paperback: 978-1-78535-699-5 ebook: 978-1-78535-700-8

In the Dust of This Planet
Horror of Philosophy vol. 1
Eugene Thacker
In the first of a series of three books on the Horror of Philosophy, *In the Dust of This Planet* offers the genre of horror as a way of thinking about the unthinkable.
Paperback: 978-1-84694-676-9 ebook: 978-1-78099-010-1

The End of Oulipo?
An Attempt to Exhaust a Movement
Lauren Elkin, Veronica Esposito
Paperback: 978-1-78099-655-4 ebook: 978-1-78099-656-1

Capitalist Realism

Is There No Alternative?

Mark Fisher

An analysis of the ways in which capitalism has presented itself as the only realistic political-economic system.

Paperback: 978-1-84694-317-1 ebook: 978-1-78099-734-6

Rebel Rebel

Chris O'Leary

David Bowie: every single song. Everything you want to know, everything you didn't know.

Paperback: 978-1-78099-244-0 ebook: 978-1-78099-713-1

Cartographies of the Absolute

Alberto Toscano, Jeff Kinkle

An aesthetics of the economy for the twenty-first century.

Paperback: 978-1-78099-275-4 ebook: 978-1-78279-973-3

Malign Velocities

Accelerationism and Capitalism

Benjamin Noys

Long-listed for the Bread and Roses Prize 2015, *Malign Velocities* argues against the need for speed, tracking acceleration as the symptom of the ongoing crises of capitalism.

Paperback: 978-1-78279-300-7 ebook: 978-1-78279-299-4

Babbling Corpse
Vaporwave and the Commodification of Ghosts
Grafton Tanner
Paperback: 978-1-78279-759-3 ebook: 978-1-78279-760-9

New Work New Culture
Work we want and a culture that strengthens us
Frithjof Bergmann
A serious alternative for humankind and the planet.
Paperback: 978-1-78904-064-7 ebook: 978-1-78904-065-4

Romeo and Juliet in Palestine
Teaching Under Occupation
Tom Sperlinger
Life in the West Bank, the nature of pedagogy, and the role of a university under occupation.
Paperback: 978-1-78279-637-4 ebook: 978-1-78279-636-7

Color, Facture, Art and Design
Iona Singh
This materialist definition of fine art develops guidelines for architecture, design, cultural studies, and ultimately, social change.
Paperback: 978-1-78099-629-5 ebook: 978-1-78099-630-1

Sweetening the Pill

or How We Got Hooked on Hormonal Birth Control

Holly Grigg-Spall

Has contraception liberated or oppressed women? *Sweetening the Pill* breaks the silence on the dark side of hormonal contraception.

Paperback: 978-1-78099-607-3 ebook: 978-1-78099-608-0

Why Are We the Good Guys?

Reclaiming Your Mind from the Delusions of Propaganda

David Cromwell

A provocative challenge to the standard ideology that Western power is a benevolent force in the world.

Paperback: 978-1-78099-365-2 ebook: 978-1-78099-366-9

The Writing on the Wall

On the Decomposition of Capitalism and its Critics

Anselm Jappe, Alastair Hemmens

A new approach to the meaning of social emancipation.

Paperback: 978-1-78535-581-3 ebook: 978-1-78535-582-0

Neglected or Misunderstood

The Radical Feminism of Shulamith Firestone

Victoria Margree

An interrogation of issues surrounding gender, biology, sexuality, work, and technology, and the ways in which our imaginations continue to be in thrall to ideologies of maternity and the nuclear family.

Paperback: 978-1-78535-539-4 ebook: 978-1-78535-540-0

How to Dismantle the NHS in 10 Easy Steps
(Second Edition)
Youssef El-Gingihy
The story of how your NHS was sold off and why you will have to buy private health insurance soon. A new expanded second edition with chapters on junior doctors' strikes and government blueprints for US-style healthcare.
Paperback: 978-1-78904-178-1 ebook: 978-1-78904-179-8

Digesting Recipes
The Art of Culinary Notation
Susannah Worth
A recipe is an instruction, the imperative tone of the expert, but this constraint can offer its own kind of potential. A recipe need not be a domestic trap but might instead offer escape—something to fantasise about or aspire to.
Paperback: 978-1-78279-860-6 ebook: 978-1-78279-859-0

Most titles are published in paperback and as an ebook. Paperbacks are available in traditional bookshops. Both print and ebook formats are available online.
Follow us at:
https://www.facebook.com/ZeroBooks
https://twitter.com/Zer0Books
https://www.instagram.com/zero.books